CONQUEST 1066

CONQUEST 1066
A History of the Norman Invasion of England

DAVID KLINKER DAHL HANSEN

McFarland & Company, Inc., Publishers
Jefferson, North Carolina

ISBN (print) 978-1-4766-9858-8
ISBN (ebook) 978-1-4766-5639-7

LIBRARY OF CONGRESS CATALOGING DATA ARE AVAILABLE

Library of Congress Control Number 2025030347

© 2025 David Klinker Dahl Hansen. All rights reserved

No part of this book may be reproduced or transmitted in any form or by any means, electronic or mechanical, including photocopying or recording, or by any information storage and retrieval system, without permission in writing from the publisher.

Front cover image: detail of the Bayeux Tapestry, 11th Century. The scene depicts the infamous death of the last Anglo-Saxon King, Harold Godwinson, as he is allegedly hit in the eye with an arrow (reproduced with the permission of the Museum of Bayeux in the City of Bayeux).

Printed in the United States of America

McFarland & Company, Inc., Publishers
Box 611, Jefferson, North Carolina 28640
www.mcfarlandpub.com

*To my father,
Michael Erik Klinker Hansen,
for always believing in me,
even when I did not believe in myself.
Your unwavering faith
has been my greatest strength.*

ACKNOWLEDGMENTS

This publication includes reproductions of selected scenes from the Bayeux Tapestry, an eleventh-century masterpiece that depicts the events leading up to the Norman Conquest of England. These images have been reproduced with the generous permission of the Museum of Bayeux.

Each image is labeled "Detail of the Bayeux Tapestry, 11th Century," and I would like to extend my sincere gratitude to the City of Bayeux for granting me the right to use these images in this work.

I am deeply appreciative of the Museum's support in bringing these historical scenes to life within the pages of this book.

I would also like to extend my heartfelt gratitude to those who have contributed to this project in various ways.

My friends Zi Siang Peter Lim, Lukas Sværke, and Jonas Sværke have been invaluable in providing numerous research articles and books that have greatly enriched my studies and understanding of the subject matter.

I am also thankful to my brother, Adam Klinker Dahl Hansen, for sharing multiple research resources, fully aware of my quest for comprehensive material for this book.

Lastly, I am deeply grateful to my father, Michael Erik Klinker Hansen, for his unwavering support. He purchased nearly all the books I used in my research and provided the critical insights that were instrumental in shaping the chronology and structure of this work.

TABLE OF CONTENTS

Acknowledgments   vi

Preface   1

Introduction   3

1. The Creation of the Duchy of Normandy   7
2. The Anglo-Saxons   16
3. The Death of King Edward the Confessor   33
4. The Northumbrian Rebellion of 1065   42
5. The Norwegian Invasion of England in 1066   49
6. The Origins of William the Conqueror   60
7. Preparations   74
8. The Invasion Unfolds   87
9. The Battle of Hastings   98
10. The Aftermath   115
11. The Bayeux Tapestry   128
12. The Harrying of the North   139
13. Domesday Book   154
14. The Death and Legacy of the Conqueror   163

Conclusion   176

Bibliography   183

Index   187

PREFACE

HISTORY HAS ALWAYS BEEN A PASSION of mine, even though I never formally studied it at university. My academic background, in fact, is rooted in a different field. I hold a Master of Science in Finance and Investments and a Bachelor of Science in International Business and Politics from Copenhagen Business School. Yet, despite these qualifications, my love for history has persisted throughout my life. The closest I ever came to a historical subject during my academic career was a course in political economy of thought, which examined the works of thinkers like Adam Smith, Karl Marx, and John Stuart Mill. But that far from satisfied my hunger for understanding the intricate events of the past, particularly the Norman Conquest of England in 1066, a subject that has fascinated me since my teenage years.

The Norman invasion, perhaps surprisingly, remains relatively unknown to many people in Denmark today, despite the deep roots the Normans had in Scandinavia just one or two centuries prior to their conquest of England. This connection sparked my interest, leading me to write my high school thesis on the topic. Admittedly, that work barely scratched the surface of what this book explores, perhaps covering only 5 percent of the material presented here. But it planted a seed that would grow over time. After finishing my MSc degree, I found myself yearning to return to history, and I began writing this book as a way to rekindle my academic writing skills and satisfy my curiosity.

What started as a casual project in September 2022 quickly evolved into something far greater. At first, I saw it as a fun challenge, a way to fill my free time while also exploring an area of history that I believed deserved more attention. However, as I progressed past the first few chapters, I realized I had the potential to create something substantial—a comprehensive work that could hopefully engage readers, expand their understanding, and bring new life to the story of 1066.

This book has been a labor of love, and while it may not align with traditional historical scholarship, my educational and professional experiences have prepared me for the meticulous research it required. I have applied the same discipline and rigorous methods from my academic career, emphasizing the importance of proper citations, source criticism, and thorough referencing. I have adhered to the *Chicago Manual of Style* author-date style of citation, drawing from primary sources where possible, often through the translations of well-accredited historians and translators, and referencing reputable secondary materials from respected scholars and peer-reviewed journals.

Writing this book has been an incredible journey, one that has pushed me beyond my comfort zone and challenged me in new ways. It is a dream come true to now present this work, the result of countless hours of research, writing, and revision. I hope it sparks the same curiosity in others that it has long sparked in me, and that it offers a new perspective on one of the most pivotal events in English history.

INTRODUCTION

THE NORMAN CONQUEST OF ENGLAND in 1066 stands as one of the most transformative events in English history, reshaping the political, social, and cultural landscape of the kingdom for centuries to come. The invasion led by Duke William of Normandy was more than a military conquest; it marked a shift from Anglo-Saxon England to a new era under Norman governance, fundamentally altering the kingdom's political, social, and cultural landscape. The ripple effects of this conquest would reach far beyond England's borders, influencing the development of law, governance, and even the language spoken in the British Isles. This book not only explores the pivotal events surrounding 1066 but also provides essential historical context, offering readers a comprehensive understanding of the forces that led to the conquest, as well as the long-term consequences that followed. The story begins long before Duke William set foot on English soil and long before the Battle of Hastings was fought. To fully appreciate the magnitude of the conquest, we must first delve into the history of both the Normans and the Anglo-Saxons.

The first chapter traces the formation of the Duchy of Normandy, revealing the Scandinavian roots of the Norman people, who were originally Vikings. Dudo of St. Quentin's writings serve as a key primary source, providing insight into the early days of Normandy. Chapter Two turns its attention to the Anglo-Saxons, beginning with their arrival in England after the fall of the Roman Empire. It explores how this group of settlers evolved into a powerful, unified kingdom under the leadership of figures like Alfred the Great. By the time of Edward the Confessor, whose life and death are examined in Chapter Three, the Anglo-Saxon kingdom was a well-established entity, but one beset by internal strife and an increasingly precarious royal succession. The succession crisis that followed Edward's death in 1066 is one of the core themes of this book. Chapters Four through Six cover the complex political and military machinations leading up to the Norman invasion. The Northumbrian Rebellion of 1065, the Norwegian invasion by Harald Hardrada, and William's own

ENGRAVING BY GEORGE VERTUE, 1733. This engraving portrays King William I, commonly known as William the Conqueror, in a formal, regal pose. The detailed engraving captures the authoritative image of the first Norman King of England, emphasizing his commanding presence. Vertue, a renowned engraver of the 18th century, created this work to commemorate William's significant impact on English history following his conquest in 1066. The plate size is 11½ in. × 7⅝ in., and it was given to the National Portrait Gallery by Sir Herbert Henry Raphael in 1913.

ENGRAVING BY JOSEPH HALFPENNY, 1831. This engraving depicts William the Conqueror seated on a throne, holding a large manuscript with a suspended seal. His nephew, Alain, Earl of Brittany, kneels before him, holding a pennant, while armed knights stand behind William. The scene is likely based on a historical moment from 1070, when William granted lands to Alain. The engraving is richly detailed with red, yellow, and dark blue watercolors or gouache paint, and is probably the frontispiece from *Fragmenta Vetusta*, Halfpenny's collection of drawings and etchings of ancient buildings in York.

preparations for conquest are all crucial elements that set the stage for the fateful events to come. The heart of the book is found in Chapters Eight and Nine, where the invasion and the Battle of Hastings are detailed extensively. These chapters chronicle the strategy, tactics, and battlefield conditions that led to William's triumph and Harold Godwinson's defeat. More than just a battle, Hastings was the decisive moment that confirmed William's claim to the English throne, reshaping the future of the kingdom forever. Chapters Ten through Fourteen explore the aftermath of the conquest, from the initial consolidation of William's rule to the far-reaching consequences for English society. The Harrying of the North (Chapter Twelve) represents the brutal measures William undertook to suppress rebellion, while Domesday Book (Chapter Thirteen) showcases his administrative prowess, creating one of the most remarkable surveys of medieval Europe. The final chapter examines William's later years and his lasting legacy. Throughout these chapters, this book offers a well-rounded picture of the conquest and its impact, combining military history with social, political, and cultural analysis. The Bayeux Tapestry, examined in Chapter Eleven, is not only an invaluable visual record of the conquest but also a symbol of how the events of 1066 were understood and memorialized in the years that followed.

This work does not merely recount the events of 1066, but rather places them within the broader context of medieval European history. It highlights the ways in which the Norman Conquest was both a climactic battle and a turning point that reshaped the trajectory of England. By weaving together the stories of key figures like Harold Godwinson, William the Conqueror, and Harald Hardrada, this book provides readers with an in-depth understanding of why the year 1066 continues to hold such significance in the annals of history.

1

THE CREATION OF THE DUCHY OF NORMANDY

THE CREATION OF THE NORMAN DUCHY was borne out of violence, much like the English kingdom that William the Conqueror would rule centuries later. Established during the height of the Viking era, Normandy arose from the brutal raids and eventual settlement of Norse warriors. What began as waves of pillaging evolved into territorial claims, laying the groundwork for a powerful, semi-autonomous state that would leave a lasting impact on European history. Initially, the Viking raiders of the eighth century sought only to loot and plunder, but their relentless success pushed them to expand their ambitions, transitioning from marauders to landholders and rulers. The success and brutality with which the Vikings carried out their raids generated so much fear that an old Anglo-Saxon prayerbook contained a plea entitled *A furore Normannorum libera nos, Domine* ("Lord, deliver us from the wrath of the Norsemen") (McLynn 1998, 7). However, as the Viking raids succeeded time and again, the raiders set their sights on gaining political power and land. Normandy epitomizes this transformation. The history of the Normans, as they were known during the time of William the Conqueror's invasion in 1066, begins around the turn of the tenth century. Back then, Normandy was not a duchy, nor did it have a duke. While this period in time is somewhat obscure, there are a multitude of contemporary sources surrounding the circumstances in which the duchy arose.

One of the earliest, and likely most accurate, sources is the *Gesta Normannorum* ("History of the Normans") by Dudo of St. Quentin. The work was written in late–Carolingian Latin, with a few isolated words and short phrases in Greek. Dudo writes in a literary language, both in prose and verse of several meters, which is divided into four parts, with the second part covering Duke Rollo of Normandy. Although Dudo has been criticized by historians, he is nevertheless a serious historian who manages to construct coherent historical narratives using both written sources and oral traditions. These criticisms have been re-examined in recent decades, with scholars recognizing that while Dudo may have made some errors, it is important to understand him within his historical context and appreciate the project he undertook. He was the only writer to manifest a coherent narrative of the early periods of the Norman duchy, meaning that even historians most critical of him still had to refer to his work (Neveux 2006, 58). The *History of the Normans* was completed around the year 1015 by Dudo, a traveling French scholar, and was meant to illustrate how once heathen Vikings came to be honored as powerful territorial rulers in France. This book will refer to the translated work of Dudo by Eric Christiansen (1937–2016), who was a medieval historian and fellow emeritus of New College, Oxford University (Bates 2016). Dudo himself was the dean of St. Quentin, born around 965. At the age of 21, Albert I, the count of Vermandois, requested that he travel to the court of Richard I, who was then the third duke of Normandy and the grandson of Rollo, the founder of the duchy. Dudo was originally sent to ask Richard I for assistance against the new French king, Hugh Capet. However, Richard I requested that Dudo remain at his court to write a history of Normandy (Neveux 2006, 58). Although Dudo remains a somewhat mysterious figure, with few known details of his personal life—except that he was born around 965 and died before 1043—his work on the history of the Normans endures as one of the most valuable primary sources on Norman history. Dudo had the advantage of being among the select few, if not the only one, to have lived so close in time to the founding of the Duchy of Normandy and to have produced a written account of it. His reliance on oral tradition, rather than prior documents, is evident in his writing. Most of his information came from Raoul, the count of Ivry and half-brother of Duke Richard I. The work that Dudo eventually crafted covers the history of the Normans from 852, prior to the establishment of their duchy, up until the death of Duke Richard I in 996 (Christiansen 1998, 1–2).

According to Dudo himself, the work was commissioned by Richard I of Normandy, and following Richard's death in 996, as the work was being written, other members of the Norman ducal house continued to pressure the author into finishing it. Given that Dudo wrote before the invention of the printing press, his work has survived through a large number of manuscripts, each uniquely crafted, unlike the mass-produced literature the modern world is accustomed to. Most of these manuscripts were copied during the eleventh and twelfth centuries, and the copy that Christiansen used for his translation was produced around 1050 at Mont-St.-Michel, a monastery near the "border" between Brittany and Normandy. This manuscript, entitled *Gesta Normannorum* or "Deeds of the Normans," is now held at the Berlin State Library (Lifshitz 1998, 3–9). When discussing the actual work written by Dudo and how the Norman duchy was established in France, an introduction to the historical figure known as Rollo is necessary. The Scandinavian Vikings were known for their ferocity in battle, so much so that the modern phrase "to go berserk" originates from these Nordic warriors. Many of these warriors were known as "berserkers," who were believed to enter an almost euphoric trance as they went into battle. The berserkers were often described as a sacred brotherhood who dressed only in animal hides, as ring mail seemed to hamper their movement, and they fought with relentless fury in a surreal battle rage. This gave birth to many myths, including that they were werewolves, whereas modern scholars believe that the berserkers may have taken some type of hallucinogenic drug just before a major battle (Finch 2003, 37). The berserkers' fighting style complemented the psychological warfare prevalent in medieval Scandinavian warfare. Scandinavian armies were notorious for being highly individualized, as noted in numerous sagas and on many rune stones. Individual valor and heroism were more highly regarded in Scandinavian society than united military action (DeVries 2000, 1999). Likewise, individual military feats were well rewarded. The National Museum of Denmark provides a good example in the case of "The Grave from Mammen." In 1868, a farmer uncovered an unusually richly furnished grave, created around the winter of AD 970–971. The warrior buried there was adorned with expensive purple and red silk clothing, a ceremonial silver-decorated axe, and a large wax candle (National Museum of Denmark n.d.). Danish archaeologist and historian Johannes Brønsted concluded that the reason for this extravagant burial must have been due to this warrior's valorous individual military service. Thus, the concept of military organization was likely quite foreign to most Scandinavian armies and soldiers. Historians agree that Scandinavian military forces did not begin to function like traditional medieval armies until the eleventh century. Prior to that, Scandinavian armies primarily consisted of small gangs of fighters (DeVries 2000, 1999).

Despite being branded as uncontrollable savages in many medieval sources, these Vikings also demonstrated a willingness to assimilate into many of the areas they raided. Rollo and the Norman Duchy provide an excellent example of this. Dudo describes Rollo as a warrior who is "vigorous in arms, well-versed in warfare, in body most fair" and "in spirit most hardy." The origin of Rollo has been the subject of much historical debate, with scholars often concluding that Rollo was either Danish or Norwegian. Most scholars from the Middle Ages argued that Rollo came from Norway, where he was known as Rolf, the son of Rögnvald, earl of Möre. This is mentioned, for example, by the famous Icelandic historian

Snorri Sturluson in his collection of sagas, *Heimskringla*, where he notes that Rolf was so large that no steed could bear him, and he had to walk everywhere, earning him the name Rolf "the Ganger." Supposedly, Rolf was then exiled from Norway due to his lawlessness and eventually came to possess a great earldom in Normandy, where he founded the Norman duchy (Douglas 1942, 417–419). Interestingly, Dudo notes that Rollo hailed from an area known as "Dacia." For those familiar with Roman history, this name should be recognizable. The Romans originally used this term to describe a province north of the Danube, corresponding to modern-day Romania. However, during the medieval era, this term was mistakenly used as the Latin name for Denmark. In fact, the first recorded instance of this error appears in Dudo's work (Encyclopedia 2018). Professor Johnny Grandjean Gøgsig Jakobsen of the University of Copenhagen provides an elaborate explanation of the origin of the name "Dacia" for what is now modern-day Denmark. During the Middle Ages, it was likely pronounced [Da-tjia], whereas the more common form *Dania* appeared later. While *Dacia* historically referred to a geographical area covering modern-day Hungary and Romania, its use for Denmark seems to have stemmed from misunderstandings by later antiquity authors. These authors likely made the correct reference, but they were misunderstood by medieval scholars. The historian and geographer Paulus Orosius (c. AD 400) noted that Dacia is "where Gothia is also located," which is between Alania and Germania. This was later copied by Isidore of Seville (c. AD 600). Both of these authors were highly renowned throughout the Middle Ages and cited by many later scholars. The Goths, who likely originated in the Nordic countries, migrated southward during the Migration Period (approximately 400–800 AD). Orosius's and Isidore's writings, from the time when the Goths occupied Eastern Europe, are accurate. However, the connection between Dacia and the migrating Goths caused confusion for later medieval scholars, leading them to misplace Dacia in the modern Danish latitudes, alongside Götaland and Gotland. A classic example of this misunderstanding occurred around the turn of the millennium when two Norman authors, Dudo of St. Quentin and William of Jumièges, referred to Dacia. Both authors were aware that the people of Dacia called themselves "Danes" and their country "Denmark," but they nevertheless referred to the area as "Dacia." The misconception was solidified around the turn of the twelfth century when a Cardinal in 1192 simply referred to Denmark as Dacia, after which the designation quickly became the Church's standard term for Denmark and the Nordic region. This tradition continued when two new monastic orders, the Dominicans and Franciscans, divided Europe into provinces in the early thirteenth century. In this division, the Nordics were referred to as Dacia, which further compounded the confusion, as both the entire Nordic region was labeled as the province of Dacia (*provincia Dacia*), and the kingdom of Denmark was called *regio Dacia* (Jakobsen 2012). Pinpointing exactly when this misconception of the term "Dacia" for Denmark faded can be difficult. However, in the Swedish writer and cartographer Olaus Magnus's work *Historia de Gentibus Septentrionalibus* ("A Description of the Northern Peoples"), published in Rome in 1555, we see one of the first uses of the term *Dania*. On page eight of the book, Magnus provides a map of the Nordic countries, including Iceland, Norway, Denmark, Sweden, and parts of modern-day Finland and Russia. On this map, Magnus clearly highlights Denmark as *Dania*, aligning with the Latin term for Denmark that most people are familiar with today (Magnus 1555, 8). This marked a pivotal shift in the way scholars and cartographers referred to Denmark, as the term Dania gradually replaced the outdated Dacia in academic and ecclesiastical circles.

While Dudo's credibility as an author can certainly be questioned, he is the earliest author to mention Rollo and the only one to have engaged in verbal conversations with individuals who may have had firsthand contact with Rollo. Moreover, most of the authors and scholars who supported the idea of Rollo hailing from Norway were born much later than Dudo and had never visited Normandy themselves. The claim that Rollo came from Norway did not emerge before the late eleventh century and did not gain much recognition until William of Malmesbury (c. 1095–1143) wrote about it in the twelfth century. Additionally, the majority of the invaders in Normandy were undoubtedly Danish and Anglo-Danish, with many being recruited from the Danish territories in England. Rollo was also known to have had a grandson, Robert II, Archbishop of Rouen (989–1037), who bore the sobriquet "Rollo the Dane" (Mark 2018). The Franks did not pay much attention to the origin of the Vikings; they simply saw the invaders as "Northmen." Given the weather and sailing conditions the Vikings faced, it also makes the most sense for the Norman invaders to have come from Denmark. The Danish Vikings tended to raid France and England, whereas the Norwegians ventured further north and established settlements in Scotland and Ireland. According to the *Historia Gruffydd*, it was even a Norwegian king, Harald Finehair, who founded Dublin (Gareth 2007, 36–84). While the origin of Rollo and the Viking settlers who followed him is still up for debate, this book will take Dudo's claims in favorable terms and ascribe Rollo's origin as Danish, viewing this as the most accurate conclusion.

Having touched upon the discussion of Rollo's origin, Dudo's introduction of Rollo can now be expanded. Dudo introduces Rollo alongside his younger brother, Gurim, describing them as two Danish warriors, sons of a mighty Danish duke. After their father's death, the Danish king declares his intent to invade their territory and exact revenge on the sons for their father's misdeeds. According to Dudo, Rollo initially defeats the king in battle, forcing him to retreat to the safety of his towns. Rollo buries his own soldiers, leaving the king's fallen army to rot. After a year of incessant fighting, the king deceives Rollo by offering a peace talk while secretly preparing a nocturnal ambush. Rollo and Gurim fight back with great ferocity as their city is set on fire and looted by the king's men. However, the Danish king ultimately prevails; many of Rollo's men, including Gurim, fall in battle, and the king besieges and subjugates the towns. Rollo is forced to flee to the peninsula of Scania (modern-day Skåne in Sweden) with six boats and the few men he has left (Dudo 1015, 62–63). During his time in Scania, Rollo allegedly experiences a divine vision in which he is instructed to visit England. He sails to England, where he battles an army of hostile peasants who have heard of "Rollo the Dane" and seek to either kill him or drive him away. Rollo defeats the peasants and begins to contemplate whether his next move should be to invade Denmark, France, or perhaps claim some of England for himself (Dudo 1015, 63–65). While in England, Rollo establishes a territory and has another dream in which he suffers from leprosy but is cured by bathing in the waters of a French mountain. Shortly thereafter, Rollo is introduced to a local Christian king named Alstem of East Anglia, whom scholars have since identified as the Danish Viking leader Guthrum (Mark 2018). King Alstem listens to Rollo's tale of misfortune in Denmark and his failed attempts to return due to the harsh winter weather. Rollo assures Alstem that he has no interest in plundering his realm and plans to depart for France in the spring. Sympathetic to Rollo's plight, Alstem pledges mutual aid in case either needs assistance (Dudo 1015, 65–69). Afterward, Rollo sails to France and begins a spree of pillaging, ravaging the lands with fire, supported by King Alstem. Dudo describes Rollo as relentless in battle, killing thousands upon his arrival in Northwestern Europe and fending off local chieftains Ragnar Long-Neck and Radbod the Frisian. Eventually, the locals agree to pay tribute to Rollo to end the attacks. Rollo then sails south into Rouen, intending to claim the land by force. French emissaries ask him why he has come and if he would submit to their king, Charles III. Rollo replies, "We are Danes. Carried here from Dacia, we have come to take Francia by assault" and "we will never subjugate ourselves to anyone." Rollo and his men then engage in fierce fighting, occupying the fortresses and towns around Rouen and Meulan. After killing a local duke named Ragnold, Rollo and his forces besiege and pillage Paris for a year. They then move on to Bayeux, where they "utterly destroy" the city. Rollo takes a maiden named Popa, daughter of the Count of Bayeux, Berengar, and she bears him a son, William (Dudo 1015, 70–82). In the midst of this, the Anglo-Saxons wage war against King

Alstem, who requests Rollo's aid. Remembering their pact, Rollo faithfully returns to England. King Alstem promises him half of his kingdom for his help, but Rollo declines the offer, returning the land to Alstem so he can resume his activities in France. Upon hearing of Rollo's return to Paris, King Charles III realizes his armies cannot match the Danish raiders. He requests a three-month truce in exchange for "the very greatest of favors." Rollo agrees, but when some of the Franks break the truce, Rollo retaliates by devastating their lands and pillaging any French province within reach. Desperate, King Charles III asks his advisors how to stop the raids. They suggest offering Rollo land from the River Andelle to the sea and marrying him to the king's daughter. Charles sends Archbishop Franco of Rouen to negotiate with Rollo, offering him land and the hand of his daughter, Gisla, in exchange for converting to Christianity. After consulting with his men, Rollo agrees. However, upon seeing the land offered, Rollo deems it too small and unworthy. He rejects the Flemish marshlands and instead accepts Brittany, which borders the lands he was promised. Rollo is then baptized, marries Gisla, and becomes the ruler of what will become known as Normandy (Dudo 1015, 99–100). Upon receiving his lands, Rollo is asked to kiss the king's foot to seal the treaty. Rollo refuses, declaring, "I will never kneel before the knees of another, nor will I kiss anyone's foot." After much urging, Rollo orders one of his warriors to kiss the king's foot, who does so by lifting the king's foot to his mouth, causing the king to topple backward, much to the amusement of the onlookers. Following this, Rollo becomes the first Duke of Normandy, converts his entire army to Christianity, and restores the land by rebuilding its churches, towns, and sanctuaries. After his death from old age, Rollo's son, William Longsword, whom he had with Popa, succeeds him as the second Duke of Normandy (Dudo 1015, 103–107).

This concludes the story of Rollo, as told by Dudo. While the historical accuracies have been challenged primarily in terms of the years in which Rollo arrived in France and the dates in which he besieged many of the cities such as Bayeux, the events which unfolded are likely to be very accurate. Rollo quickly changed the demographics of Normandy, where the treaty he made with King Charles III allowed Scandinavians to settle in the area. This caused the native population to live alongside their new Scandinavian neighbors, which was unacceptable to many of the monks and clerics that had taken shelter in Rouen, and many of them decided to go into exile. The few clerics from Coutances who remained in Rouen ended up assisting Rollo in going beyond the status of a foreign settler isolated within the Frankish world, but rather one with established relations and a strong network of alliances (Neveux 2006, 60–61). In geographical terms, it seems that the entire east and north of the diocese of Rouen were handed over to the Norman conquerors, with the surrounding territories such as Le Mans and Bayeux coming into Norman hands in 924. As Normandy was founded as a duchy under Rollo, it seems to mark the end of a long process of raiding and pillaging from the Scandinavian Vikings, with Rollo receiving royal authority while keeping his de facto independence and enjoying equal status to the other dukes and counts of France. This also gave King Charles III a strong defense going forward, as he would now only have to deal with a single Scandinavian, who would in turn help protect his realm against any new raids that may be undertaken by foreign Nordic invaders. This agreement, which ensured Rollo's legitimacy, his conversion to Christianity, and his fealty to the French king, would go down in history as the Treaty of Saint-Clair-sur-Epte and the creation of the ecclesiastical province of Rouen, which would preserve its relative independence as a part of the French Kingdom for almost three centuries (Neveux 2006, 68). This strategic alliance not only solidified Rollo's position but also marked a significant shift in the relationship between the Frankish Kingdom and the Scandinavian world, fostering a period of relative peace and stability in the region.

Following this, Normandy continued to be shaped by Rollo's successors through the tenth and eleventh centuries, who managed to unite, with great difficulty, the Scandinavian, Breton, and Frankish populations within the duchy. While the rulers of Normandy are often referred to as "dukes" by most historians, the title was not fixed until the middle of the eleventh century, and most texts often use the titles of "marquis" or "count." While the Normans became integrated and civilized from a Frankish perspective, it did not happen overnight either. Rollo continued expanding his principality by raiding Flanders and seizing Bessin in 924. However, he kept his oath of fealty to the French king by keeping a watch on the lower Seine and protecting it from Viking raiders, so they could no longer use it to penetrate the heart of the kingdom, as he had himself once done (Neveux 2006, 69–70). Following Rollo, his son William I, known as William Longsword, ruled from around 927 until 942 and managed to stabilize the realm under his rule. William I then had his son Richard I succeed him, who, despite troublesome beginnings, ruled the realm for more than fifty years from 942 until 996, during which Dudo entered the Norman realm. Richard I was then succeeded by his son Richard II, who was not the son of Richard I's French wife Emma but instead the son of a Danish woman named Gonnor, who belonged to a family that had settled in Pays de Caux. Richard II was very religious and strengthened the alliance with the French king Robert the Pious, assisting him in conquering Burgundy, as well as forming a new alliance with Brittany through an exchange of marriages, in which his sister married Duke Geoffrey of

Brittany, and Richard II married Geoffrey's sister Judith. Under Richard II's rule, Normandy's borders at last became more or less fixed, and while these borders may have seemed artificial, they were largely based on the old Roman boundaries (Neveux 2006, 71–74). After Richard II, his son Richard III ascended to the throne for a single year from 1026 to 1027. While Richard III was no more than around twenty years old, and his death has been shrouded in mystery, many later historians, such as the twelfth-century monk William of Malmesbury, argue that his brother Robert the Magnificent poisoned him to usurp the throne. In reality, it is difficult to ascertain the truthfulness of this accusation given the absence of convincing documentation, and given how fragile life was in the Middle Ages, it would not be preposterous to claim that the young duke may have died from some other unfortunate circumstance. Nevertheless, the death of Richard III allowed his brother Robert the Magnificent to accede to the throne at the age of seventeen. Robert the Magnificent continued to rule Normandy for around seven or eight years until 1035, and despite his short career, he has gone down in history as an exceptional figure who managed to assert his authority within and outside the Norman duchy, undertaking expeditions to England and pilgrimages to the Holy Land. Following his premature death at the age of approximately twenty-five, Robert left his realm to his young son William, who was only eight years old, which led to a long period of unrest. William would, however, as history has shown us, overcome these challenges and assert his authority over his lands, and later on over foreign lands as well with his conquest of England, which led to him going down in history as William the Conqueror (Neveux 2006, 96–110). By the time of William the Conqueror's birth, the Norman descendants from Rollo had mingled with their French subjects for over a century and integrated themselves into the society that they conquered. In addition to this, the Normans abandoned their Scandinavian languages and chose to willingly adopt the French social structure and administrative legal system, leading to a much more diverse and multicultural duchy by the turn of the eleventh century.

2

THE ANGLO-SAXONS

WHEN DOES THE HISTORY OF ENGLAND as a sovereign nation truly begin? At what point in time did this island nation begin to assert itself as a significant political player within European politics? The answer lies in the Anglo-Saxon period. This period typically refers to the time at which the Angles and the Saxons began arriving and settling in serious numbers on the British Isles, which began happening around the fifth and sixth centuries AD. It should be noted that it is currently being debated whether the term "Anglo-Saxon" is fair to use when referencing early medieval England, as the earliest occurrence of the term can be found in the late eighth-century *Historia Langobardorum* by Paul the Deacon, who mentions it in a passage describing the way early Lombards would dress with the garments worn by the Anglisaxones of Paul's time. The current usage of the term by modern scholars most likely originates from a sixteenth-century resurrection (Tinti 2021, 3). Nevertheless, it was during this time that England achieved unification under a single ruler and began to engage actively in the diplomatic and military affairs of Europe. This era marked the birth of England as a cohesive political entity, setting the stage for its significant role on the continental stage. While the Norman Invasion of 1066 ensured that the Anglo-Saxons were effectively erased from history as an independent people ruling their own nation, their legacy must not be undermined. The modern country of England derives its name from the expression "land of the Angles," and while most people might argue that modern English is vastly different from the language spoken by the old Anglo-Saxons, now referred to as "Old English," the current English language is still a direct descendant of this speech. The entire English regional system, consisting of shires and hundreds, originated during the time of the Anglo-Saxons and essentially lasted until the local government underwent significant reorganization in 1974 (Higham & Ryan 2013, 1–4). Moreover, many cultural and legal foundations established during the Anglo-Saxon period continue to influence contemporary English society and governance, reflecting the enduring impact of this formative era.

2. The Anglo-Saxons

The land that is now referred to as England has existed for ages, with the earliest signs of habitation by the predecessors of *Homo sapiens* dating back around 800,000 years, a time when the land was more of a tropical peninsula. Nevertheless, the predominantly lowland part of the archipelago has been continuously occupied by human settlements for about 11,500 years, of which 1,300 years could fairly be described as "English." It was not until around the eighth century that the concept of an "English people" began to emerge. Additionally, the creation of an English kingdom with its own land ("eard") did not come into being until the ninth century, and this land acquired its name, England ("Englalond"), around the year 1000. While ancient empires and their successor states, such as China and Iran, did exist, the Old English people were pioneers in building a political community characterized by a sense of kinship, shared culture, and participation in representative institutions and government (Tombs 2016, 4–9).

Eventually, the island faced its first imperial invasion at the hands of the Roman Republic under Julius Caesar, who justified his invasion in 55 and 54 BC by claiming that the warriors of the English island had allied themselves with the Gauls. Despite this assertion, the famous Roman historian Tacitus later commented that the Romans had a competitive advantage when facing their foes due to their inability to create alliances: "Nothing has helped us more in war with their strongest nations than their inability to co-operate. It is but seldom that two or three states combine to repel a common danger." Nevertheless, Caesar withdrew from England due to a revolt in Gaul, and the island managed to maintain its autonomy for another century. Eventually, after the Roman Republic transitioned into an empire under Augustus, the island faced a massive invasion of around 40,000 troops under the emperor Claudius in the year AD 43. Complete control of the island, which the Romans referred to as Britannia, would take several decades, and it was not until the year AD 60 that the last significant resistance to Roman occupation was overcome (Tombs 2016, 12–13). It should be noted that the Romans did not attempt to govern the entire island; the northern part was sealed off, in part by the famous Hadrian's Wall, consisting of 300 smaller fortlets and towers. Under Roman rule, towns, trade, and administrative governance flourished. It was during this period that famous cities such as Londinium (London), Eboracum (York), Corinium (Cirencester), and Lindum (Lincoln) emerged. However, the island still contained a predominantly rural population, with about eighty percent living in small settlements and estates of various sizes (Tombs 2016, 14). The Roman conquest of Britain was largely driven by the island's mineral wealth, leading to the establishment of certain industries, specifically tin in Cornwall and gold, silver, and lead in Wales, along with salt in Droitwich, coal in the East Midlands, and iron in the Weald. Unfortunately, the management of these industries was largely through imperial monopolies, resulting in minimal profits reaching local communities (Higham & Ryan 2013, 25). The link to the Roman Empire also brought an influx of literacy, the Latin language, and Christianity in the fourth century, when this became the official religion of the empire. Nevertheless, the British colony faced various crises of the empire, including multiple attempted military coups—some originating from the army in Britain—epidemics, economic decline, and uncontrollable movements of peoples. Before the Western Roman Empire's final fall in 476 AD, the western provinces became autonomous kingdoms ruled by "barbarians" or natives. As the Huns began moving west in the late fourth century, the Romans recruited "barbaric" mercenaries, and the province of Britain was exposed to foreign influences seeking to trade, raid, or settle in the region. Picts from northern Britain and Scots from Hibernia began raiding the Romanized areas of Britain. Notably, from the third century onward, Roman Britain faced invasions from the people referred to by the Romans as the "Saxons" (people from northern Germany and southern Scandinavia) (Tombs 2016, 15). The Saxons persistently carried out attacks on both sides of the North Sea and the Atlantic coast of Gaul. To curb the looting and forced enslavements resulting from these raids, the Romans began stationing numerous troops in Britain and constructed some of the largest fortifications in the empire. This area, including the Fortress of Eboracum and other massive forts and naval stations, came to be known as "the Saxon shore" (*litus saxonicum*). In 367, the Picts, Scots, and Saxons united in a coordinated attack on southern Britain. While these attacks were resisted, the invaders remained steadfast. In 408, the Saxons launched another significant attack, shortly after Rome itself was sacked by the Goths under the Visigoth king Alaric. As the empire began to crumble, Roman rule in Britain quickly disintegrated around the year AD 410, with imperial governance rapidly replaced by local leadership (Tombs 2016, 15).

By the fifth century AD, the Saxons began migrating into southeastern and central Britain, marking the beginning of their settlement rather than sporadic raids. While Saxon pirates had been raiding Roman territories since the late third century, leading to the construction of the Saxon Shore forts for protection, their settlement differed from these earlier incursions. Initially entering as allies under agreements with local rulers, such as the figure known as Vortigern, the Saxons eventually revolted and expanded their hold over much of England, eastern Scotland, and areas like the Solway Plain. The land they entered was heavily forested and dotted with marshlands, with limited arable land except on chalk and oolite plateaus.

Roman infrastructure, including roads and towns, had largely fallen into decay following the decline of centralized Roman governance and urban economies. Many Roman cities were abandoned or sparsely inhabited, and the Saxons, unfamiliar with stone construction and urban living, established timber-based settlements outside these remnants. Over time, even in its deteriorated state, Roman architecture left a lasting impression on the new settlers, who referred to it in their poetry as the "work of giants" (Whitelock 1972, 13–16). This marked a significant turning point in the demographic and cultural landscape of Britain, as the incoming Saxons not only established new settlements but also laid the foundation for the development of a distinct Anglo-Saxon identity that would shape the future of the island.

Whether the Saxon move into England was a series of violent invasions, potentially culminating in the ethnic cleansing of the pre-existing Romano-British population, or a more peaceful settlement remains a topic of debate; if one were to ask the old Norman historians, they would likely have argued that it was the former. The half–Norman Henry of Huntingdon rewrote the history of the English island as a succession of legitimate governments beginning with the Romans and ending with the Normans. As each chronological region would eventually grow weak, it would succumb to a stronger culture. Henry argued that the Anglo-Saxons had gained control over the English island in a violent manner, similar to the Normans, and were thus also originally invaders of foreign territories. He posited that each of these cultures had the right to conquest and sovereignty. William of Malmesbury, who was also half–Norman and wrote around the same time, contended that the arrival of the Norman invaders was simply a civilized progression of sovereignty that was necessary given the savage nature of areas such as Yorkshire, where the barbaric Danes and Saxons had strongholds. Geoffrey of Monmouth (ca. 1095–1155), writing from a pro–Norman perspective, asserted that British civilization had reached a high point under King Arthur and Camelot, but due to later weakness and corruption, combined with Saxon invasions, the English island had descended into barbarity, and the Norman invasion was necessary to restore the island to a golden age (Karkov 2020, 73–75). While the Normans may seem biased given the nature of their own violent invasion in 1066, their arguments are supported by the monk Gildas, who provides the oldest surviving narrative from around 540 AD; this account, preserved through two medieval manuscript copies, describes the Saxon invasion: "The first wave landed on the eastern side of the island ... and there they fixed their terrible claws, as if to defend the country, but in fact to attack it. Their German mother-land, seeing them successfully installed, dispatched a wonderful collection of hangers-on and dogs, who, arriving by the boatload, joined up with their misbegotten comrades" (Tombs 2016, 16). Some archaeologists believe that the migration of Saxons in the 3rd and 4th centuries, and the Angles in 449, according to the Anglo-Saxon Chronicle, was a less traumatic process that included gradual settlement in underpopulated areas and voluntary cultural emulation from the natives. Tombs (2016) suggests that perhaps as many as 200,000 Germanic war bands, equal to around twenty percent of the native British population at the time, invaded the fertile lowlands of southern and eastern Britain without displacing the existing population, but still forcing out the relatively small Romanized elite (Tombs 2016, 16). It should be noted that Gildas himself was British, and in his work *De Excidio et Conquestu Britanniea* ("On the Ruin and Conquest of Britain"), he argued that the Romano-British population had brought the invasions upon themselves due to their moral and religious failings. Gildas compared the ruin of Britain by the Saxons to the destruction of Jerusalem by the Romans, likening the defeat of the Britons to that faced by the Jews (Karkov 2020, 8–9, 112). He noted that the Saxon settlers were "tyrants" who "plundered and terrorized the innocent" and surrounded themselves with "many wives and whores" while waging unjust wars. One should examine Gildas's account with a critical eye, as he was most likely relying on oral tradition rather than written records; although his narrative is the only one available concerning the period of the Anglo-Saxon settlements, it contains inaccuracies, such as assigning the building of the Antonine and Hadrian Walls to the fourth century (Yorke 1990, 2).

The settlements of the Saxons and Angles eventually led to the creation of three predominantly Germanic kingdoms by the end of the seventh century: Northumbria, Mercia, and Wessex, along with several smaller kingdoms, including East Anglia, Kent, Essex, and Sussex (Tombs 2016, 18). The eighth-century monk Bede provides two lists of "tribes" representing the settlers; the short list mentions the Angles, Saxons, and Jutes, while his longer list includes Frisians, Huns, Rugii, Bructeri, and Old Saxons. Ethnic interpretations of archaeological finds support Bede's short list but also suggest the presence of Franks in southern England, at least one Goth in southwestern England, and Scandinavians from southern Norway in eastern England. Nevertheless, it was the Saxons and Angles who primarily emerged as the dominant faction of the invaders, and whose emerging kingdoms and regional identities would play a significant role in the evolution of Anglo-Saxon England, while other groups, such as a Frankish faction of immigrants in southern England, appeared to be subsumed in the regional identity of the new West Saxons (Härke 2011, 11). This dominance laid the groundwork for the distinctive cultural, political, and social structures that would characterize England in the centuries to come, ultimately influencing the formation of a unified English identity.

The British philosopher Thomas Hobbes famously described life in the state of nature as "solitary, poor, nasty, brutish, and short." While the early Anglo-Saxons did have governmental structures, studies from the Buckland cemetery near Dover, which was in use from around 480 to the 750s, provide insight into what life was like during that period. Approximately twenty percent of the population died before reaching adulthood at age eighteen, and female remains are more numerous than male remains, likely because men died away from home while engaged in wars or hunting. Despite this, women had a lower life expectancy due to the dangers associated with childbirth, with the average age of death being thirty-one, compared to thirty-eight for men. Only six percent of people lived past the age of sixty, and those who did often faced serious dental issues, disabling joint damage, endemic diseases like tuberculosis, and poorly healed fractures. While women of the warrior nobility enjoyed better living conditions and were less likely to die from childbirth, the men were more susceptible to violent deaths (Tombs 2016, 18). This stark contrast in mortality rates highlights the harsh realities of life in early Anglo-Saxon society, where social status could afford some individuals a degree of security, while others faced greater risks in both daily life and conflict.

According to Gildas, the Romano-British resistance around the year 500 was led by a mysterious and possibly fictitious "King of Britain" named Ambrosius Aurelianus, who achieved a notable, albeit temporary, victory over the Saxon invaders at Mons Badonicus (Mount Badon). Later authors, such as the eighth-century monk Bede of Jarrow and the ninth-century writers of the Anglo-Saxon Chronicle, attempted to elaborate on Gildas' account of this resistance, during which vague references to King Arthur first appeared in British records. Arthur is depicted as a military leader who carried a cross as his emblem at Mount Badon and who met his end at Camlann in 537. These early references would eventually evolve into the Arthurian legend, greatly expanded by the cleric Geoffrey of Monmouth in the twelfth century, who claimed to have derived his information from "a certain very ancient book" in Oxford. Subsequently, French writer Chrétien de Troyes, writing in the late twelfth century, introduced chivalric themes such as tournaments, quests, the knightly exploits of figures like Perceval and Lancelot, damsels in distress, and the tale of the Holy Grail. King Arthur continued to hold a significant place in British folklore throughout the late Middle Ages, with later figures like Richard the Lionheart claiming possession of Arthur's sword, Excalibur. The legend was further developed by subsequent authors such as Thomas Malory in 1470, Lord Tennyson in the nineteenth century, and, in a reimagined form, J.R.R. Tolkien in the twentieth century. Early Welsh writers viewed King Arthur as a symbol of pre–Anglo-Saxon civilization, believing in his eventual return as "the once and future king" (Tombs 2016, 18–19). These mythical tales from Britain's transition from Romano-British rule to Anglo-Saxon dominance endowed Britain with a distinctive cultural identity that transcended its status as merely a conquered Roman province, transforming it into the heart of a mystical epic with a unique heritage.

It is difficult to establish exactly when Anglo-Saxon history began; however, many scholars argue that a key milestone occurred with the arrival of Augustine and his group of around forty monks at the court of King Æthelbert of Kent in 597, as Pope Gregory the Great had dispatched Augustine and his followers to "preach the word of God to the English race." Unsurprisingly, given his Christian and monastic background, Bede begins the history of the Anglo-Saxon kingdoms at this point in time as well. With the arrival of Augustine, the Anglo-Saxons were introduced to a new religion and learned the arts of reading and writing. It should be stressed that while the arrival of the Gregorian mission did indeed mark an important stage in the history of the Anglo-Saxons, most of the Anglo-Saxon kingdoms and their political systems were already in existence by 597 (Yorke 1990, 1). The Angles, Saxons, and Jutes had arrived over several generations from northern Germany and southern Denmark, and these people were not homogeneous ethnic units, tribes, or nations; they often consisted of polyglot armed bands. It was often only after they had settled into a territory and established a stable grip on power that they began to develop a distinct identity and a dialect that, in some cases, became a written language. Unlike other former Roman provinces such as Gaul and Italy, or distant nations like the Chinese Empire, which faced reunification under the Tang Dynasty, England ended up in a fragmented state with multiple kingdoms rather than under the power of a single Germanic conqueror (Tombs 2016, 23). Most archaeological and linguistic research from the twentieth century argued that the immigration of Germanic immigrants (primarily Anglian, Saxon, and Jutish) into post–Roman Britain brought with it a new culture and language, leading to the establishment of multiple new ethnic kingdoms that replaced the pre-existing structures of the native Britons to such a significant extent that it would, from a modern perspective, constitute ethnic cleansing (Härke 1, 2011). Since the 1980s, however, an opposing perspective has taken root, arguing that the written sources for the fifth and sixth centuries in Britain are unreliable in both content and chronology. This was followed by an argument, manifesting during the 1990s, that the Anglo-Saxon invasion had not been a "folk migration" but rather consisted of smaller groups of warriors and a few families. According to Härke

(2011), who has based his research on modern DNA samples extracted from ancient skeletal remains, the Anglo-Saxons appeared as an outcome of ethnogenetic processes, where the assimilation and acculturation of the native British population played a significant role. Härke argues that the Germanic immigration was a "minority immigration" on the scale of around ten to twenty percent of the pre-existing native British population, and rather than a simple invasion, it was a series of immigrations and intrusions over a considerable period, estimating the total number of immigrants to have been around 100,000 to 200,000 over about a century (Härke 2011, 19). This perspective challenges the traditional narrative of a swift and overwhelming conquest, suggesting instead a more complex process of cultural exchange and gradual transformation within the existing societal framework.

If one were to look at a milestone for early Anglo-Saxon history prior to the Gregorian mission, Bede gives a noteworthy description in his *Ecclesiastical History* from 731. Despite relying on Gildas' work, which never identifies the early Saxon leaders that arrived in Britain, Bede identifies them as two brothers named Hengist and Horsa, who founded the royal house of Kent. This information likely came from Abbot Albinus of Canterbury, who Bede used as his chief Kentish informant. Hengist and Horsa are also mentioned in greater detail in the *Anglo-Saxon Chronicle* and in the "Kentish Chronicles," included in the *Historia Brittonum*, a British compilation written around 830 and attributed to the Welsh ninth-century monk Nennius. In the *Anglo-Saxon Chronicle*, there are accounts of the arrival of Cynric and Cerdic, Wihtgar and Stuf, and Ælle and his sons—individuals who respectively founded the kingdoms of the West Saxons, the Isle of Wight, and the South Saxons. These kingdoms were established after some years of fighting against local British leaders, and similar patterns seem to have followed for Northumbria and the Jutes settling in mainland Hampshire. While Bede's account, like most other historical accounts of the time, relied on often unverifiable oral tradition, he does often refer to information about Hengist and Horsa with the phrase "they are said...," indicating that much of the information regarding the two brothers should be examined with caution. Most notably, the sources describing the early arrivals of the Angles, Saxons, Jutes, and other Germanic peoples in Britain are not contemporary with the events they describe. While Bede argues that Cerdic and Cynric arrived around 494 AD, British historian David Dumville suggests that other versions of the West Saxon regnal list imply that Cerdic's reign lasted from 538 to 554. Following the time sequence of the *Anglo-Saxon Chronicle*, this would place the arrival of Cynric and Cerdic in 523. Even if the stories of Cerdic and Hengist were devoid of inaccuracies, it is nearly impossible to separate them from the later reworkings that these tales have received. Nevertheless, Cerdic was the founding king of the West Saxon dynasty, from whom all subsequent West Saxon kings claimed descent. Bede also notes that the kings of the East Angles were known as Wuffingas, named after Wuffa, the grandfather of King Rædwald, who ruled around the turn of the seventh century. Given that Rædwald died around 625, his grandfather presumably ruled in the middle of the sixth century. As for the East Saxons, the key figure was Sledd, from whom all subsequent East Saxon kings claimed descent, and whose son ruled in 604. Thus, Sledd must have come to power around the latter half of the sixth century (Yorke 1990, 3–4). This suggests a gradual establishment of royal lineages during this period, reflecting the complexities of political authority and cultural integration in early Anglo-Saxon England.

The majority of the significant Anglo-Saxon kingdoms therefore seemed to be creations of the sixth century rather than the fifth century, and it was at this point in time that Britain began its transformation into what would later become a unified Anglo-Saxon Britain. During the early sixth century, the British islands evolved into a multicultural region with multiple languages, religions, and ethnic and cultural origins. The five main language groups consisted of Germanic in the eastern and southern regions, Brittonic, Gaelic, and Pictish in the western and northern regions, and Norse in the northeastern region. While these regions were not necessarily united, and the northern and western parts were divided into rival kingdoms, certain powerhouses did appear, with Northumbria, situated between the Humber and the Forth, and its main city of York, becoming the most powerful in the north. In the south, Mercia emerged as a dominating force, with its royal seat located at Tamworth. The kingdoms of the East Angles, Kent, and the West Saxons in the southwest also rose in prominence. Despite the fractured political landscape and cosmopolitan structure of Britain, as well as the lack of a shared ethnic origin at the time, the people settling on the isles would come to be known as the English, leading many historians to argue that the English emerged as one of the first nations due to their common administrative and political institutions and a growing shared identity (Tombs 2016, 25–26). It was also during this time that England began to unify on religious grounds. Bede notoriously described the pre-existing British church in mostly negative terms, partly due to its alleged refusal to convert the newly arrived pagan Germanic immigrants. While he praised the Irish missionaries active in Northumbria during the seventh century, he indirectly criticized them for their stance on the dating of Easter. This issue was resolved at the Synod of Whitby in 664, where the Northumbrian king Oswiu ruled that his kingdom would calculate Easter according to the Roman system, which Bede also supported. This decision championed the unity of the early English church and elevated the church of Canterbury as the religious capital of England, which maintained a continuous relationship with Rome throughout the Anglo-Saxon period. In the seventh century, this relationship extended to deliberate imitation of Rome, evident in the construction of early churches in Canterbury dedicated to saints with Roman links, such as Peter and Paul, and by adopting Roman liturgy (Tinti 2021, 12). For almost a century after Augustine's arrival as part of the Gregorian mission, all the bishops of Canterbury were chosen by the Roman papacy and sent from Rome, with one short-lived exception. Wighard, the first native English bishop-elect, was sent to Rome around 667 to be consecrated by Pope Vitalian. Unfortunately, Wighard died of the plague, and the Pope replaced him with a monk from Tarsus in Cilicia, Theodore, who was living in Rome. Theodore's pontificate lasted from 669 to 690 and transformed the structures of the English church. He introduced a new mode of metropolitan authority by adopting the title of archbishop and receiving the archiepiscopal pallium from the Roman pope, which granted him the right to consecrate bishops in his province. The pallium, a white woolen band marked with crosses, was worn during the celebration of Mass on specific days and would come to represent the principal symbol of the archbishop's authority derived from the papacy (Tinti 2021, 13). Under Theodore's leadership, the English church became more organized and hierarchically structured, strengthening its ties with Rome and laying the groundwork for a unified ecclesiastical framework that would influence the governance of the church in England for centuries to come.

This leads to the question, If a shared English identity began to emerge due to religious unification, what led to the English identity merging into a shared political and national form? The answer to this question lies in the emergence of a shared common threat; the Vikings, which was the old Norse expression for "pirate" or "sea adventurer." These warbands had already been ravaging Europe for several centuries, but they would soon begin to make serious incursions into the British Isles beginning with the notorious incident in which Viking raiders looted the holy site of Lindisfarne in June 793. Alcuin of York, Charlemagne's court theologian, saw it as divine punishment for monkish self-indulgence and described the sacrilege in brutal terms: "The blood of saints poured out around the altar … the bodies of saints trampled on … like dung in the streets." Following this, there was a brief period of respite with only small, sporadic raids until the 830s. During this time, mass attacks began to rise in prominence, involving as many as one hundred raiding ships. These raiders carried out their activities with ruthless ferocity, exemplified by the legendary ritual known as the "blood eagle." This gruesome practice involved chopping through the ribs and pulling out the lungs so they draped over the back like scarlet wings. It is said that this was also the fate of King Ælla of Northumbria in 867. The brutal attacks by the Viking raiders would transform the British Isles. The common peasantry would suddenly, beyond their everyday hardships, face potential enslavement or violence from the raiders. On a political scale, some local warlords and rebels thought they could use the Vikings as allies in factional struggles, but many of them would soon find that these ferocious allies would not come without a cost. This was exemplified in the north, where an aggressive Norse lordship established a colony that became the Kingdom of Dublin, which would later turn into the main base for slaving and raiding in Britain, and eventually part of a Viking kingdom that included York. The Vikings would eventually conquer two of the four major kingdoms, East Anglia and Northumbria, and partition a third, Mercia. Wessex, the kingdom of the West Saxons, would remain as the only intact Christian power and with its annexation of the remnants of western Mercia around 880, the geographical and ideological step towards a unified English kingdom began to turn into reality (Tombs 2016, 30).

To go into further detail on how this devastation came about, closer examination of the Viking invasions in the later part of the ninth century is needed. The Viking invasion that truly broke the political structure of England was the one conducted by what has since become known as "The Great Heathen Army," "The Danish Great Army" or "The Viking Great Army." This army consisted of a notoriously large Viking army who invaded England in 865 and encamped on the Isle of Thanet. Year after year the army would conduct nonstop campaigns on the Anglo-Saxon kingdoms with devastating consequences. The army was, as noted by the name by which it is often referred to, "The Danish Great Army," mostly composed of Danish Vikings. However, some of its members also came from neighboring Scandinavian countries such as Norway and Sweden. According to legend, the army was originally led by the five sons of Ragnar Lodbrok: Ivar the Boneless, Sigurd Snake-in-the-Eye, Björn Ironside, Ubba, and Halfdan. According to old Norse-Icelandic sources, King Ælla of Northumbria had captured and tortured the Viking Ragnar Lodbrok in a snake-infested pit, and in order to avenge their father, Ragnar's sons, most notably Ivar the Boneless, began conducting ruthless raids into Northumbria (Mueller-Vollmer and Wolf 2022, 125–126, 265). The size of the Great Heathen Army has been a topic of considerable debate among scholars, but a reasonable estimate suggests that it comprised at least a couple of thousand soldiers. While the army certainly profited from its successful raids, its primary goal was to occupy and conquer the four English kingdoms of East Anglia, Mercia, Northumbria, and Wessex. The campaign began with raids in eastern Kent, followed by their occupation of East Anglia. In late 866 or early 867, the army continued its advance by conquering York and all of Northumbria, which was soon followed by the conquest of Nottingham in Mercia. When Mercia, aided by Wessex, failed to lay siege to Nottingham, they opted to resort to tribute payments to the Vikings instead (Mueller-Vollmer and Wolf 2022, 126). After a series of successful campaigns across the English Isles, the Great Heathen Army decided to spend the winter of 868–869 in York and then moved to Thetford in East Anglia for the winter of 869–870. In 869, St. Edmund of East Anglia (ca. 841–869) broke the peace treaty he had established with the Vikings and was subsequently captured and brutally killed. Shortly after, Viking reinforcements arrived from Scandinavia in 871 to support the Great Heathen Army in their attack on Wessex, where they faced their first significant defeat at the Battle of Ashdown. Following this loss, the Viking invaders spent the winter of 871–872 in London before returning to York, where their control was beginning to weaken. The following year, they wintered in the Kingdom of Lindsey (modern-day Lincolnshire) and, in 873, collected another payment from Mercia before spending the winter of 873–874 in Repton in Derbyshire. In 874, they successfully conquered Mercia and decided to split their formidable force into two armies. One half, led by Halfdan Ragnarsson, went north to raid Northumbria, Strathclyde, and Scotland before settling in the Danelaw in 876. The other half, under Guthrum, occupied Cambridge during the winter of 874–875 and subsequently raided the area around Wareham and other parts of Wessex. Eventually, this faction faced defeat when they clashed with King Alfred the Great of Wessex in 878 during the legendary Battle of Edington, after which the remnants of the Viking army settled in East Anglia (Mueller-Vollmer and Wolf 2022, 126–127). This decisive battle, coupled with the rise of King Alfred, later known as "the Great," paved the way for the emergence of a united Anglo-Saxon kingdom. King Alfred the Great played a pivotal role in unifying England, not only against the Viking threat but also in establishing it as an autonomous nation.

The man who would later become known as King Alfred the Great, the first "King of the Anglo-Saxons," was born in Wantage, Oxfordshire, in 849 as the youngest of five brothers. His father was Æthelwulf, the king of Wessex, and his mother, Osberh, was described as "a most religious woman, noble in character and by birth" (Anlezark 2021, 13). Royal Anglo-Saxon names typically included the component "Æthel-," meaning "noble," and often had specific meanings, as seen in the case of Æthelwulf, which translates to "noble-wolf." Although Alfred's name does not start with "noble," his contemporaries likely pronounced it as "Ælf-ræd" (elf-counsel), reflecting someone endowed with insightful counsel (Anlezark 2021, preface). Alfred's family was no stranger to the Viking threat, as his grandfather, King Egbert, had defeated a combined army of local Britons and Danish Vikings in Cornwall in 838, eleven years before Alfred's birth. Following Egbert's death in 839, his dominion was divided between Alfred's father, Æthelwulf, who received Wessex Proper, and Alfred's eldest brother, Æthelstan, who was given Essex, Kent, Sussex, and Surrey, ancient kingdoms absorbed under West Saxon dominion. By the 850s, the Vikings began altering their tactics; previously, they had been mere raiders, coming with fleets of thirty to thirty-five ships for pillaging before returning home for the winter. However, in 850, the year after Alfred's birth, the Anglo-Saxon Chronicle notes that the Vikings decided to remain in England during the winter for the first time. By 851, the Chronicle reported an invasion involving 350 ships, which caught the Mercian king Beorhtwulf by surprise, forcing him to flee across the river into Surrey to seek West Saxon assistance. The English ultimately won this battle with the aid of Alfred's father, Æthelwulf, and his brother Æthelbald, but it was clear to the Anglo-Saxon populace that the raiders had evolved into a significant invasion threat (Anlezark 2021, 14). This alarming shift in Viking strategy underscored the urgent need for a unified response among the Anglo-Saxon kingdoms to confront the growing danger and safeguard their territories from further incursions.

One of the most significant sources for understanding the life of King Alfred the Great is the *Life of King Alfred*, written by the Welsh monk Asser, a contemporary and biographer of Alfred. This work provides a detailed account of Alfred's reign, personal struggles, and achievements, offering invaluable firsthand perspective despite reflecting certain biases and the historical limitations inherent in medieval historiography. For example, Asser describes Alfred's youth as marked by intense piety alongside sexual scruples, noting that he found it difficult to "act against God's will with uncontrollable sexual urges." To manage his desires, Alfred would rise early at dawn to visit churches and pray for an illness that could help him suppress his sexual impulses while being tolerable enough not to incapacitate him. According to Asser, God responded to his plea by granting him piles (hemorrhoids), although the affliction proved too painful, prompting Alfred to visit the shrine at Saint Gueriir to request relief from his suffering (Anlezark 2021, 27). This account, likely based on Alfred's own testimony, underscores a lack of critical scrutiny in medieval historiography, where oral traditions often went unchallenged.

Alfred first enters the historical narrative when he was sent to Rome on a pilgrimage in 853, at just four years old. According to Asser and the *Anglo-Saxon Chronicle*, Pope Leo IV consecrated Alfred as king, declaring him his "adoptive son," and a letter from Pope Leo confirms that the young prince was instituted as a Roman consul. When Alfred was six, he returned to Rome with his father, Æthelwulf, who, as Asser noted, loved Alfred more than his other sons. Despite the growing Viking threat in Wessex, they remained in Rome for two years. Before departing, King Æthelwulf gave a tenth of his land to the Church, likely hoping to secure divine assistance in the battles ahead. Alfred returned home at seven, and on the way, his father married Princess Judith, the twelve-year-old daughter of Emperor Charles of France, after the death of his first wife, a union likely motivated by political ambition, serving both to recognize Æthelwulf's dominance in Britain and to forge an alliance with the powerful Frankish Empire. In 858, when Alfred was nine, his father died, and Alfred's older brother, Æthelbald, married Judith, an act that Asser condemned as against God's law and a "great disgrace." This marriage was seemingly arranged without Emperor Charles the Bald's approval, and after Æthelbald's death, Judith was confined to a convent in Senlis, north of Paris, only to elope with Count Baldwin of Flanders. Neither Æthelwulf nor Æthelbald fathered any children, and Asser described Æthelbald's reign until his death in 860 as "lawless," while the *Anglo-Saxon Chronicle* remains silent on the matter. Following Æthelbald's death, Alfred's other older brother, Æthelberht, ruled the entire kingdom of Wessex. During Æthelberht's five-year reign, the Great Heathen Army attacked Winchester and established a permanent base in Thanet, Kent. Asser described Æthelberht with much more affection than Æthelbald, characterizing his reign as one of "peace, love, and honor," with his death causing "great sorrow." After Æthelberht's death, Alfred, at sixteen, watched his last surviving brother, Æthelred, assume control of Wessex, where Alfred was granted the status of crown prince. Æthelred's reign was marked by continual conflicts with Viking invaders, and after Easter (April 15, 871), King Æthelred died of unspecified causes, leading to Alfred, the last of the five royal brothers, ascending to the throne of Wessex at the age of twenty-two (Anlezark 2021, 38). This would leave Alfred facing the daunting challenge of uniting a kingdom that had suffered extensive Viking raids and division, a task that would ultimately define his reign as he sought to restore stability and resilience in Wessex.

Despite Alfred's later successes as a king, he inherited a kingdom in devastation. Between Christmas and Easter, the Wessex army fought the Vikings five times, losing three of those battles, and after King Æthelred's death, the Great Heathen Army was bolstered by a "great summer host," leading to the near annihilation of the English army commanded by Alfred by 871, as reported by Asser. The Vikings also experienced losses, with nine of their jarls and one of their kings slain in battle. By the end of 871, the West Saxons reached a peace agreement with the Vikings, likely involving tribute payments, ushering in a period of relative tranquility for the next eight years. However, in early January 878, while Alfred celebrated Christmas at his royal estate in Chippenham near Bath, the Vikings launched a brutal invasion of Wessex. According to the *Anglo-Saxon Chronicle*, the Vikings "rode over Wessex and occupied it," causing many West Saxons to flee overseas while those who remained were forced into submission. As the Vikings prepared to besiege the stronghold at Cynuit, the West Saxons launched a surprise attack, resulting in the deaths of Viking leader Ubbe and over 800 of his soldiers. Alfred's army later confronted the formidable Viking forces at Edington, where Asser notes that Alfred "destroyed the Vikings with great slaughter." The astonished Vikings eventually surrendered unconditionally to Alfred, offering hostages in exchange for peace and a promise to leave Wessex. Viking king Guthrum also vowed to receive baptism, with Alfred acting as his sponsor. Three weeks later, Guthrum and thirty leaders of the Great Army came to Alfred at Aller, where Guthrum was baptized. Following twelve nights of festivities, Alfred gifted Guthrum and his companions richly, and in 879, Guthrum and his men left Alfred's kingdom, staying in Cirencester for a year before departing for East Anglia, which they subsequently colonized (Anlezark 2021, 43–46). Despite this crushing victory, Danish armies secure in their northern and eastern territories continued to invade whenever they felt strong enough. In response, Alfred implemented a comprehensive restructuring of Wessex's economic and urban landscape into a regular system of large fortified settlements known as "burhs." Some of these burhs were established at old forts from Roman or even Iron Age times, while others were newly constructed, all situated within twenty miles—approximately a day's march—of each other. During times of danger, these burhs would be garrisoned by organized local defense forces and a field army known as the "fyrd," alongside a royal fleet. This defensive strategy proved largely successful, culminating in Alfred's seizure of London in 886, a pivotal moment many scholars mark as the birth of the English kingdom. According to the *Anglo-Saxon Chronicle*, it was at this time that "all the English race turned to him," with the exception of the captive Danish men. Alfred began referring to his people as "Angelcynn" ("Englishkind") rather than Saxons, and he was acknowledged in royal charters as rex Saxonum, which evolved into rex Angul-Saxonum ("King of the Anglo-Saxons") to signify the union of Wessex and Mercia. While Alfred argued that he was restoring the English, it could also be posited that he was inventing them (Tombs 2016, 31). Unlike many of his contemporaries and predecessors, Alfred aspired to be a philosopher-king, akin to the renowned Roman emperor Marcus Aurelius, and he became one of the first monarchs to personally reflect on the moral duties of kingship. He translated (with assistance) the Psalms and several classical works, most notably Boethius's *Consolations of Philosophy*, to which he added his own reflections. In the thirteenth century, historians began referring to him as "the Great," and in the fifteenth century, there was even an attempt to canonize him, though it was unsuccessful. By the eighteenth century, he was celebrated as a patriot-king of Britain, inspiring the British patriotic song "Rule Britannia," which emerged from the masque and later opera *Alfred* (1740). Alfred became exalted as a symbol of Anglo-Saxon liberties and future imperial greatness, and the Victorians revered him as an ideal Christian ruler, erecting monuments and statues in his honor (Tombs 2016, 33–34).

Was Anglo-Saxon England and the birth of the English autonomous nation ruled under one monarch created during Alfred's time? No. Alfred achieved significant work in uniting the kingdoms of Wessex and Mercia against the Viking invasion and in fostering a unified Anglo-Saxon identity under the title of *rex Angul-Saxonum*. Additionally, it was during Alfred's reign that efforts began on the now-famous *Anglo-Saxon Chronicle*, which he sponsored as a continuation of Bede's *Ecclesiastical History of the English Peoples* (Vincent 2011, 5). While cultural and national identity made substantial progress, geographical issues persisted. England remained divided among the kingdoms of the Anglo-Saxons, Northumbrians, Mercians, Britons, and pagans. The Danes in the northern and eastern regions were unreconciled, and a sense of English "national" solidarity was still lacking. Many nobles and peasants readily allied with or supported the invaders, and when Alfred died in 899, his nephew Aethelwold attempted to enlist Viking support to claim the crown. Despite these challenges, progress continued. In 910, Edward the Elder conquered Danish-ruled areas up to the River Humber and successfully repelled numerous invasions from Scandinavia and the Viking kingdom of Dublin. By 920, all the rulers of Britain collectively recognized Edward the Elder as their "father and lord," a term denoting status rather than dominion. England would ultimately see its long-coveted unification under Edward the Elder's son, Æthelstan, who succeeded him in 924 and subdued the Danish northeast. Æthelstan became paramount king, famously defeating a coalition invasion led by the Dublin Vikings, Britons, and Scots at the Battle of Brunanburh in 937 (possibly located in modern-day Bromborough, Cheshire). This victory solidified Æthelstan's claim as *rex Anglorum* ("King of the English"), a title he was the first to assume, symbolizing the ruler of a unified Britain (Tombs 2016, 34). This pivotal moment not only established Æthelstan's dominance over the British Isles but also laid the groundwork for the future political landscape of England, fostering a sense of shared identity among its diverse peoples.

Despite Æthelstan's notable achievements, he is often overshadowed by his predecessor Alfred, the legendary King Arthur, and his later successor Edward the Confessor. Fortunately for the Anglo-Saxons, the unity they achieved under Æthelstan appeared to be enduring; the kingdom did not fracture into warring principalities, unlike the Carolingian Empire across the Channel, and civil war was averted despite factional conflicts and blood feuds. A potential civil war almost erupted in 1051 but was averted by protests that it was "hateful to men to fight their own kin" and warnings that such conflicts would leave them vulnerable to foreign adversaries poised to seize the opportunity. By the year 1000, the nation had acquired the name "Englalond" and boasted a growing population of over 1.5 million, with roads, bridges, and harbors maintained by royal authority. Investment had also accumulated, resulting in the kingdom having over 6,000 water mills, the most complex machinery of the time, which positioned the English kingdom as one of the richest and most powerful nations in Europe. Alfred's descendants would go on to rule the nation for more than a century (Tombs 2016, 34–38). Unfortunately, this stability also revealed a significant flaw within the kingdom: its inability to provide a secure and orderly succession. When Edward the Confessor, who was Alfred the Great's great-great-grandson, died in 1066, the nation faced its greatest succession challenge yet, ultimately leading to its conquest by a foreign power.

3

THE DEATH OF KING EDWARD THE CONFESSOR

THE NORMAN INVASION OF ENGLAND in 1066 was essentially a war of succession. To understand the root cause of the conflict between Anglo-Saxon England and the Duchy of Normandy under William the Conqueror, it is essential to examine the origins of the succession crisis that arose in 1066. A natural starting point is the reign of the penultimate Anglo-Saxon monarch, King Edward the Confessor, who preceded both William the Conqueror and Harold Godwinson, the latter of whom William would face during the invasion. King Edward, known for his deep piety, a characteristic that earned him the epithet "the Confessor," is often seen as the pivotal figure whose death triggered the succession struggle that would forever alter the power dynamics of Western Europe (Tombs 2016, 42). His passing in January 1066 without a direct heir left a vacuum that sparked competing claims to the English throne, ultimately leading to the Norman Conquest and the reshaping of England's future.

In 2005, Westminster Abbey celebrated the 1000th anniversary of the birth of its founder, King Edward the Confessor, who remains buried in his stone shrine at the heart of the Abbey. However, the exact year of Edward's birth is not precisely known; scholars generally place it sometime after the 1002 marriage of his parents, as he is recorded as a child-witness in a charter from 1005 (Mortimer 2009, ix). In this royal charter, Edward's father, Æthelred, is depicted condemning the Norse Vikings for their relentless raids, which had become a constant threat to his kingdom. Æthelred's reign marked a stark contrast to that of his father, King Edgar, whose rule was regarded as a golden age for the Anglo-Saxons. The Viking attacks during Æthelred's time grew increasingly brutal, and according to the Anglo-Saxon writer Wulfstan, some Englishmen even renounced Christianity in favor of the Norse gods Thor, Odin, and Frey.

The situation deteriorated further when, in 1013, Sweyn Forkbeard, King of Denmark, conquered England, establishing a maritime empire that included Denmark, Norway, and England. Although Æthelred briefly regained the throne after Sweyn's death in 1014, he died shortly after, in April 1016, passing the crown to his son Edmund. Edmund held the throne for only seven months before his death, at which point Cnut, already controlling Danelaw and Mercia, secured the submission of Wessex, marking the beginning of a 26-year period of Danish rule over England, lasting until 1042 (Barlow 1970, 4–36). Edward the Confessor, Æthelred's son, was born into this turbulent period. His mother, Queen Emma, was the daughter of Richard I, Duke of Normandy, and her Norman lineage introduced a lasting Norman interest in the English crown. The initial aim was for one of Emma's children to rule England, but since both of her sons died childless, the Norman ambitions had to adapt to new circumstances (Barlow 1970, 7). When Cnut, then a Danish prince, conquered the Anglo-Saxon kingdom in 1016, Edward and his brother Alfred were forced to flee to their maternal uncle, Duke Richard II of Normandy. According to the *Inventio et miracula sancti Vulfranni*, written at Saint-Wandrille in the early 1050s, Duke Richard welcomed the brothers warmly, treating them as if they were his own sons (van Houts 2009, 64). Meanwhile, their mother, Emma, returned to England in 1017 and married Cnut, the very man who had usurped her former husband, Æthelred. This marriage was not considered scandalous by the nobility or the church, as political marriages of this nature were commonplace during that period. The union offered mutual benefits: Cnut gained a crucial alliance with Normandy, exerted some control over Æthelred's sons, and drew on Emma's experience in ruling the Anglo-Saxon kingdom. In turn, Emma retained her queenship and could influence events to protect her sons in Normandy. However, it was likely stipulated in Emma's marriage contract that the succession of England and Denmark would favor any children she had with Cnut, rather than her sons from her previous marriage to Æthelred (Barlow 1970, 37).

The earliest contemporary source that references Edward the Confessor is the *Encomium Emmae*, a work commissioned by Edward's mother, Queen Emma, around 1041, after Edward returned to England following the death of his half-brother, King Harthacnut. Edward grew up in turbulent times, as the *Encomium* notes, highlighting the Danish invasions and subsequent conquest of England under Cnut the Great, whose sons, Harthacnut and Harold Harefoot, succeeded him as kings of England, alongside their mother, Queen Emma (Mortimer 2009, 1–2). According to the *Encomium*, Edward had been sent to Normandy as a child, where he was raised with his brother Alfred. The text recounts a chilling plot devised by King Harold Harefoot to eliminate his half-siblings. Harold forged a letter, purportedly from Emma, asking one of her sons to return to England to help her overthrow the usurping king. Alfred responded to this false call, sailing to England with a small force from Boulogne. Upon arrival, Alfred was intercepted by Earl Godwin of Wessex, who imprisoned him and his men. Under the cover of night, Godwin left Alfred under minimal guard, allowing Harold's men to capture him. The next morning, Alfred's men were either killed or enslaved, while Alfred himself was taken to Ely, where he was humiliated, put on trial, blinded, and subsequently murdered. Edward, on the other hand, remained cautious. The *Encomium* records another instance in which Emma fled to Flanders after Harold seized power, seeking Edward's assistance. However, Edward refused to help, citing his lack of authority and legitimate claim to the throne, as the English nobles had not yet sworn allegiance to him. He advised his mother to seek help from his half-brother Harthacnut, the son of Emma and Cnut. Ironically, soon after these events, Harold Harefoot died, enabling Emma to return to England with Harthacnut, who was crowned as the new king (Mortimer 2009, 2–3).

Despite Harthacnut's ascension to the throne in his early twenties on the 17th of March 1040, the Norman guardians of the young Duke William continued to support Edward's claim. Notably, a charter for Mont Saint-Michel, which was unfortunately destroyed during World War II in 1944, referred to Edward as "king." This title was likely a deliberate move by Duke William's guardians, not only to promote Edward as a legitimate ruler but also to signal his ambitions for the throne, making his aspirations known on both sides of the English Channel (D. Bates 2016, 66–67). However, Harthacnut's reign was brief; he died in 1042, likely from illness or a stroke, at the age of 24 (Barlow 1970, 27). Harthacnut's death marked the end of the Danish line of kings in England. With Cnut dying in 1035, Harold Harefoot in 1040, and Harthacnut in 1042, Edward the Confessor claimed the throne through his birthright (Neveux 2006, 129). One of the key contemporary Norman sources detailing these events is William of Jumièges' chronicle. As a monk at Jumièges in the Seine valley, William extended and updated the *History of the Normans* by Dudo of Saint-Quentin in the 1050s. He likely used information from Robert, abbot of Jumièges, one of Edward's Norman companions who accompanied him to England in 1042, became bishop of London in 1044, and later archbishop of Canterbury in 1051 before fleeing back to Normandy that same year. Though vague on many details of Edward's rule, William of Jumièges provides significant insights into key events that shaped his reign. For instance, he accuses Earl Godwin of treachery for betraying Edward's brother Alfred by handing him over to Harold Harefoot, though Harold was ultimately responsible for Alfred's death. William of Jumièges also recounts that Harthacnut allowed Edward to return from Normandy and live with him following his ascension to the throne in 1040 (Mortimer 2009, 4).

While little is known about Edward's long exile in Normandy from King Cnut's ascension to the English throne in 1016 and until King Harold Harefoot's death in 1040, his rule in England for the next 24 years from 1042 until his death in 1066 would prove to be decisive for the future of the Anglo-Saxon Kingdom. One question would continue to plague the nobility of England, as well as her foreign neighbors, during King Edward's reign as monarch: who would succeed him? And even more significantly, whom did Edward favor as his successor? William of Malmesbury addressed this issue in his *Gesta Regum Anglorum* in 1120s, where he concluded that the evidence was so problematic that he felt compelled to inform his audience of the difficulties that it posed by addressing that he himself was somewhat in doubt as to what truly happened given how vastly different the Anglo-Saxon and the Norman sources presented their facts. Malmesbury directly noted that "it is of these differences of opinion which, as I have said, put my narrative at risk, since I cannot decide what precisely is the truth." This has since proven to be quote accurate, as the English and Norman sources differ vastly, and many scholars argue that it is impossible to determine the truth of who Edward wanted to succeed him as king and the subject has since then become a great controversy in English history (Baxter 2009, 77).

Upon Harthacnut's death, Edward the Confessor was summoned from Normandy and swiftly crowned king by the Archbishops of Canterbury and York. His coronation was met with widespread approval, as the English population celebrated, and rulers in Germany and France offered high praise. The only notable opposition came from King Magnus of Norway and Denmark, who allegedly sent Edward a letter warning of his intentions to invade England with Viking forces (Larsen 2015, 114). However, Magnus became preoccupied with a civil war against Sweyn II in Denmark (Mortimer 2009, 8), preventing any immediate threat. Despite initial support for Edward's accession, tensions soon arose within the English monarchy, particularly with Earl Godwin of Wessex. Godwin had gained prominence as a chief advisor to King Cnut but now sought to expand his influence under Edward's reign. Although Godwin had backed Edward's rise to power, their relationship became strained, even after Edward married Godwin's daughter Edith in 1044 (Tombs 2016, 41–42). Edward and Earl Godwin maintained a tenuous relationship, largely due to Godwin's involvement in the death of Edward's brother during Harold Harefoot's reign. The House of Godwin was a source of significant turmoil, exemplified by the scandal in 1046 when Earl Sweyn abducted the abbess of Leominster in an attempt to marry her, which led to his exile. After returning in 1049, he murdered his cousin Beorn in a failed bid to reclaim his earldom, resulting in another exile, though he was restored by 1050. In 1047, Earl Godwin sought military support from Edward for his nephew, the future King Sweyn of Denmark, in a conflict against King Magnus; however, Edward declined the request. He also rejected Godwin's later plea to appoint a kinsman as archbishop of Canterbury, instead selecting the Norman monk Robert Champart. The mounting tensions between Godwin and Edward nearly erupted into civil war in September 1051, ultimately leading to Godwin and his sons being exiled, while Edward's wife and Godwin's daughter, Edith, was sent to a nunnery (Baxter 2009, 86). This crisis provided Edward with a chance to rebalance power within his kingdom, reducing his reliance on the House of Godwin (Baxter 2009, 86–87). Godwin eventually returned as earl when he and his son Harold sailed a fleet up the Thames, compelling King Edward to restore their earldoms and Edith as queen. In William of Poitiers's work, *Gesta Guillelmi*, he claims this was the moment Edward began to contemplate new succession plans. By this time, Duke Robert I of Normandy had been succeeded by his son William, and Edward had not forgotten the support he received from his Norman kin during Harold Harefoot's rule. Consequently, Edward designated Duke William of Normandy as his heir and arranged for prominent figures in England to pledge allegiance to William upon Edward's death. This agreement was initially conveyed by Robert, the Norman archbishop of Canterbury. To further secure this arrangement, Edward, wary of Earl Godwin's treachery, ensured that Wulfnoth, Godwin's son and brother to the future King Harold Godwinson, along with Hákon, Godwin's grandson, were taken as hostages to the Normans to guarantee peace. Edward also had Harold Godwinson affirm this grant with an oath, and during a visit to Normandy, Harold purportedly swore fealty to Duke William to uphold his claim upon Edward's death. However, it is essential to note that *Gesta Guillelmi* was written by the pro–Norman William of Poitiers in the 1070s to laud Duke William and legitimize his conquest of England in 1066. Furthermore, Norman historians disagree on the details of the oath's location—whether it was at Rouen, Bonneville-sur-Touques, or Bayeux—and whether it occurred before or after Harold's campaign in Brittany, leaving the nature of the ceremony, public or private, unspecified (McLynn 199, 170–171).

There is compelling evidence that Edward the Confessor favored his Norman counterparts, as charters issued by Duke Robert of Normandy indicate that the Normans regarded Edward as an expatriate king, likely intensifying his sense of gratitude toward the ducal house. Additionally, Edward had failed to produce an heir with his wife, Edith, and had severed ties with the house of Godwin, making it imperative for him to seek new allies to strengthen his regime (Baxter 2009, 87–96). However, neither Harold Godwinson nor Duke William appeared to be Edward's initial choice for succession.

The sudden death of Earl Godwin on April 15, 1053, likely delighted King Edward, who swiftly seized the opportunity to reorganize his earldoms by granting Harold Godwinson his father's earldom in Wessex while giving East Anglia to Ælfgar, son of Leofric, Earl of Mercia, thereby creating a more balanced power dynamic among the earls. Furthermore, Edward reached out to Edward "the Exile," the son of the former Anglo-Saxon King Edmund "Ironside," who had died in 1016. After Cnut the Great's conquest of England, Edmund Ironside's sons, Edward and Edmund, were exiled and eventually found refuge at the royal court in Hungary. As a direct descendant of Alfred the Great and the West Saxon royal line, Edward was classified as an "ætheling," a title denoting eligibility for kingship. By 1054, Edward the Exile and his son Edgar were the last surviving æthelings, and in 1057, Edward the Exile returned to England, where he died under mysterious circumstances shortly after his arrival. This left Edgar Ætheling, around five years old in 1057, as King Edward's only hope for a successor from his own dynasty. However, Edgar was notably absent from the witness list of royal diplomas issued during the last nine years of Edward's reign, indicating that he was "marginalized" in the king's final years. This suggests that Edward either chose to abandon the idea of naming Edgar as his successor or was compelled to do so due to shifting political dynamics, particularly the resurgence of the house of Godwin.

Between 1055 and 1059, Edward appointed three of Harold Godwinson's brothers as earls, leading to a significant shift in power back toward the Godwins, despite Godwin's death in 1053. Tostig became Earl of Northumbria, Harold absorbed the earldom of the former Earl Odda in the southwest Midlands, and Leofwine succeeded Earl Ralph's earldom in the southeast Midlands. By 1059, the Godwin family controlled nearly all of England's earldoms, raising questions about why Edward allowed this consolidation of power. Evidence suggests that Edward began withdrawing from political life around this time, as described in the Vita Ædwardi Regis ("The Life of King Edward"), which states that while Harold and Tostig maintained peace in the realm, Edward focused on caring for the poor and infirm and indulging in leisure activities like hunting and prayer. This withdrawal is further illustrated by the annals of 1063, which record that Earl Harold and Tostig subdued Wales, culminating in the death of the Welsh king Gruffudd ap Llewellyn, whose severed head Harold brought to Edward as proof of their military success (Baxter 2009, 96–106). However, according to Norman sources, Edward was sufficiently

3. The Death of King Edward the Confessor

powerful and, prior to his death, summoned Harold to Normandy in the early summer of 1064 to reaffirm his oath to William.

The English perspective on Harold's visit to Normandy emerged much later, through the writings of the Canterbury monk Eadmer in the early twelfth century. Eadmer claimed that Harold went to Normandy against King Edward's wishes to negotiate the return of the Godwin hostages, who had been held since Earl Godwin's exile in 1051. While setting sail, Harold encountered a storm that forced him off course, resulting in his shipwreck and capture by Count Guy of Ponthieu. With Duke William's intervention, Harold was released but learned of Edward's promise to William regarding succession. He was compelled to swear an oath to Duke William in exchange for his nephew's release, while his brother's freedom was contingent upon William's coronation. Facing limited options, Harold agreed and returned to England with his nephew. Upon Harold's return, Edward was reportedly furious and exclaimed, "Did I not tell you that I knew William, and that your going might bring untold calamity upon this kingdom?" (Baxter 2009, 108; Lawson 2003, 26–30). The twelfth-century Anglo-Norman writer Orderic Vitalis presents a contrasting narrative, asserting that upon Harold's return, he deceived King Edward by claiming that Duke William had offered him his daughter in marriage and renounced his claim to the English throne in favor of his new son-in-law. William of Malmesbury, who was familiar with both the Norman and Eadmer's accounts, recounts that Harold ostensibly embarked on a fishing expedition in the English Channel, was blown off course to Ponthieu, and imprisoned by Count Guy, where he convinced Duke William to release him by falsely asserting that he had been sent to Normandy to confirm King Edward's promise. While there is a general consensus among various accounts—Norman, English, or otherwise—that Harold did visit William in Normandy, discerning the truth among these narratives proves challenging, particularly when considering the impact of the Norman Conquest in 1066 on later writings.

Nevertheless, on January 5, 1066, King Edward the Confessor succumbed to illness. Harold Godwinson possessed a tenuous hereditary claim to the throne, being related to Edward solely through his sister's marriage to the king; however, the Godwinson family had fortified their influence within the English realm. John of Worcester, writing several decades later, notes that Harold was named successor prior to Edward's death and was subsequently elected by the principal men of England as monarch. According to The Life of King Edward, written at the behest of Edward's wife, Edith, during Edward's final moments, four individuals were present: his wife, the queen, her brother Earl Harold, Robert the steward of the palace, and Archbishop Stigand. Edward addressed Harold, instructing him to protect both his wife and kingdom. The interpretation of this moment as Edward designating Harold as his heir or merely reiterating Harold's duty to safeguard the realm remains subjective. Additionally, The Life of King Edward was completed after the Norman Conquest, thus colored by hindsight. The iconic Bayeux Tapestry visually narrates the events surrounding Edward's death but notably omits mention of those present at his deathbed, instead depicting Edward addressing his most loyal subjects (Baxter 2009, 115–116).

The set of related annals now known as the Anglo-Saxon Chronicle, particularly in the manuscripts referred to as C, D, and E, also references Edward's purported deathbed speech. These manuscripts are interrelated in complex ways, and their discussions continue today. Often, versions C and D echo each other with similar or identical phrasing, while D and E share some overlaps yet diverge at other points. Additionally, these chronicles are marked by vagueness and significant gaps, with certain years—such as 1064—receiving no coverage at all. The location where these annals were composed remains a topic of debate among historians. However, the C version's manuscript can be traced back to Edward's reign, having been initially written in 1044 and subsequently updated in 1045, 1047, and 1048, with further entries extending until 1065 and then again after the Battle of Hastings in 1066. Notably, the poem in versions C and D indicates that Edward "entrusted" his realm to Harold, while a comment in E states that he granted it to Harold.

According to Anglo-Saxon law, a deathbed bequest, referred to as *verba novissima* ("the latest words"), was considered significant and could supersede earlier claims to the same property, thereby nullifying them. Viewed from this legal standpoint, Harold's claim to the succession after Edward could be regarded as legitimate (Baxter 2009, 115–116). Later Norman chroniclers emphasized the importance of legitimizing power through royal consecration, a focus that not only supported William's claim to the English throne after his conquest in 1066 but also posed a challenge in discrediting Harold, who had also been crowned king. William of Poitiers put forth several arguments against Harold's coronation, suggesting that the ceremony had lacked legitimacy due to the sparse attendance of nobles—an implausible scenario given the Christmas court and the consecration of the new abbey church at Westminster. He further contended that Archbishop Stigand, the last surviving oath-taker from 1051 to 1052, had been stripped of his "priestly ministry" by a papal curse, thereby invalidating his anointing of Harold and implying that Harold's coronation lacked divine approval. However, the prevailing consensus among historians is that Archbishop Ealdred of York, rather than Stigand, was the individual responsible for performing Harold's coronation. While Stigand appears next to King Harold in the Bayeux Tapestry, he is not depicted conducting the coronation; rather, Harold is shown post-coronation, with the crown already on his head. The rapidity of Harold's coronation, which took place on January 6, 1066, just one day after Edward the Confessor's death, also raised suspicions, as no previous king had been so hasty; typically, coronations would occur months after the ascension to the throne, as evidenced by Edward, who succeeded in the summer of 1042 but was not crowned until Easter of the following year.

It can be assumed that Harold anticipated conflict with Duke William of Normandy, but his quick coronation likely aimed to quell domestic opposition within England rather than preempt an invasion, which would have required greater preparation. Harold's concerns were validated when the Northumbrian population, as noted in William of Malmesbury's twelfth-century biography *The Life of Wulfstan*, initially refused to accept him as king. Alongside Wulfstan, Harold traveled to York shortly before Easter 1066, where he successfully rallied the Northumbrian populace at a gemot, an Anglo-Saxon gathering, to unite against the impending invasions from both Earl Tostig and Harald Hardrada of Norway, as well as Duke William. With Harold's coronation came considerable turmoil, making it clear to the Norman Duchy that conquest was the only means to secure the English throne (Morris 2013, 132–142). This urgency for unity against external threats not only solidified Harold's position as king but also set the stage for the tumultuous events that would soon follow, culminating in the pivotal battles that would determine the fate of England.

In summary, the primary issue that precipitated the invasion of England in 1066 was the contentious question of succession following the death of King Edward the Confessor and who would inherit the Anglo-Saxon Kingdom of England. The Normans, through their blood connection with Queen Emma, the sister of Richard II, Duke of Normandy, and the great-granddaughter of the Viking Rollo, positioned themselves as legitimate contenders for the throne. In contrast, the house of Godwin wielded significant power within the English realm, having established an almost absolute monopoly over it and purportedly being promised a similar right to succeed Edward upon his death. This clash of claims between the Normans and the Godwins not only highlighted the intricacies of dynastic ties and political maneuvering but also set the stage for the dramatic events that would unfold in 1066, ultimately leading to the Norman Conquest.

4

THE NORTHUMBRIAN REBELLION OF 1065

THE DEATH OF EDWARD THE CONFESSOR on January 5 had a profound impact on the ensuing conflicts of 1066, but prior to this pivotal event, another significant occurrence known as the Rebellion in Northumbria would prove disastrous for Harold Godwinson's claim to the throne. By 1055, the earldom of Northumbria was under the rule of Earl Siward, who, from an Anglo-Saxon perspective, was far from the ideal earl due to his Danish origins, raising concerns about his loyalty to King Edward in the face of foreign or domestic threats. Although Earl Siward had risen to power under King Cnut, Edward allowed him to maintain control of his earldom when he ascended the throne in 1042, likely due to the political difficulties of removing him without inciting significant conflict. The removal of one earl would also potentially bolster the power of neighboring earls. Consequently, the ever-present threat of Earl Siward defecting to the opposing side in the event of a Danish invasion lingered in the background. Nevertheless, Earl Siward was preoccupied with monitoring the Danes of York and repelling Scottish raids, which kept him engaged in his duties (Kapelle 1979, 27–29). His modern legacy is perhaps best captured in Shakespeare's play *Macbeth*, where he plays a crucial role in the battles against the Scottish king, reflecting his significant historical impact (Kapelle 1979, 46–47). Following his victorious campaign against Macbeth, Earl Siward returned to England with considerable gains but died a year later in 1055 at York. Despite his success in the war against the Scots, the victory came at a significant cost, as both Siward's nephew, the younger Siward, and his eldest son, Osbeorn, were killed in battle, leaving no adult heir to inherit his earldom upon his death (Kapelle 1979, 48–49).

Until this point, most earls of Northumbria had been of Anglo-Danish or Scandinavian descent, and a West Saxon had never directly ruled over the northern earldom. However, in 1055, this practice came to an end with the appointment of Tostig, the younger brother of Harold

Godwinson and the third son of Earl Godwin, as Earl of Northumbria. Tostig, born around 1029 to Earl Godwin and Gyða of Denmark, first appears in the Anglo-Saxon Chronicle, which records that he commanded one of Edward the Confessor's ships against Count Baldwin V of Flanders in 1049 (DeVries 1999, 169). This appointment marked a significant shift in the power dynamics of Northumbria, as the Godwin family sought to consolidate their influence in the region amidst the growing political tensions that would soon erupt into open conflict following Edward's death. Despite being half Danish through his mother, Tostig's primary Danish characteristic was his name, and he was not known to have any connection with the old ruling family of Northumbria and was by consequence seen as an outsider in the North. As to why Tostig was appointed earl, it is likely due to the influence of his family, with his brother Harold ruling as earl of Wessex and his sister as queen. In addition, there was likely a wish to integrate the North more closely into the rest of the Anglo-Saxon kingdom (Kapelle 1979, 88–89).

Tostig would find himself in quite a predicament as he took over the unstable position as earl of Northumbria. While Earl Siward was not universally liked in his earldom, he did seem to possess a significant amount of charisma that left behind a notable legacy. One such example is a thirteenth-century manuscript from Crowland Abbey in Lincolnshire that describes Earl Siward in a style akin to the Icelandic sagas. Earl Siward is depicted as a fierce warrior who would hunt and slay literal dragons while also besting a man named Tostig in combat. While this is most certainly a mythological tale given the supernatural elements and Tostig succeeding Tostig as earl rather than preceding and losing his life in a fight against him, the tale serves as a structured account of how Earl Siward rose to power and obtained his earldom in England. The oral narrative underlying this written piece of work was likely composed after Siward's death, which would serve as a testament to his legacy as a fierce and respected leader (Parker 2014, 481–486). Given the reputation of his predecessor and the qualities demanded by his subjects, it is unsurprising that Tostig would find himself in an unstable position ruling as the earl of Northumbria. Indeed, as Tostig began his rule, he would turn the traditional resentments and the passive disloyalty of his subjects into an actual rebellion. Tostig had been chosen over the youngest of Earl Siward's sons, Waltheof, as well as Cospatric, the eldest surviving member of the Bamburgh family, which had ruled Northumbria before Earl Siward (Kapelle 1979, 87–88).

Tostig faced a series of disastrous decisions, such as choosing an extremely unpopular bishop in Durham and facing fierce raids from Scotland, which had been largely united under King Malcolm III, who had succeeded Macbeth. Rather than retaliate against the Scottish raids, Tostig chose to seek negotiations with the Scots, which many may have seen as a sign of weakness (Kapelle 1979, 89–92). This was a much different approach compared to his predecessor Earl Siward, who had utilized a strong military presence combined with intimidation tactics to keep the Scots away from the English border. Additionally, he had entered into a Scottish civil war in 1054 by supporting Malcolm against the then–Scottish king, Macbeth, who had usurped the throne from Malcolm's father, Duncan, fourteen years prior (173–174). While Tostig achieved a diplomatic victory at a summit with Malcolm in 1059, Malcolm chose to invade Cumberland and raid Northumberland in 1061 while Tostig was away on a trip to Rome with his archbishop. Surprisingly, Tostig accepted the loss of Cumberland and traveled to Scotland to make peace with Malcolm, resulting in an agreement that left Malcolm in possession of Cumberland and marked an end to Earl Siward's earlier efforts to create a strong defensible border in the North (Kapelle 1979, 93–94).

While it certainly seems strange that a vigorous, warlike man like Tostig, who was seemingly not afraid of engaging in military conflict, would accept such terms, it may well have been possible that his hold over the North was so weak that it would be too risky for him to engage in an invasion of Scotland. The Northumbrians would eventually rise against Tostig for many of the aforementioned reasons. Florence of Worcester, an English chronicler of the eleventh–twelfth century known for his chronicle of English history entitled *Chronicon ex Chronicis*, notes that the northerners rose against Tostig as vengeance for his alleged murder of three important Northumbrian nobles in 1063. At this point, Tostig had supposedly had two of these nobles assassinated in his own chamber at York while they were visiting him under a safe-conduct, and he later had the third noble murdered in 1064 at the king's Christmas court. Some of these nobles were collaborators of Earl Siward and members of the house of Bamburgh, which would have given them a legitimate claim to the earldom of Northumbria, possibly prompting their assassination. Furthermore, according to King Edward's biographer, many men argued that Tostig had exploited the courts to amass wealth. Florence adds that Tostig had supposedly collected enormous taxes contrary to the customary practices in the North, and it is widely accepted that taxation was one of the primary reasons for the revolt (Kapelle 1979, 94–96). As a result, Tostig's actions not only alienated key local leaders but also fueled widespread discontent among the general populace, leading to a significant breakdown of trust in his leadership.

When examining ancient texts on this matter, the *Anglo-Saxon Chronicles* serve as an excellent source. This collection of historical documents, written in Old Anglo-Saxon English, chronicles the history of the

4. The Northumbrian Rebellion of 1065

Anglo-Saxons from around the 9th to the twelfth century. It is important to note that the Chronicles were authored by different writers over multiple centuries, resulting in a decentralized production where events may be described repetitively from varying perspectives. Despite this, the various manuscripts within the Anglo-Saxon Chronicles universally agree on the emergence of the rebellion in Northumbria under Earl Tostig, indicating the event's significance in Anglo-Saxon history. The Peterborough Manuscript, a major version of the Chronicles, explains that in 1064, the Northumbrians united to outlaw their earl Tostig, killing all men in his court, regardless of their English or Danish origins. They seized his weapons in York and looted his gold, silver, and any other valuables. Following this uprising, they sent for Morcar, son of Earl Ælfgar, and elected him as their new earl (Swanton 2000, 190). The Worcester Manuscript and The Abingdon Manuscript convey essentially the same account regarding the rebellion in Tostig's earldom (Swanton 2000, 190–191). The Abingdon Manuscript further details that after the rebellion, a significant meeting was convened at Northampton and Oxford, where Earl Harold sought reconciliation but ultimately failed. Consequently, Tostig's earldom unanimously deserted him and anyone who aligned with him due to his reportedly harsh policies, with descriptions of him "despoiling the life and land of all those he had power over." Morcar was then elected as earl, and Tostig went into exile with his wife, initially seeking refuge with Baldwin, the Count of Flanders (Swanton 2000, 192). This uprising in 1065 not only marked a turning point for Tostig but also set the stage for the tumultuous events of 1066, culminating in the Norman invasion.

The *Anglo-Saxon Chronicles* provide an accurate but somewhat superficial account of the Northumbrian rebellion's origins and development. To elaborate, the revolt began on October 3, 1065, during Tostig's absence from the North, when a group of insurgent thegns launched a surprise attack on York. The men in York quickly joined the revolt, uniting to slay the leaders of Tostig's housecarls as they attempted to flee the city. Following this, as noted in the Anglo-Saxon Chronicles, Tostig lost all his treasury, money, and weapons to the rebels, likely suffering significant losses in his command structure due to the elimination of many important subordinates. Subsequently, the rebels outlawed Tostig, elected Morcar as their new earl, and marched south, their forces growing along the way. Upon reaching Northampton, Morcar's brother Edwin joined them, merging an army from his earldom with some Welsh auxiliaries into the rebel army, creating a formidable force that compelled King Edward to negotiate with the rebels through Tostig's older brother, Earl Harold. By the month's end, King Edward and Earl Harold accepted the rebels' demands, consenting to Morcar's appointment as earl of Northumbria (Kapelle 1979, 98–99). Although

Morcar had no clear connection to either Earl Siward or the house of Bamburgh, he appeared to be a suitable compromise for the Northumbrians, who desired a representative of the house of Bamburgh as earl, and for the Yorkshiremen, who favored Earl Siward's younger son Waltheof as their ruler. Additionally, under Morcar, Osulf of Bamburgh was granted rule over Northumbria, while Waltheof seemingly received Northampton and Huntingdon. Thus, the revolt of 1065 represented a conservative reaction against the changes the English monarchy sought to impose by appointing Tostig as earl, transferring power back to the traditional ruling families from the house of Bamburgh and Earl Siward's lineage (Kapelle 1979, 101). This pivotal moment in Northumbrian history marked a significant shift in local governance, reinforcing the desire for leadership that resonated with the traditional values and lineage of the region.

The *Vita Ædwardi* portrays the Northumbrian uprising negatively, characterizing Tostig's leadership as assertive and just, praising his loyalty to King Edward and dedication to the royal courts, which explained his frequent absences from Northumbria. In this account, the Northumbrian rebels are depicted as savagely rash and wicked, destroying Tostig's properties with fire and sword. Tostig is credited with establishing peace and justice in a previously lawless earldom (Dockray-Miller 2021, 292). However, it is important to consider that the *Vita Ædwardi* was commissioned by King Edward's wife, Edith—Tostig's sister—suggesting a bias in its favorable portrayal of him. In contrast, historians like William of Malmesbury align with the rebels, accusing Tostig of "habitual ferocity" and framing the Northerners' actions as a declaration of their status as free men, rooted in their traditions (Dockray-Miller 2021, 294). These contrasting narratives highlight the complexities of Tostig's rule and the deeply rooted tensions between Northumbria and the southern elite, illustrating how historical perspectives can shape our understanding of leadership and rebellion.

The ousting of Tostig Godwinson as earl of Northumbria and his subsequent exile ignited a bitter conflict between him and his older brother, Harold Godwinson, which is chronicled in various contemporary sources that offer differing perspectives, some sympathizing with Tostig while others favor Harold (DeVries 1999, 168). Tostig's frustration was palpable, particularly because he had previously provided critical support to Harold during his successful campaign against the Welsh king Gruffudd ap Llywelyn in 1063, which resulted in Gruffudd's head being presented to King Edward in London (DeVries 1999, 176–177). Chronicles by John of Worcester, William of Malmesbury, and the *Vita Ædwardi* assert that King Edward initially refused to depose Tostig and that Harold attempted to suppress the rebellion with military force. However, the sheer size and ferocity of the Northumbrian rebel army proved overwhelming, as they ravaged the countryside and violently coerced those who resisted joining their cause. Ultimately, Tostig, filled with anger, was compelled to leave England on November 1, 1065 (DeVries 1999, 180–181). This familial discord not only highlighted the tensions within the Godwinson family but also set the stage for the tumultuous events that would follow in the lead-up to the Norman Conquest.

After Tostig's exile, he found himself without a title or income, making it difficult to support his household. His first course of action was to travel to Flanders with his wife Judith, where they were warmly welcomed by Count Baldwin V, who provided them with a house, an estate, and a battalion of knights. Baldwin also appointed Tostig as the castellan of St. Omer, a position that required him to defend the town as part of Baldwin's territory while allowing him to collect taxes and maintain a degree of power and income (Dockray-Miller 2021, 291–295). Initially exiled in November 1065 while Edward the Confessor was still alive, Tostig likely hoped to make a powerful return and regain his position. However, following Edward's death on January 5, 1066, and Harold Godwinson's coronation, Tostig's ambitions expanded, leading him to covet the English throne, even if he did not intend to claim it himself. In the spring and early summer of 1066, Tostig attempted to establish a stronghold in southern England, but his small-scale invasion ended in chaotic raids along the English coast, which further diminished any support he may have once had in England. Recognizing the futility of his efforts, Tostig likely understood that he would need to seek foreign assistance to return to England and reclaim a legitimate seat of power in his homeland (Dockray-Miller 2021, 297). Tostig eventually expanded his raids into the north, prompting Morcar, the new earl of Northumbria, and his brother Edwin, the earl of Mercia, to mobilize their forces against him. In response, Tostig retreated further into Scotland before ultimately abandoning the English kingdom to return to mainland Europe. According to Orderic Vitalis, Tostig sought to ally himself with Duke William of Normandy, pledging his loyal support in securing the English crown. Vitalis claimed that Tostig and Duke William were good friends due to their wives being sisters, a statement that is inaccurate; Tostig's wife Judith was the daughter of Count Baldwin IV of Flanders, while Duke William's wife Matilda was the daughter of his son, Count Baldwin V of Flanders (Rex 2011, 34). Duke William convened his Norman nobility to discuss the situation, while Tostig attempted to return to England from the coast of Normandy on William's behalf but was thwarted by adverse weather that forced him towards Norway (Dockray-Miller 2021, 298–299). It is important to note that Orderic Vitalis wrote his accounts nearly a century after the conquest, and discrepancies exist regarding how

Tostig ended up in Norway and whose assistance he sought for an invasion of England. Snorri Sturluson, in the 78th chapter of his saga of Harald Hardrada, asserts that Tostig traveled to Denmark after leaving northern France, seeking help from King Sweyn II of Denmark. Tostig's journey took him across the Lower Lorraine and Friesland, eventually reaching Bremen and then the Elbe, proceeding through North Saxony until arriving at the Danish frontier. Despite Tostig's insistence on a collaborative invasion to dethrone Harold Godwinson, King Sweyn showed little enthusiasm for the proposal, though he offered Tostig a substantial earldom in Denmark should he choose to remain. Tostig, unsatisfied, pressed Sweyn further, promising to support his claim as King of England and his legacy as a descendant of Cnut the Great. Sweyn's humble retort highlighted his struggle to consolidate his power in Denmark against Norwegian attacks, contrasting his precarious position with Cnut's more fortunate circumstances. Tostig's ungracious reaction to Sweyn's honest assessment resulted in their departure on unfriendly terms (Butler 1966, 66). Notably, despite Sweyn's initial refusal in 1066, he would later launch his own invasion of England in 1069–1070, ultimately facing defeat against the Anglo-Norman forces (Rex 2011, 34–35). Following his unsuccessful attempts to forge an alliance with the Danes, Snorri Sturluson records that Tostig continued northward to seek out King Harald Hardrada in Norway (Sturluson [c. 1230] 1964, 643–644). Regardless of whether one subscribes to Vitalis' narrative, Sturluson's account, or another perspective, it is clear that Tostig Godwinson ultimately arrived at Harald Hardrada's court to discuss the possibility of invading England.

During Tostig's visit, which likely took place in late 1065 or early 1066, he successfully rekindled the warrior spirit in Hardrada, persuading him that England was ripe for conquest. This campaign would not only enable Harald Hardrada to expand his empire but also serve as a form of retribution against Cnut the Great, who had slain Hardrada's brother and seized Norway at the battle of Stiklarstaðir in 1030. Moreover, Hardrada resented that Cnut had allowed England to slip back into Anglo-Saxon hands following Edward the Confessor's coronation in 1042 (DeVries 1999, 67). In a show of loyalty, Tostig swore fealty to Hardrada as his subordinate, agreeing to recognize Hardrada's claim to the English throne should the invasion prove successful (Dockray-Miller 2021, 299). Thus, it appears that Tostig's motivations were heavily influenced by a desire for vengeance against his brother Harold Godwinson, who he believed had betrayed him following his loss of the Northumbrian earldom. Tostig's quest for vengeance was not merely a personal vendetta but also a pivotal moment that would set in motion the events leading to the tumultuous year of 1066, ultimately reshaping the course of English history.

5

THE NORWEGIAN INVASION OF ENGLAND IN 1066

TOSTIG'S ALLEGIANCE TO HARALD Hardrada laid the groundwork for the Norwegian invasion of England in 1066, a pivotal moment in the power struggle for the English throne between its Anglo-Saxon ruler and the Norman and Norwegian claimants. This invasion is often seen by historians as the final chapter of the Viking Age, as its failure, combined with the subsequent Anglo-Saxon victory, marked a significant turning point. To fully understand this event within the broader context of England's history of invasions over the preceding two centuries, one must consider the intricate royal ties that connected England not only to Normandy but also to Denmark and Norway. These connections contributed to the complex web of claims on the English throne. Viking raids on the British Isles, which began as early as 793 with the devastating sack of Lindisfarne, are well documented in sources like the *Annals of Ulster* and the *Anglo-Saxon Chronicle*. These records detail the havoc wrought by Norse raiders on coastal monasteries and settlements across northern Britain and Ireland, including Iona, Rechru, Skye, and others (Katherine 2007, 32–33). The onset of Viking naval invasions in the late eighth century can be attributed to practical motivations rather than the divine punishment perceived by the monks of Lindisfarne at the time. Monasteries like Lindisfarne were dual-purpose sites, functioning as both treasure houses and places of worship, but were poorly defended and located in isolated areas, making them prime targets for opportunistic Viking raiders. Alcuin, a Northumbrian monk and scholar serving under Charlemagne, wrote extensively about the raid on Lindisfarne in 793, describing how the monks were caught entirely off guard as the Viking raiders slaughtered many, drowned others, and looted the monastery's treasures (Lyons 2021, 26). This attack is widely regarded as the beginning of the Viking Age, a period lasting roughly two and a half centuries during which Scandinavian Vikings dominated the northern seas and executed numerous successful and brutal invasions across Europe. The Viking Age is also closely tied to Scandinavia's eventual claims to the English throne, paralleling the naval strategies that would later be employed by Duke William of Normandy.

Initially motivated by wealth, Viking raiders like those who attacked Lindisfarne soon shifted their ambitions towards acquiring political power and land. Over time, many Vikings, particularly from Denmark, began settling in England and subjugating large portions of the country, especially north of the Thames. This led to the establishment of "Danelaw," a region governed by Danes independent of West Saxon rule. As Denmark itself underwent Christianization under King Harald Bluetooth around 965, as evidenced by the inscriptions on the Great Stone of Jelling (Lausten 2002, 3), Danish settlers in England began to integrate into Anglo-Saxon culture. This process of integration saw Danelaw absorbed into the Kingdom of Wessex by the turn of the millennium (Vincent 2011, 7). However, tensions remained, as Anglo-Saxon rulers viewed Danelaw as a threat to their authority, culminating in the infamous St. Brice's Day Massacre of 1002.

By 1002, England was ruled by King Æthelred II, also known as Æthelred "the Unready," an epithet given to him due to the misinterpretation of the Old English term *"unræd,"* meaning "poorly advised" or "ill-counseled." Rather than suggesting that Æthelred was unprepared, the nickname was a pun on his name, as Æthelred means "noble counsel" or "well-advised." The irony in the epithet reflects the perception that he frequently made ill-advised decisions during his reign, particularly in his handling of Viking invasions and internal political crises, such as his reliance on paying Danegeld to buy off Viking raiders. By 1002 Æthelred had been on the throne for a little over two decades, and had experienced numerous Viking raids on his country, eventually finding himself in the unfortunate situation of having to pay off the invaders on an annual basis to stall off any further invasions. These payments have since been referred to as "Danegeld," which in modern Danish still roughly translates into "Danish debt" (Crowcroft and Cannon 2015). The humiliating nature of these payments, combined with the gradually increasing presence of Danes within England, led Æthelred to take drastic action to address what he saw as the problem of the Danes festering in his kingdom. In 1002, Æthelred decided to carry out what can be described in modern terms as ethnic cleansing by issuing a charter that justified the brutal massacre to follow. Æthelred compared the Danes to weeds in a wheat field that needed to be rooted out for the survival of the crop. Additionally, later sources somewhat humorously suggested that the Anglo-Saxons viewed the Danes as a threat due to their long, well-combed hair and their habit of bathing every week for seductive purposes. Some have even suggested that the massacre was carried out on November 13, 1002, because it was a Saturday, a day the Danes called "Laugar-dagr," or "Bath-day" (Vincent 2011, 21–22). Alongside this act of genocide against the Danish settlers in England, the St. Brice's Day Massacre had an unforeseen political consequence for Æthelred: among the victims was Gunhilde, the sister of King Sweyn Forkbeard of Denmark. She had initially been held as a hostage but was later executed on Æthelred's orders during the massacre (Williams 2003, 54). This fateful act would ultimately provoke retaliation from Sweyn Forkbeard and his forces. Following the massacre, and seemingly as a sign of immediate divine retribution in the eyes of many Englishmen, a great famine ensued. As news of the massacre and the death of Gunhilde spread across the North Sea, King Sweyn Forkbeard decided to avenge his fallen countrymen and sister by launching his own invasion of England in 1013. This culminated in Sweyn defeating the armies of England that same year, forcing Æthelred into exile with his wife's family in northern France. Æthelred made a brief return to the throne following Sweyn's death in 1014, and his son, Edmund Ironside, succeeded him shortly after. However, this victory was short-lived, as the Danes returned under Sweyn Forkbeard's son, Cnut, in 1016, ultimately conquering all of England for good. This generated considerable chaos within the English realm, as the former ministers of Æthelred found themselves in an incredibly unstable political environment, forced to negotiate settlements with the Danish victors to secure their positions. Cnut, who would go down in history as Cnut the Great, solidified his reign over England and entered into a marriage with Æthelred's widow. After this, England remained largely under Danish control until around the middle of the eleventh century when it gradually returned to Anglo-Saxon rule, ultimately culminating in the invasions of 1066 (Vincent 2011, 22).

While 1066 is, in modern times, mostly remembered as the year in which the Normans under William the Conqueror launched their successful invasion of England, it also witnessed another similar invasion carried out by the Norwegian king Harald III Sigurdsson, commonly known by his name Harald Hardrada ("the Hard Ruler"). Harald Hardrada has historically been described as a tall, battle-hardened career warlord with broad shoulders. Snorri Sturluson describes Harald as a great warrior with exceptional skill in arms, who was stronger and more dexterous than any other man. Specifically, Sturluson portrays Harald Hardrada as a man of "an imperious nature" who made it worse than useless for anyone to oppose him or promote matters that went against his wishes (Sturluson [c. 1230] 1964, 607–610). Harald Hardrada spent 35 years honing his martial skills in the royal court of Kiev and the palaces of Byzantium. He lived a life rife with battles and wars, having invaded Denmark almost immediately after he succeeded to the Norwegian throne in 1047, and by 1066, he was hungering for a new conquest (Manley 2008, 39). Despite his royal advisor, Ulf Ospaksson, voicing his concern about the alliance with Tostig Godwinson and the battle prowess of the Anglo-Saxon warriors (Rex 2011, 35), Hardrada nonetheless decided to seek out a re-enactment of the conquests that his Viking ancestors, Sweyn Forkbeard and Cnut the Great, had carried out several decades beforehand.

One may ponder why Harald Hardrada believed he should succeed to the English throne. Despite nominally being a Christian, Harald had several wives, one of whom was allegedly related by blood to Cnut the Great. Through this connection, Harald believed he had a legitimate claim to the throne of England, despite the fact that Cnut's line had always been regarded as foreign invaders in England and had passed out of history back in 1042. While Harald's claim was spurious, it garnered enough local legitimacy to convince his fellow Norwegian warriors that he had a valid claim to the English throne. Following this, Harald gathered an incredibly diverse army of warriors from all over Scandinavia, including Danes, Letts, Geats, Norse-Irish, Finns, Friesians, Swedes, Icelanders, Rus, Orkneymen, and Shetlanders. Most of these Viking warriors gathered their troops and ships at Sogne Fjord near Bergen or at the base of Harald's power in Trondheim (Finch 2003, 34–40).

What did the Norwegian army of 1066 look like? Modern film and literature often depict Vikings as large, muscular Scandinavian warriors with long blonde hair underneath horned helmets, carrying massive two-handed battle axes. In reality, while the Scandinavian Vikings were well-equipped, this image is rather romanticized when examining the Norwegian army in 1066. Most adult males were trained for military service, and their weapons were made of fine materials, often adorned with gold, silver, or jewelry ornaments if the soldier could afford it (DeVries 1999, 193). Life as a Scandinavian warrior required a great deal of physical fitness combined with good weapon skills. The Scandinavians excelled at training their youth from a young age, irrespective of their social rank. Training would start around age five or six, and once a boy reached the age of ten, he would be expected to partake in athletic competitions alongside adults. By age twelve, the expectation was that he would have become a fully developed athlete. The Scandinavian youth would engage in various sports to harden their bodies and prepare for the challenges they would face in adulthood (Hjardar & Vike 2019, 84). This is noted in the Heidarviga Saga, which tells us that it was customary for the Northmen to practice games by day and come together for wrestling. Wrestling was seen as an extremely important skill for Viking warriors. Two types of wrestling had been developed: normal wrestling and glima. In normal wrestling, opponents would grasp each other around the waist with their hands clasped behind the opponent's back in an effort to throw the opponent to the ground without the use of external aid. Glima wrestling was developed in Iceland and is still practiced in modern times. Here, opponents grasp each other's trouser bands with their right hands, leaving their left hands free for use. The aim is to topple your opponent and throw him to the ground, which can be achieved with several rapid moves using one's legs or hands. Many children would learn this from childhood, and in a man-to-man fight on the battlefield, it would later prove useful when needing to throw an opponent to the ground if it ever came to hand-to-hand fighting (Hjardar & Vike 2019, 89). Perhaps one of the most infamous Vikings, Egil Skallagrimsson (c. 910–c. 990), is noted in his saga to have killed his first sports opponent, a boy named Grim, who was approximately ten years old when Egil himself was just seven years old. The saga mentions that Egil's father, Skallagrim, was indifferent to what had happened, and Egil's mother, Bera, even praised him, saying that he had the makings of a true Viking (Scudder 2015, 157–158). In reality, this would likely have been looked down upon, as most Vikings were taught self-control, and while the sports they played were brutal, a deliberate attempt to injure an opponent would have been seen as a violation (Hjardar & Vike 2019, 85). Thus, while the training and competitions were intense, they also instilled a sense of respect and honor among warriors that was fundamental to their identity.

By 1066, all freemen in Norway had the right to possess weapons, which would often include a sword, axe, shield, or spear, typically supplemented by a bow and two dozen arrows. The large two-handed battle axes often seen in modern depictions were not the primary weapons of the Vikings. This weapon, referred to as "the Danish axe," had indeed been used by Scandinavians, but it was not as popular as one might think. For the Norwegian army in 1066, the most favored weapon was by far the pattern-welded iron sword with steel edges, which typically measured around 95 centimeters in total length, with 75 centimeters of that being the blade length. Aside from the sword, many warriors would use the spear, with most opting for either a throwing spear or a thrusting spear depending on their preferred means of combat. In terms of defense, all Norwegian males were required to have a shield. These wooden shields were large, flat, and round, typically measuring about a meter wide. They were painted with bright colors, designs, and animal motifs, and featured an iron rim around the edge. A large iron boss was placed in the center of the shield's front, secured with an iron grip on the underside of the board. While kite-shaped shields may have been used by the Norwegian army in 1066, they were not common Scandinavian equipment and would likely have been acquired from the English or Normans, who at the time preferred to use them (DeVries 1999, 193–197). Another important piece of defensive equipment was the helmet. Modern media typically portrays Vikings wearing horned helmets, but in reality, most Scandinavians would wear a much simpler helmet designed for practicality rather than decoration. Excavations in Scandinavia and England from the eleventh century show that these helmets often consisted of several parts. The first part was the cap, followed by two hinged cheekpieces, and then a section of mail that protected the back and sides of the neck. Holes were sometimes cut in the front of the helmets for the eyes, but the helmets often ended with a thick and wide brow band that covered the eyebrows. Others had a long and thin piece of metal that descended between the eyes and served as a nose guard (DeVries 1999, 197–198). In terms of armor, the most popular defensive clothing in Europe around the eleventh century was chain mail, or mail shirt (*hringsekr* or *hringskyrta* in Old Norse). This was made of interlocking iron rings braided together over a leather jerkin and would cover the body from the neck down to the knees, with long sleeves for the arms (DeVries 1999, 198). These mail shirts were sometimes given names as well. Snorri Sturluson noted that King Harald Hardrada himself wore a coat of mail called Emma, which was reported to be so long that it reached below his knees and so strong that no weapon had ever been able to pierce it (Sturluson [c. 1230] 1964, 654). If a warrior could not afford chain mail armor, they would often wear lamellar armor, which descended from Roman armor designs and was generally made of numerous metallic scales attached to each other by wire or leather laces and affixed to a linen undergarment (DeVries 1999, 199).

Following the gathering of his warriors in Trondheim, the Norwegian Viking warriors boarded their ships to set sail for England. The Norwegian fleet consisted of 300 dragon ships, which were large longships with carved dragon heads mounted on their stems, and around 12,000 warriors set sail. By early September 1066, they arrived on the northeastern coast at the Tyne estuary, where they met up with Tostig and Scottish levies that Tostig had secured from the Scottish king, Malcolm. The army commanded by Harald Hardrada wasted no time in sailing along the Humber River, plundering and looting as much as possible. However, this was not mere theft, as Hardrada was well aware that devastating the surrounding area would prevent any large Saxon force from launching a surprise attack. Additionally, the looting would provide ample provisions for the army's men and animals, as the campaign might very well take a long time, given that many Viking armies had been defeated by the English in the past due to English scorched earth tactics. As the Norse army advanced into the English countryside, they left behind a substantial force to guard the fleet, consisting of Harald Hardrada's son, Olaf, and one of his favorite warriors, Eystein Orri, who had been betrothed to Hardrada's daughter, Maria (McLynn 1999, 204–205). Harald's army established themselves in the small Yorkshire town of Riccall, from which they quickly started marching to York, a journey they covered in just a day. Here, Harald Hardrada faced off against the English earls Morcar and Edwin, who commanded a relatively weak army of around 2,000 men. The battle was quickly decided, resulting in over 1,000 dead English warriors, and York surrendered to Harald's demand to be recognized as the new king of England. Following this, the Viking army withdrew northeast to a place called Stamford Bridge. Shortly thereafter, King Harold Godwinson of England marched toward Stamford Bridge with his army of 6,000 men from the south, gathering local levies along the way and eventually reaching an army size of close to 10,000 men. Harold reached York on the early and hot Monday morning of September 25, where he found the beaten earls Edwin and Morcar with what little remained of their armies (Finch 34–40, 2003). The stage was now set for a confrontation that would not only determine the fate of the English crown but also mark a pivotal moment in the history of England.

Surprisingly, it seems that the Norwegians never posted any scouts in or near York, and the march of Harold Godwinson's army through York came as a complete surprise to both them and the local townspeople of York, who had just surrendered to their Norwegian invaders. However, rather than stopping in York, King Harold decided to march directly through the town and onward toward the battlefield of Stamford Bridge, where he took the Norwegian army completely by surprise (DeVries 268–269, 1999). Once the Norwegians realized that the Anglo-Saxons had managed to sneak up on them, Tostig immediately argued in favor of a retreat back to Riccall, where they could gather reinforcements. Unfortunately, the English had surrounded them and occupied the only possible route back to Riccall. Hardrada stood fearless and refused to retreat, although he did send his fastest riders back to the Norwegian fleet, guarded by Eystein Orri, urging him to come with reinforcements as quickly as he could muster. Before the battle began, there were allegedly a series of verbal clashes. According to some accounts, Hardrada was thrown from his horse when it became skittish, and he supposedly dismissed the incident with a comment about how a fall is lucky for a traveler. Harold Godwinson, on the other hand, noticed this stumble and asked his men who had just fallen from the horse. Upon learning that it was Hardrada, he supposedly retorted that the Norwegian king's luck had deserted him. After this, Harold is said to have ridden up to the foot of Stamford Bridge with twenty of his housecarls in order to parley with the Norwegians (McLynn 1999, 209). Harald and Tostig, flanked by a small bodyguard, rode over to meet Harold Godwinson. Harold allegedly promised Tostig that if he returned to the Anglo-Saxon side, he would be given back his earldom as well as one-third of all of England. Tostig asked what would happen to Harald Hardrada in return, to which his brother Harold uncompromisingly responded that the large Norwegian king would be given seven feet of ground to be buried in. Tostig replied that he would not be known as the person who brought the king of Norway all the way to England just to betray him, after which he turned his horse around and rode away. Harald Hardrada, who hardly spoke any Old English, asked what had just occurred and who the Anglo-Saxon individual on the other horse was. When Tostig responded that it was his brother King Harold, Hardrada said he would have cut him down on the spot if he had known this. Tostig quickly exclaimed that he would also not wish to go down in the annals of history as the dishonorable brother who killed his own brother just after said brother had offered him dominion and renewed friendship (McLynn 1999, 210). According to one story, the Viking warriors had seemingly left their ring mail coats due to the warm weather back in Riccall and were caught with a divided force at the convergence of four roads, which was known as Stamford Bridge. The battle itself has been described in somewhat legendary terms, with a lone Norse berserker holding the English at bay for a considerable time, cutting down a score of English soldiers until he was eventually overrun. Despite the time purchased and the evenly matched armies, the Norse army was outflanked and taken by surprise. Harald Hardrada went out in a fury, as could be expected from a man of his legendary renown. As the shield wall around him was breached by the numerous Anglo-Saxon warriors, he rushed into the open in berserker fury, where he was slain almost immediately by an arrow to the windpipe. Supposedly, Harald Hardrada still held his love for poetry as he neared death's door, and in a final act of defiance, he dictated a poem to his scribe: "We march forward in battle array without our corselets to meet the dark blades; helmets shine, but I have not mine, for no war armor lies down on the ships." Ironically, Harald Hardrada soon decided that it was a bad poem and would not provide his men with the inspiration they desperately needed. He then yelled out a composition that was much richer in kennings and metrically superior, which was recorded thus: "We do not creep in battle under the shelter of shields before the crash of weapons; this is what the loyal goddess of the hawk's hand commanded us. The bearer of the necklace told me long ago to hold the prop of the helmet high in the din of weapons when the valkyrie's ice met the skulls of men." Upon seeing the death of their king, Harold Godwinson offered the Norsemen favorable terms if they surrendered. However, Tostig stood in refusal to surrender, and his men roared with defiance alongside the remaining Norwegians, declaring they would rather die in battle with their slain king. The second, and much bloodier part, of the battle then commenced, where Tostig was shortly thereafter slain (McLynn 1999, 211). King Harold was victorious after only a couple of minutes, following which the final showdown against the Norwegians would come. Having heard word of the ongoing engagement, Eystein Orri hurried to the battlefield with his reinforcements. Unlike Harald Hardrada, Orri chose a different route. While Hardrada would have taken him into the English rear, Orri's improvised path led the Norsemen through Wheldrake to the bridge at Kexby. From there, they crossed the countryside through either Catto or Wilberfoss until they reached the Stamford Bridge-Gagfoss road, where they rushed into battle against the Englishmen from the south. Despite their long march in the heat, the Norsemen made a ferocious charge, which has since been immortalized as "the storm of Orri." The Norsemen almost broke the English, but Harold Godwinson's men stood firm and engaged them head-on until nightfall, at which point Eystein Orri and most of his high-ranking soldiers were dead. As darkness fell, the remaining Norsemen fled, and King Harold was at long last victorious, but the losses he faced were far more severe than he could afford (McLynn 1999, 212). Harold Godwinson claimed complete victory on September 26, when his army captured the ships at Riccall, parleyed with Harald Hardrada's surviving son, Bishop Olav, and allowed the remaining Norsemen to sail back to their homelands with all of their dead, including Harald Hardrada, in peace. According to the sagas, the Norse army had suffered such slaughter that it only took 24 ships to carry them back (Finch 2003, 34–40). This devastating defeat marked the end of Norse ambitions in England.

Most medieval battles typically lasted between one and two hours, with one army usually forcing the other side to flee from the battlefield. The Battle of Stamford Bridge undoubtedly lasted more than a few hours, primarily due to the fighting occurring in four stages: first on the western side of the river, then with the Norwegians trying to defend the bridge, followed by skirmishes on the right side of the river, and concluding with a final showdown against Norwegian reinforcements. A good estimate is that the battle lasted around four to five hours (DeVries 1999, 270–271). While Stamford Bridge still exists as a small village in the United Kingdom today, the exact location of the battlefield is not known. Original sources, including the Norwegian Kings' Sagas, are vague regarding the topography of the battlefield. The only indication they provide is the prominence of the Derwent River, a tributary of the Ouse River, which ran through the battlefield with a narrow wooden bridge crossing it. It is noted that the western side of the river, approached by Harold Godwinson's army, had a wide, slightly sloped meadow, while the eastern side, where Harald Hardrada likely placed his camp, featured higher ground with a sharper slope rising from the riverbank. However, the river has changed since 1066 and is now more like a narrow, sluggish stream. The original wooden bridge has also disappeared, replaced by a wide two-lane stone bridge used to cross into the town. Without certain knowledge of the river or the location of the wooden bridge, it is nearly impossible to pinpoint exactly where the western part of the battle occurred. However, if the area named Battle Flats can be trusted—located in an area of higher ground southeast of the present town's center—it is likely that the eastern part of the battle took place there (DeVries 1999, 269).

Despite the overwhelming Norwegian loss at the Battle of Stamford Bridge, it indirectly assisted William the Conqueror by weakening the English army and allowing the Norman forces to securely establish a base on the southern coast of England (Cannon and Crowcroft 2015). As the Norwegian invasion ended and the Viking Age, which had dominated the North Sea for centuries, came to a close, the defeat at Stamford Bridge severely weakened the Norwegian kings for decades. The people of southern Britain and western Europe could finally breathe a sigh of relief as the Viking raiding parties from the north began to cease. The battle also confirmed the cautious approach of King Sweyn II of Denmark and solidified the national divisions in Scandinavia, divisions that persisted despite later unions such as the Kalmar Union, Denmark-Norway, and Sweden-Norway, and remain to this day (Butler 1966, 193–194). While King Harold's army was left exhausted with significant casualties, the victory conditions were not entirely without merit. The Norwegians had left behind a large cache of loot, including gold that Harald Hardrada had brought from Norway and plunder seized during their raids in England. Additionally, a portion of the Norwegian fleet passed into Anglo-Saxon hands. Initially, King Harold kept the treasure under his own control, as compensating and resettling the civilian victims of the invasion was not a pressing concern (Butler 1966, 194). The victory over the Norwegians was seen as such a significant achievement that Harold enjoyed almost a week of victory celebrations in York (Butler 1966, 203), and it solidified his legitimacy and rightful claim to the English throne. However, as October began, Harold's celebrations would be cut short. On Sunday, October 1, an exhausted rider arrived in York with urgent news. Pushing through the narrow streets, he reached the hall where Harold was dining. The tranquility Harold had enjoyed immediately vanished upon hearing the messenger's news: William, the bastard Duke of Normandy, had landed with an invasion force at Pevensey and was devastating the surrounding countryside (Butler 1966, 203). King Harold was understandably shocked at the revelation. Less than a month ago, he had been assured by his trusted naval commanders that the southern enemy had been destroyed in a grand mixture of a naval engagement culminating with the fierce storm that took both fleets by surprise. King Harold reportedly reacted with great sadness for his citizens in the southern provinces, lamenting his inability to be there to defend them against the invading Normans. Butler (1966) concludes that the sudden Norman landing was not only completely unexpected but also gravely underestimated by Harold and his commanders. Despite the strength of the Norman forces, Harold initially held to the belief that the invaders would soon be expelled (Butler 1966, 203–204). Fortune had favored the Anglo-Saxons in their recent encounter with the Norwegian invaders, but less than two weeks later, King Harold Godwinson would face his ultimate challenge when he confronted Duke William of Normandy at the Battle of Hastings on October 14, 1066.

6

THE ORIGINS OF WILLIAM THE CONQUEROR

THE NAME WILLIAM THE CONQUEROR is almost synonymous with the conquest of England in 1066 in modern times. But who was the man with the awe-inspiring epithet? The man who would become Duke William of Normandy, and eventually King William of England, was born in Normandy around 1028. The earliest known source indicating this is the tract known as *De Obitu Willelmi* ("On the Death of William"), which was composed soon after William's death on September 9, 1087. In this historical document, William's age was recorded as fifty-nine. This would indicate a date of birth between September 10, 1027, and September 9, 1028 (D. Bates 2016, 2, 25). While the man who would become King William was born into nobility, he was, in fact, born a bastard. This has led many scholars to somewhat spitefully refer to him as "William the Bastard" rather than by his more popular epithet, "the Conqueror." William's father was the Duke of Normandy, Robert. On the other hand, his mother was neither his father's wife nor of noble origins. She was instead a poor peasant girl named Herleva (or Arlotte, depending on the source), who was the daughter of a tanner in the commune of Falaise in Normandy (Abbott 1902, 22). Supposedly, Robert became acquainted with Herleva after returning home to his castle from an expedition one day when he set his sight upon a group of barefooted peasant girls wearing disheveled dresses and washing their clothes on the margin of a brook. One of these girls, Herleva, immediately caught Robert's attention, and he gazed at her with great admiration. According to medieval royal etiquette, Robert would not have been able to marry Herleva, but nothing could keep him from inviting her to his castle to live with him. Robert thus sent a messenger to ask Herleva to come to the castle, which led to an intimate love affair between the two (Abbott 1902, 22–24). According to legend, when William was born, his first exploit was to grasp a handful of straw with such tenacity that the nurse could hardly take it away from him. The nurse, astonished by his infantile strength, considered it an omen and made the prediction that the babe would one day seize and hold great power (Abbott 1902, 24). This tale first appeared in the *Brevis Relatio* ("short account"), which is an early twelfth-century narrative written at Battle Abbey covering the events surrounding the Norman conquest of 1066. William of Malmesbury further repeated this tale and even noted that the midwife proclaimed that William's infantile prowess was a sign that he was destined for kingship (D. Bates 2016, 29). This symbolic tale of William's infancy would later serve as a fitting prelude to his rise as one of the most formidable rulers in European history, reinforcing the notion that his destiny for power had been evident from birth.

Pilgrimages were very common in the Middle Ages and were often undertaken to Santiago de Compostela, Jerusalem, or Rome. Naturally, the most difficult of these would be the one to the Holy Land, with many of the holy places remaining under the control of the Fatimid caliphs of Egypt, who were not particularly fond of Christian pilgrims. Nevertheless, Duke Robert of Normandy decided to embark on a pilgrimage to Jerusalem in 1035. While the exact reasons for his departure are unknown, beyond what one can assume about his devotion to his faith, he did not leave Normandy without making certain preparations first. The primary issue to be addressed, in case anything went wrong, was that of his immediate successor. Robert was just twenty-five years old and had no legitimate heir, save for a bastard son around age seven or eight. Robert had trained William somewhat in the formal duties of the court and had even asked William to put his own signature on several of his father's documents. The next step for Robert was to convince his vassals of his son's claim to legitimacy and power regarding the Norman duchy. He did so by holding a great assembly in Fécamp on 13 January 1035. The attendees of this assembly included the Archbishop of Rouen, other bishops of the province, and the great secular lords. At this meeting, two things happened: first, the abbey of Montivilliers was founded, and secondly, Duke Robert announced his departure for the Holy Land while naming his illegitimate son William as his immediate heir. The barons supposedly raised no objection to this and all pledged an oath of loyalty to William. While all seemed well for the young William, his childhood would certainly not turn out to be very easy. Duke Robert did, in the end, manage to complete his pilgrimage and reach Jerusalem. Nevertheless, on his return journey, he fell ill and died at Nicaea, which unsurprisingly led to a conflict regarding who should rule in Normandy (Neveux 2006, 109–110). Thus, the stage was set for a turbulent power struggle, ultimately shaping William's path to becoming one of history's most formidable rulers.

Duke Richard I, the great-great-grandfather of William and the grandson of Rollo, had a son named Robert, who became the archbishop of the Church in Normandy. As a senior member of the royal family, Robert initially claimed and held power with much legitimacy. However, by this time, Robert was already an elderly man, and he died just two years later, in 1037. As was often the case in medieval times when power was disputed, a rebellion broke out following his death, with the rebels initially targeting William's closest allies. William had three notable allies: his tutor Turold, his guardian Gilbert of Brionne, and his steward Osbern of Crépon. These three did all they could to protect the young bastard, with Osbern even sharing a bed with him. Nevertheless, all three were assassinated, with Osbern falling victim while sleeping next to the young William, who remained surprisingly untouched—likely due to the oath of loyalty that the assassins' employers had sworn to the young duke earlier at Fécamp (Neveux 2006, 112). William of Jumièges explains that the period following Archbishop Robert's death was utter chaos, as many Normans forgot their oaths and loyalties, building unlicensed castles and fortified strongholds all over Normandy. From these fortresses, they plotted rebellions, and the duchy was engulfed in constant violence as rivals fought each other. Orderic Vitalis provides an example of an unlucky Norman nobleman, William Giroie, who was kidnapped at a wedding feast and then tortured by having his nose and ears cut off and his eyes gouged out. With no law and order in place, Normandy had essentially descended into anarchy. While it remains questionable why the rebels allowed the young William to live, it was most likely an attempt to control him. Notably, William of Jumièges refused to name the murderers of William's closest allies, referring to them only as "the very men who now surround the duke." However, Orderic Vitalis, writing several generations later and free from the threat of retaliation, identified one of the murderers as Rodulf of Gacé, who was later described as William's guardian and the leader of the Norman army (Morris 2013, 51–52). William was seemingly pushed into the foreground around the age of fourteen in 1042, when, according to Jumièges, he made his uncle William, Count of Arques. Jumièges further attributes William's first military activity to the capture of Falaise from a rebel named Thurstan Goz, typically dated to around 1043 (D. Bates 2016, 53). These early experiences of betrayal and bloodshed undoubtedly shaped William's character, preparing him for the ruthless political and military maneuvers that would later define his career.

The young William also faced pressure from external forces. According to the French monk and chronicler Ralph Glaber, William had his status as the heir of Duke Robert legitimized by the king of France, Henry I, who had been restored to power in 1033 thanks to Norman assistance.

6. The Origins of William the Conqueror

This was not atypical, as the kings of France often looked to the Norman dukes for military support, while in return providing them with legitimization. Strictly speaking, "France" did not exist at this point in time, and references to the "Kingdom of France" only began appearing around a hundred years later. The kings of France did not claim this title either, using instead the title Rex Francorum ("king of the Franks") and viewing themselves as the successors of Charlemagne. In reality, France had crumbled since the rule of Charlemagne, splitting into two: Eastern Francia, which would eventually become Germany, slipped out of their control, while Western Francia, what is France today, remained in a constant state of chaos for centuries afterward (Morris 2013, 44–48). Despite legitimizing the young William in 1035, Henry I apparently aided the rebels, who, according to Jumièges, "scattered the firebrands of Henry, king of the French." King Henry quickly demanded that the Normans surrender the castle of Tillières, which was close to the French border. The regents agreed and assisted the king in besieging it until the garrison surrendered.

Around a year later, for unknown reasons, King Henry sponsored another rebellion in the heart of Normandy by supplying soldiers to a viscount who seized William's birthplace, Falaise, and began invading the southern part of the duchy. This revolt was eventually abandoned, the viscount fled into exile, and the French king withdrew his attention from Normandy. Jumièges attributes all decision-making on William's side to his regents up until this point, after which William seemingly summoned troops and laid siege to the viscount (Morris 2013, 52–53). It seems that in the years following Archbishop Robert's death in 1037, William's regents held considerable sway over the administration of the Norman duchy. However, ducal rule was revived when William began to formally act as duke around 1042, having reached the canonical age where marriage could be considered to enhance his political standing (D. Bates 2016, 54).

From this point, when William started to truly rule as duke, until his invasion of England, more than twenty years would pass. During this period, William took on responsibilities such as governing the duchy, suppressing insurrections, improving infrastructure, building towns and castles, waging war with neighboring states, regulating civil institutions, and performing all the functions of government (Abbott 1902, 44). Once Duke William fully assumed his role, he secured the stability of his rule through careful selection of close allies and dismissed those who had self-appointed during his absence from power. Any counts or viscounts who had become accustomed to disregarding ducal authority during the rebellious years were swiftly dealt with. Naturally, this provoked a hostile reaction from William's opponents, and by 1046, a new rebellion had emerged in Normandy. Unlike previous uprisings, this one had the explicit goal of assassinating William and replacing him with a more favorable ally. Chroniclers named the leader of this rebellion as one of William's cousins, Guy, who had been raised alongside him and ruled over Brionne. However, it is equally likely that Guy was merely a puppet, manipulated by the many viscounts and nobles displeased with William's increasing authoritarianism and the reduction of their autonomy. Unfortunately, there are no contemporary sources that provide significant details about this challenge to Duke William's rule. One source, writing over a century later, was the Norman historian Wace. According to Wace, William was desperately outnumbered by the viscounts and left Normandy to seek assistance from the king of France. This may seem surprising, given the French king's opposition during the previous rebellion, but it is supported by both William of Poitiers and William of Jumièges and likely reflects how desperate the duke was at the time.

This turned out to be a brilliant move, as King Henry agreed to help him. Early in 1047, the king summoned his army and rode to William's aid. They confronted the rebel forces southeast of Caen, at Val-ès-Dunes. According to William of Poitiers, the duke "spread such terror by his slaughter that his adversaries lost heart and their arms weakened," while Wace noted that William "fought nobly and well" (Morris 2013, 54–58). At the beginning of the battle, one of the key figures of the rebellion, Ralph Taisson, who had vowed to "strike" Duke William, changed his allegiance. Supposedly, he approached the duke, struck him with his glove to fulfill his oath, and then offered his and his soldiers' support. Duke William achieved a decisive victory, with most rebels being driven back toward the Orne River, where many drowned. Most of the rebellion's leaders were captured or sent into exile. William's cousin Guy, who had led the rebellion, sought refuge in his castle at Brionne. Shortly after, Duke William besieged it successfully, forcing Guy into exile in Burgundy.

At just 19, Duke William had secured a major victory and legitimized his rule in the face of long-standing adversaries. Without delay, he organized a peace council in Caen, where a new "Peace of God" was established with the Church's assistance (Neveux 2006, 116–118). The term "the Peace of God" or "the Truce of God" has historically been seen as a movement used by secular political leaders in order to reassert their responsibility for social order. This movement was spearheaded by monks in order to reform the church and society and scholars have since then seen it as everything from the most significant transformative medieval movement to a lesser occurrence. This also means that defining "the Peace of God" has been a difficult task to undertake without defining its significance as well. Geoffrey Koziol, professor of history at the University of California, Berkeley, defines it as a program originating in the last decades before the tenth century that, in broad terms, protected the church and its environs. This movement began in Aquitaine in France, but quickly spread across the rest of the country and eventually to Normandy as well. It should be noted that the Peace of God was not used as a tool to end violence, but rather to establish measures that could prevent future violence (Koziol 2018, 1–3). The peace established at Caen in 1047 had the demand that it should be "frequently repeated and firmly held" and entailed a demand that on Sundays and feast days priests would curse those who violated the peace, but bless those who obeyed it (Koziol 2018, 91). William of Poitiers later wrote that conclusion of the Battle of Val-ès-Dunes in 1047 "brought civil war in Normandy to an end for a long time" (D. Bates 2016, 49). The peace thus served Duke William as a measure to prevent future violence, while simultaneously giving the Church and its dominion a permanent peace.

With peace secured in his realm, Duke William now turned his attention to marriage, which would ensure the longevity of his dynasty. Unlike his father, who had fathered a bastard, the young duke was determined to enter into a royal marriage blessed by the Church. Matilda of Flanders seemed the perfect choice for William. Born around 1031, Matilda was approximately three years younger than her future husband. She was the daughter of Baldwin V, Count of Flanders, and Adela of France, sister to the French king Henry I. Baldwin's connections to both the French monarchy and other royal houses in Europe made this alliance highly advantageous for William. Although no early images of Matilda exist, William of Malmesbury described her as "a singular mirror of prudence in our day, and the perfection of virtue." Initially, Matilda had been infatuated with an Anglo-Saxon nobleman named Brihtric Mau, who had visited her father's court on a mission from Edward the Confessor. Though Brihtric was of noble lineage through his father Algar, lord of Gloucester, he, for reasons unknown, was not interested in courting Matilda (Strickland, A., and E. Strickland, 23–25). According to legend, Brihtric supposedly turned her down because he did not find her attractive enough. After Brihtric returned to England, Matilda married Duke William of Normandy. Years later, after William conquered England and became king of the Anglo-Saxon realm, Matilda, still bitter about the rejection, asked her husband for revenge, which he agreed to. Although Brihtric had already made peace with the Normans, he would ultimately pay the price for refusing Matilda's hand in marriage. He was arrested at his manor in Hanley, Gloucestershire, taken to Winchester, and murdered while imprisoned. Following his death, Matilda seized his inheritance, dividing it between herself and a Norman baron named Robert Fitzhamon. While the story remains dubious, it is known that Brihtric's father, Aelfgar, owned vast lands in western England, spanning from Dorset to Cornwall and north to Worcestershire. By 1086, all of these properties had passed into other hands, particularly those of Queen Matilda. Whether Matilda's revenge is fact or legend, it's possible that Brihtric's forfeited estates were a consequence of his participation in King Harold Godwinson's final campaign against the Normans (Butler 1966, 220). Regarding Matilda's later marriage to Duke William of Normandy, the initial proposal had been made by William, who sought her hand to strengthen his ducal position and form an alliance with the County of Flanders. The young duke sent his envoys to Flanders to ask Matilda's father, Baldwin V, for her hand in marriage. While Baldwin happily accepted William's offer, Matilda reportedly refused due to William's illegitimacy. According to the chronicler Ingerius, this enraged William, leading him to allegedly confront Matilda while she attended mass, drag her into the streets, beat her, and then ride off at full speed. Matilda, bedridden for several days, eventually changed her mind, perhaps impressed by his strength or out of fear of further violence, and agreed to marry him (Strickland, A. and E. Strickland 23–25). Shortly thereafter, in either 1049 or 1050, Matilda and William were married against the wishes of Pope Leo IX, who objected to the union due to consanguinity. Consanguinity, the sharing of common ancestors, was a significant concern for the Catholic Church. In medieval times, the Church prohibited marriages between individuals related within seven generations. Both Matilda and William descended from Rollo, and Matilda's mother, Adela, had briefly been betrothed to William's uncle, Duke Richard III of Normandy. Moreover, both William and Matilda traced their lineage to Fulk II the Good, Count of Anjou from 940 to 962. The shared descent from Count Fulk and Rollo placed Matilda and William within the fourth and fifth degrees of consanguinity, making their marriage problematic under canon law. This issue had previously affected William's sister, Adelaide, whose marriage to Count Enguerrand II of Ponthieu was annulled on similar grounds (D. Bates 2016, 99–100). Ironically, in earlier periods, such marriages were often overlooked by the Church. However, during this time, the Church was undergoing a moral reform that aimed to set higher standards for both clergy and laypeople, and rulers were expected to lead by example. Pope Leo IX, appointed by Holy Roman Emperor Henry III (an enemy of Matilda's father, Baldwin V), condemned the marriage. Moreover, the pope was engaged in conflict with the Normans who had settled in southern Italy, complicating relations with Normandy. Despite the papal disapproval, William and Matilda proceeded with their wedding around 1050 in Eu, on the northern border of William's duchy. The ceremony appears to have been a private affair, attended only by close family, with no Norman barons present (Neveux 2006, 119–121). Their defiance paid off when Pope Nicholas II eventually sanctioned the marriage in 1059. Despite the initial troubles surrounding their union, the marriage was seemingly affectionate. In 1051, Matilda gave birth to their first son, Robert (Izzard 2023). Over the years, Matilda bore William a total of four sons and six daughters (Strickland, A. and E. Strickland 94), helping to secure the future of William's dynasty.

Following the Battle of Val-ès-Dunes and his marriage to Matilda, William began his formal rule as Duke of Normandy. He continued to face rebellions, primarily from members of the ducal family. Most of these rebellions came from a specific branch of the ducal family known as the "Richardides"—family members related to Duke Richard I of Normandy—who were left unsatisfied with the ascension of a bastard to the ducal throne. William nevertheless successfully repelled all of these rebellions, with the three most noteworthy ones ending as follows: Richard I's great-grandson William Werlenc, Count of Mortain, was forced into exile in Italy; Richard I's grandson, William Busac, Count of Eu, was exiled to King Henry I's court, yielding his county to his brother Robert; and the third rebellion, which lasted from 1052 to 1054, concluded with Count William of Arques, the son of Richard II, being exiled to the court of Eustace, Count of Boulogne (Neveux 2006, 123–124). Despite facing some familial rebellions at home, Duke William seemed to feel secure in his position following the peace he had secured in 1047, allowing him to focus on external affairs. This led to William agreeing to assist King Henry I in besieging the fortress of Mouliherne, held by Geoffrey Martel, Count of Anjou. The siege did not succeed in defeating Geoffrey Martel, and the Count continued to conquer the County of Maine, located between Normandy and Anjou, as well as taking control of two border strongholds that once belonged to the estate of Bellême. In response, William went on the offensive, attacking both the Count of Anjou and the Lords of Bellême. He captured the castle of Domfront and annexed the region of Passais into his realm. Following this, William besieged Alençon, which was under the control of the Count of Anjou at the time. This event was of significant importance, as Alençon was located on the borders of Normandy. According to William of Poitiers, Duke William supposedly showed great benevolence toward the defenders of the town and castle after conquering it. However, Wace, writing in the twelfth century, recounts that a group of defenders mocked William's heritage due to his mother being the daughter of a tanner, by beating animal hides used for protection at the top of the castle's tower while yelling, "The skin, the skin of the tanner that belongs to his trade." While William had previously punished royal enemies for similar acts with exile, he had no such patience for commoners, and when the town was conquered, he ordered the soldiers who had insulted him to have their hands and feet cut off (Neveux 2006, 124–126). This brutal punishment not only instilled fear among his enemies but also solidified William's reputation as a formidable and uncompromising leader in his quest for power.

Duke William had proven himself to be both a successful leader within and beyond the Norman borders. Two of the most prominent contemporary writers on Norman history, William de Jumièges and William de Poitiers, noted that as William's influence began to grow, every person with a significant amount of power in Northern France—ranging from the French king down to smaller princes and dukes—was fearful of the Norman duke and would have been more than happy to see him overthrown. It seemed that William was so successful that he instilled a level of fear so great in his former ally, King Henry I of France, that the king decided to do something that had never been done before: invade Normandy. Ironically, King Henry had started out on extremely favorable terms with the young Duke William. The French king had been on good terms with William's father, Robert, who ruled as the sixth Duke of Normandy from 1028 to 1035. Duke Robert had assisted the young Henry in the beginning of his reign against his rebellious little brother. When William's father, Duke Robert, later set out on his pilgrimage to Jerusalem, he wanted to keep his son William safe and established him in King Henry's court. William was received at the royal court in a grandiose ceremony and was made to kneel and do homage to the king. At the behest of a nobleman named Alan, whom Duke Robert had appointed as regent in Normandy while he was gone, King Henry also allowed the young William to return to Normandy, where he would be installed as duke (Abbott 1902, 20–34). As noted earlier in this chapter, the king also returned the loyalty that William had shown him when he assisted him at Val-ès-Dunes in 1047. However, the king grew increasingly jealous of the young duke's success and began to view him as a threat to his sovereignty.

Historically, Normandy had, since its foundation in 911, only fallen victim to military conflicts and warfare within its own borders and from its own citizens. This changed in 1054 when King Henry I decided to team up with his and William's former shared enemy, Geoffrey Martel, whom the king now viewed as the lesser evil, to launch a military campaign into Normandy (Neveux 2006, 126). The royal armies split up, with one entering the Norman duchy from the north and another from the south of the Seine, while King Henry I and Geoffrey Martel decided to assault Évreux in the south of Normandy. In response, Duke William rode out with his army to face the king, while his cousin, Count Robert of Eu, was sent to lead the main Norman army against the assault from the French king's brother, Odo, in the north, where they were pillaging the town of Mortemer. The battle there ended in a devastating defeat for the invaders under Odo, whose soldiers had taken little precaution and had gotten intoxicated while leaving their camp unguarded. The entire army was taken by surprise in their sleep, and most were killed or taken as hostages, with only a few men, including Odo, managing to escape (Neveux 2006, 127). Duke William triumphantly had a messenger inform the French king of the disastrous defeat of his brother in the north, which caused the French king to make a rapid retreat from the duchy and conclude a truce with Duke William (Crouch 2007, 70). With a strong hold over his duchy, William solidified his reputation as a fearsome general who should not be trifled with. This strategic victory over the French king brought William some peace for a while, but King Henry's ambition to topple the up-and-coming young duke would not wane in 1054.

Following the king's invasion of Normandy in 1054, Duke William decided to go on the counteroffensive for once and wage war outside his own duchy. This began with an extensive campaign to secure Maine as a buffer against Anjou. William had a castle erected in Ambrières, about 20 kilometers south of Maine's northern municipality of Domfront. This threatened the neighboring lord of Mayenne, who sought assistance from the Count of Anjou, Geoffrey Martel. They attempted to conquer the castle, but the arrival of Duke William and his army deterred them (Crouch 2007, 72). After successfully destabilizing Maine and demonstrating that he should not be trifled with, the Count of Anjou, Geoffrey Martel, began to scheme with King Henry of France once more. Despite their previous failures, they decided to push into Normandy again, and in August of 1057, they resolved to attempt the seemingly impossible once more: invade Normandy (Crouch 2007, 73). This renewed aggression would set the stage for a pivotal confrontation between William and his adversaries in the years to come.

The Count of Anjou and King Henry merged their armies into one and entered Normandy from the south, advancing deep into the duchy's interior down the Orne Valley. William waited patiently before striking, while the French army laid waste to the countryside as it continued marching through his lands. Eventually, an opportunity arose when the Franco-Angevin army sought to cross the Dives marsh east of a village named Varaville, situated in the southern reaches of Normandy. Here, the invading army had to cross a narrow passage along the sea wall that separated the marsh from the sea, which eventually led to the "Dives ford," a crossing point across the River Dives. This forced the Franco-Angevin army to stretch out, and although King Henry and Count Geoffrey Martel, who were at the head of the column, reached a hill overlooking the site early, a significant portion of their army was still in the midst of crossing the narrow passage. It was at this moment that Duke William decided to strike. The Norman soldiers had purposefully waited for high tide to meet the rearguard, and the Franco-Angevin army was easily routed, with many drowning in the sea or marshes as their king looked on helplessly from the top of Bassebourg Hill (Neveux 2006, 127). This decisive victory not only showcased William's strategic brilliance but also marked a turning point in the struggle for control over Normandy.

While William had proven himself to be a clever military strategist who time and again outwitted his foes, the Battle of Varaville did successfully fend off the invaders from his duchy for a while; however, the struggle for Norman independence would not end in 1057. It was not until 1060 that William managed to gain true peace and stability regarding both internal and foreign interlopers for his duchy and could start to look outward to foreign affairs. Nevertheless, Duke William would eventually see the French region turn in his favor politically, as both of his main enemies, Count Geoffrey Martel and King Henry I, died in the same year, 1060. A clerk of Chartres noted that this year marked the end of the civil war between King Henry and Count William (Crouch 2007, 73). Additionally, Duke William's luck shone once more, as Geoffrey Martel had no children, which meant that his inheritance became disputed between his two nephews, Fulk Rechin and Geoffrey the Bearded, who would fight against each other until Fulk Rechin emerged victorious in 1068 (Paul 2012, 52). Similarly, while King Henry I's inheritance was not disputed, the new king, Philip I, was a mere child aged eight when he took the throne in 1060 and was in no position to engage in warfare with his powerful ducal subjects. Furthermore, William's father-in-law through his wife Matilda, Count Baldwin V of Flanders, had been designated as the guardian of the young French king while Philip was being accustomed to the duties of monarchy (Neveux 2006, 128). This left William in a political climate where he could achieve complete peace in his duchy, should he wish to do so. However, unsurprisingly, the duke's ambition would always come first. Additionally, the duke enjoyed a great deal of praise and admiration within his duchy in the late 1050s and early 1060s. The morale among the Norman populace received a significant boost from William's many military victories, and as seen in contemporary writings, the Norman golden age that emerged under Duke William extended into the fields of literature and music as well. The famous Norman chroniclers and historians William of Poitiers and William de Jumièges were writing during this period, both intending to commemorate the Norman successes for the glory of the population living under Duke William's rule. Additionally, references were made to Duke William's successes being celebrated in verse and song for the benefit of a larger and potentially illiterate audience. The church also seemed to attract prominent figures who wished to immigrate to Normandy. The celebrated teacher from Pavia, Lanfranc, operated one of the most famous schools in northern Europe, where, in 1059, he attracted the young intellectual St. Anselm into a Norman orbit. The recognition and prominence of Norman identity, distinct from French identity, thrived within the duchy like never before (Crouch 2007, 74).

With his rule secured and little competition left in the greater French region bordering Normandy, William was largely free to do as he pleased. His enemies had all been subdued, neutralized, or humbled, and a pro-William aristocracy had been installed in all key positions of power within the Norman duchy. Duke William had made the offices of constable, chamberlain, butler, and steward permanent, appointing his most trusted counts to these posts (McLynn 1999, 104). The success with which William—who, on top of everything, had been born a bastard—managed to centralize Normandy and essentially create a personal power resembling the absolutism of monarchs that would arise much later in Europe was quite impressive. The eleventh century in Europe marked a period of splintering and decentralizing authority, which was both a result of and a contributing factor to the intense brutality of that time. Many regions of Europe experienced what has been described as "feudal anarchy," where private lords in fortified castles increased their power at the expense of those who had previously worked as agents for the central government. While scholars still debate to what extent Normandy prior to 1066 could have been considered a feudal society, the imperialism that arose under Duke William had been unprecedented up until this point in time in the duchy (McLynn 1999, 106). This shift in power dynamics not only reshaped the governance of Normandy but also set the stage for the dramatic changes that would follow in the wake of the Norman Conquest.

Naturally, the ambitious duke had no hesitation in using his new strong and fortified position to his advantage. The final count of Maine, Herbert II, had been exiled when the Count of Anjou, Geoffrey Martel, drove him and his family from their county. Duke William, who had long been at war with the Angevins, supported the exiled Count Herbert on the condition that he would become his vassal and that, if he died childless, he would allow the Norman duke to succeed him in all rights and possessions (David 1920, 7). Count Herbert II did indeed end up dying without any children in 1062, and his county was thus bequeathed to Duke William. A potential heir was left in the form of Herbert's sister Margaret, but Duke William quickly arranged for her to be married to his eldest son, Robert Curthose, who was around twelve years old at the time. Unfortunately for the young ducal son, Margaret would die at Fécamp, where she was buried in the monastery of La Trinité, before either she or Robert reached a marriageable age. Nevertheless, Robert continued to be referred to as count, and Duke William maintained his hold over the county

(David 1920, 10–11). Maine had almost been secured, but Duke William still faced a threat from Geoffrey, Lord of Mayenne. Duke William laid siege to Lord Geoffrey's castle, and in another devious scheme, the Norman duke supposedly let two children slip into the castle and set fire to it from the inside. Successful in his conquest, Duke William effectively conquered and secured a stable hold over Maine in 1063 (Neveux 2006, 128).

With the county of Maine secured under William's domain, the Norman duke once again let his ambition determine his next course of action: Brittany. At the time, Brittany was ruled by Duke Conan II, who was actively trying to wrest his domain free of any Norman control or influence. Naturally, Duke William would have none of this, and he launched an expedition into the duchy in 1064. William's aims were not to conquer all of Brittany, but rather to weaken the hostile duke and provide support to one of Conan's vassals, the Lord of Dol, Ruallon, who had rebelled against the duke. Most notably, as mentioned in the second chapter of this book, Harold Godwinson, then Earl of Wessex, had supposedly entered Normandy to free his family members who had been held hostage in the duchy since 1051. Here, the Earl supposedly swore his fealty to Duke William. Additionally, a famous scene in the Bayeux Tapestry depicts the earl rescuing two Normans, who were seeking to enter Brittany as part of William's military campaign into the duchy, from drowning in the quicksand located in the River Couesnon. Harold's features are distinguishable as he is depicted with a "pudding-bowl" haircut and a mustache, unlike his then–Norman allies, who are portrayed with the backs of their heads shaved and without facial hair. Harold is depicted valiantly carrying one of the Norman soldiers "piggyback" while dragging the other, who has seemingly fallen, with his right hand. The Latin inscription in the tapestry also notes, "Here Duke William and his army came to Mont St Michel, and here they crossed the River Couesnon. Here Duke Harold pulled them out of the sand."

This scene is notably intriguing in that it portrays the Anglo-Saxon earl in a very positive light as a life-saving ally—an act to which no extant contemporary sources make reference. Additionally, the scene seems to draw direct inspiration from Virgil's *Aeneid*, where the Trojan hero Aeneas is depicted fleeing the city of Troy while carrying his father, Anchises, on his back and pulling his son Ascanius/Iulus by the hand (Rollason and Lewis 2020, 203–205). The Anglo-Saxon earl was therefore supposedly present as an ally during William's invasion of Brittany. The invasion, whose primary aim was to lift the siege of Dol to aid Ruallon, was successful, and Duke Conan II was forced to flee by seemingly sliding down a rope. The Norman army continued to chase down Conan as it advanced into Brittany, reaching as far as the cities of Rennes and Dinan.

The Normans would eventually engage Conan at Rennes, where he surrendered, and according to the Bayeux Tapestry, it was at this point that William "gave arms to Harold" and Earl Harold "swore a sacred oath to Duke William." The content of the oath is unknown, but it is generally thought that Harold promised to assist William in becoming King of the English upon the death of Edward the Confessor. Although Conan II was not decisively defeated, and William of Poitiers even suggested that Duke William had gained a "limited victory," his weakened state led William to largely disregard him (Rollason and Lewis 2020, 208). Furthermore, the Norman duke had his own allies in Brittany, the most significant of whom was Conan's uncle, Odo of Penthièvre, who would also go on to supply Duke William with substantial forces for his later invasion and conquest of England (Neveux 2006, 128–129). Following William's success in Brittany and Earl Harold's return to England, approximately one and a half years would pass before the duke received news of Edward the Confessor's death.

However, with this news also came an insidious side note: Harold Godwinson had betrayed the oath that he had supposedly sworn to Duke William and decided to crown himself King of England on January 5, 1066. When news of this broke, the Norman duke hesitated little. Such an act of treachery meant that the English realm would have to be taken by force, and Duke William quickly began to plan his invasion.

7

PREPARATIONS

IF ONE IS TO BELIEVE THE NORMAN sources, such as the writings of William of Poitiers, Edward the Confessor made a promise to designate Duke William of Normandy as his heir around 1051. In 1066, the Norman duke would have gone around for fifteen years believing himself to be the rightful successor to King Edward, and this belief would have been emboldened by Earl Harold's supposed oath of fealty to him following his visit to Normandy approximately two years earlier. The duke had not only knighted Harold and bestowed lavish gifts upon him, but he had also honored him as a guest during his triumphant campaign in Brittany and released his nephew Hakon. In return, Harold, breaking the supposed oath he had sworn to William, claimed the very prize that had been the focus of William's desires for decades (McLynn 1999, 173). The shock of Harold's rapid coronation, with no warning or consultation with the Norman duke, must undoubtedly have left him furious. The Norman duke wasted no time in sending a message to the newly crowned King Harold immediately. Exactly what the message entailed, whether it was delivered orally or in writing, and in what tone is unknown, but Duke William certainly wanted to confront Harold regarding what had just unfolded. Harold, in turn, gave a resolute response: he had been chosen as king by the witan, and the church had anointed him (Howarth 1977, 70).

Duke William wasted little time considering his options, and his first move was to hold a meeting with his most significant Norman allies to discuss what had just transpired in the British realm with King Harold's coronation. This meeting gathered the most important people in Normandy at the time, including Duke William's brother Robert, Count of Mortain; Richard of Evreux; Roger of Beaumont; Hugh of Grandmesnil; William FitzOsbern; Odo of Bayeux; Roger of Montgomery; Hugh of Montfort; Walter Giffard; and William of Warren. These individuals all held titles of nobility, had close ties to the duke himself, held great military and political power within Normandy, as well as landholdings and wealth, and many of them had participated in prior gatherings of great importance alongside Duke William. They would play pivotal roles if William were to gain the support of his countrymen. Those assembled listened to Duke William's plans and ambitions for conquering England, and eventually, it was agreed that a second meeting, which would include the entire Norman nobility, should be held, where the members of this first meeting would provide support for William's ambition to conquer England (McLynn 1999, 189–190). In the meantime, while Duke William awaited the delivery of his summons, he sought to negotiate with the newly crowned King Harold Godwinson. Initially, the duke sent an embassy to England to remind Harold of the promise he had made to William in 1064. Harold responded callously that Edward had named him as his successor on his deathbed, and the council of Anglo-Saxon nobles and clergy, known as The Witan, had supported Harold in his claim to the throne. According to William of Malmesbury, Duke William, cunning as always, sought to reach out to the papacy in Rome prior to his second assembly (Morris 2013, 143). Duke William therefore sent the Bishop of Lisieux, Gilbert, as an envoy to parlay with Pope Alexander II. After listening to Gilbert's arguments in favor of William and wishing to extend his papal influence in the northern parts of Europe, the pope decided to give the Normans his blessing for an invasion of England. One may wonder why King Harold did not send an envoy of his own to show the pope that there are often two sides to a story. Most likely, Harold figured that it would be a hopeless cause, as the method by which the Anglo-Saxons elected their kings had nothing to do with the papacy, and the papacy would, regardless, be expected to support the Normans in their military aspirations, as it had done with prior Norman expeditions in the 1060s (McLynn 1999, 190–191). Regardless, Harold's failure to engage with the papacy would ultimately prove to be a significant miscalculation in the escalating conflict between the two rivals.

Some scholars suggest that another reason for Pope Alexander II's blessing of the Norman expedition was related to the Archbishop of Canterbury, Stigand, who was considered the principal religious leader in England. Stigand had ruled as archbishop of Canterbury since 1052 and continued in this role even past William's Conquest until 1070. Supposedly, the papacy may have seen his position as uncanonical. However, during the papacy's investigation of the English church in 1062, no action was taken against the Archbishop of Canterbury. William of Poitiers hinted that Stigand's influence made the future King William hesitant to move against him for a while, until he replaced him with the pro–Norman Lanfranc of Pavia in 1070. While Stigand did not seem to be popular with the papacy, there is little evidence to suggest that he was the reason for the papal blessing that Duke William received (Morton 1975, 363–364, 378–379). Duke William's ally, Lanfranc, is often credited with advising the Norman duke to seek a blessing from the papacy. Lanfranc, an Italian figure, earned renown as a revered scholar and churchman. However, akin to numerous contemporaries, he was also a political operator and would not shy away from employing questionable tactics to advance his ideals. Duke William was likely grateful to Lanfranc, given that he was the one who had advised Pope Nicholas II to sanction the duke's marriage to Matilda in 1059. Many scholars argue that it was likely Lanfranc who identified the fundamental issue in William's claim to the English throne. Harold may not be worthy of the throne, but why would the Norman duke be a legitimate contender? What right did he have to overthrow the Anglo-Saxon king, whose legitimacy was backed by the Anglo-Saxon church and the witan? Duke William's great-aunt Emma had been the wife of Æthelred and Cnut, as well as the mother of Edward. However, this was the only familial relationship that the Norman duke had to the royal house of England. The invasion was therefore presented not simply as a secular conquest, but as one whose highest aim should be the reformation of the errant English church in order to bring it back into the fold of the Roman papacy (Howard 1975, 99–100).

The claim that Pope Alexander II gave his blessing to Duke William's expedition in 1066 is further reinforced by the account of William of Poitiers, who was a contemporary witness to the events of that year. William of Poitiers is often cited as the originator of the story of Rome's favor toward the expedition. While William of Poitiers had a very pro–Norman perspective on the events that unfolded in 1066, subsequent chroniclers in the following century, like William of Malmesbury and Orderic Vitalis, who were half-English and boasted less bias toward a solely Norman viewpoint compared to William of Poitiers, echoed the tale told by William of Poitiers in his work *Gesta Guillelmi*. Furthermore, it is often claimed that the Bayeux Tapestry depicts the papal banner that Pope Alexander II allegedly sent to the Norman duke as a token of his papal approval of the expedition. On a final and decisive note, Alexander II's successor, Pope Gregory VII, sent a letter to then–King William on 24 April 1080 to confirm the approval that he had secured from Alexander II prior to his conquest in 1066 (Morton 1975, 363). This endorsement not only legitimized William's claim to the English throne but also underscored the pivotal role of papal authority in shaping the political landscape of medieval Europe.

While the idea of priests and the church may invoke a feeling of pacifism in most contemporary readers, this was absolutely not the case when it came to the papacy during medieval times. Pope Alexander II had personally organized what was essentially a crusade in Spain against Islamic foes a few years earlier. He had also granted papal banners to supporters of the papacy fighting wars in Italy in the decade before 1066. This was not the first time he had given his blessing for an invasion to a Norman, as he had done so earlier in 1063 for the Norman nobleman Roger de Hauteville and his invasion of Sicily (Rex 2011, 30). While the papal blessing for Duke William's invasion plans granted the duke no favors in terms of sheer army strength, it was a significant diplomatic victory for the Normans. With the church's blessings on his side, William could legitimize his invasion by arguing that he was leading a crusade against the Anglo-Saxon heathens. Normandy would rise as the sword of a confident Christianity, going on the offensive for the first time in centuries after facing oppression from Vikings in the North, Hungarians in the East, and Islam in the South. This trend would continue three decades later when the Normans rose as the vanguard of the First Crusade against the rising Islamic communities settled in the Holy Land. Furthermore, the interference of the papacy in the upcoming invasion would also mean that any other major European powers that sought to intervene on Harold's side would be doing so against the blessed Christian army of the Normans (McLynn 1999, 191).

At some point after the delegation from Rome returned, Duke William summoned his second council at Lillebonne. Here, he presented his case for an invasion of England and requested his barons' assistance. Convincing his own vassals turned out to be one of the most difficult tasks to complete before embarking on the expedition. Although Duke William's vassals were bound to him by their feudal obligations, they were not obligated to serve him across the sea. William thus framed the case from his perspective, portraying Harold as a faithless vassal and a perjurer who must be punished for his treachery. However, the barons were unconvinced, and many of them feared the might of the English nation, which arguably possessed a powerful navy and a great army to defend itself (Rex 2012, 30).

While making a complete comparison between the naval forces of England and Normandy at this time is challenging, historical material suggests that the English navy was certainly not one to be trifled with. During the reign of Edward the Confessor in the 1040s, England repeatedly commanded large fleets used to defend against Viking attacks. At the request of the German emperor, Edward the Confessor also instituted a naval blockade of Flanders around this time. The Godwines seemed to have only added to this naval power, as they had forced their return from exile in 1052 thanks to the large fleet they managed to recruit. Additionally, when Harold subdued Wales and ended the life of their king, Gruffudd ap Llewellyn, in 1063, he did so largely due to his ability to draw upon powerful naval support. Whenever Normandy was mentioned during this time, it was almost solely in relation to wars waged on land borders (Morris 2013, 144). In addition to the oceanic challenges a Norman fleet would face in crossing the English Channel, the Norman barons pointed out that

England was much richer than the Norman duchy. They worried that the ships could not be prepared in time, and even if they were, they would lack oarsmen. Duke William countered this argument, asserting that wars are won by courage, not numbers, and while Harold would be fighting to retain what he had stolen from the Norman duke, his army would fight to regain the gift he was rightfully owed and should lawfully have acquired (Rex 2012, 30–31). The invasion was not only ambitious; it was also the first time someone would attempt to take a chivalric army across the sea. The Vikings never took horses with them when they crossed the sea to pillage, and while the Greeks of the Byzantine Empire transported mounted troops, they had much larger ships that were more advanced in their design. Additionally, if the ships did not have favorable winds and rowing became a necessity, two shifts of oarsmen would be required for the distance that Duke William had in mind. This meant that essentially everyone on the ship would have to be willing and able to row. For example, a fifty-foot ship would require twenty-four oars and, therefore, forty-eight oarsmen, which left little room for passengers. If horses were to be taken aboard, rowing would become impossible. Duke William was, however, undeterred by this and would have to rely on favorable winds, risking everything in case of a change in the weather. Too much wind would destroy the fleet, while too little would leave it stranded. The duke would seemingly need his good fortune if the transportation prior to the invasion were to be successful as well (Howarth 1977, 91–93).

In the end, the Norman nobles present at Lillebonne made the mistake of asking William FitzOsbern, a staunch supporter of the invasion and one of Duke William's guardians in his youth, to act as their attorney and argue their case for why it would be ludicrous to stage an invasion of the Anglo-Saxon nation. However, William FitzOsbern cunningly tricked the nobles, and when the meeting reconvened and he was supposed to act as an intermediary between the nobles and the duke, he stood up from his chair and delivered a speech promising Duke William that each of the nobles would indeed double their contingency due under the feudal bond and be willing to let it bind them to Duke William's service even across the sea. Naturally, the nobles quickly erupted in cries of protest. Duke William used this as an excuse to adjourn the meeting once more, taking this time to call the nobles in for personal interviews with him one by one. Likely fearful of the duke's retaliation, they all accepted the obligation laid upon them by FitzOsbern, subject to the condition that the exceptional double military requirement should not serve as a standard for future feudal obligations (McLynn 1999, 192). Duke William was pleased to agree to this, as he now had the domestic support he needed to stage an invasion. The Norman historian Wace recorded an account that historians have since referred to as "the Ship List." The title comes from its simplicity; it is no more than a list of fourteen names, including how many ships each individual contributed to William's fleet in 1066. This list had long been regarded as inauthentic because many historians argued that such a precise statement of military service would have been unknown at this point in time, especially given that Wace lived 100 years later in the twelfth century. However, modern scholars tend to agree that it is a genuine résumé originally created in the year 1066 and drawn up shortly after the Conquest. The figures mentioned in the Ship List were most likely minimum requirements, but the numbers were quite impressive. Duke William's closest advisors, Roger of Montgomery and William FitzOsbern, who had served him since the beginning of his reign, both pledged to provide him with sixty ships according to the list. Duke William's half-brothers, Robert and Odo, were respectively required to provide him with 120 and 100 ships (Morris 2013, 144–146). This collective commitment underscored the significant resources and alliances that Duke William was able to rally in preparation for his ambitious campaign.

Furthermore, the great Norman houses of Eu, Beaumont, Avranches, and Montgomery each offered to provide the duke with sixty ships. The house of Évreux offered eighty, and the house of de Montfort offered forty. The duke's wife, Duchess Matilda, provided her husband with the largest ship in the entire fleet, named the *Mora* (Rex 2012, 31). Walter Giffard supplied the duke with thirty ships and one hundred knights, while Nicholas, the abbot of St-Ouen, offered twenty ships and a hundred knights (McLynn 1999, 193). The army that Duke William ultimately assembled could be described as very cosmopolitan in its composition, and it would be a hasty conclusion to refer to it solely as a Norman army. This would overlook the amalgamation of soldiers from different regions, backgrounds, and languages that comprised the army that the Norman duke gathered. Unlike the English army it would end up fighting, this Norman-led army can be described as an impromptu force whose sole purpose was the conquest of England, after which it would be dissolved. While primarily organized for the specific purpose of conquering England, the Norman-led army was deliberately assembled for this campaign rather than being a standing force. Its main objective was conquest, yet its formation involved prior planning, resources, and troops gathered for this specific endeavor.

Numerous historical sources cover the cosmopolitan composition of Duke William's army, and most agree on the diversity of his fighting force. The Bishop of Amiens, Guy, wrote in his history of the Norman invasion of England, entitled *Carmen de Hastingae Proelio* ("Song of the Battle of Hastings"), that before the Battle of Hastings, Duke William addressed men from Francia, Brittany, Maine, and Norman men from both the Norman Duchy in France and the Norman settlements in Italy. William of Poitiers likewise lists men from Maine, France, Brittany, Aquitaine, and Normandy. The annals from the monastery of Nieder-Alteich on the Danube and the twelfth-century chronicle from the abbey of St. Maixent in Poitou also confirm the presence of men from Aquitaine in Duke William's army. William of Jumièges, however, does not cover the backgrounds of the men in Duke William's forces. When Orderic Vitalis revised his work, he referred to the army as a great assembly of Norman, Flemish, French, and Breton soldiers. However, when he wrote his *Historia Ecclesiastica*, the soldiers were described as men of Gaul, Brittany, Poitevins, Burgundy, and others from north of the Alps. In Wace's work, *Roman de Rou*, which also contains *The Ship List*, he notes that he is unable to list the names of all the Norman and Breton barons in the army but mentions that many also came from Anjou, Maine, Thouars, Poitou, Ponthieu, and Boulogne, as well as what were most likely mercenaries seeking land and money. John of Worcester argues that William included auxiliaries from all of Gaul. In the Bayeux Tapestry, Duke William's men are described twice during the Battle of Hastings, and in both instances, they are referred to as Franci ("French"). While the sources show some minor disagreements, most tend to agree that Duke William's army was cosmopolitan in nature (Lawson 2003, 173–174). There is little reason to disbelieve these statements.

William of Poitiers notes that as rumors of the duke's expedition spread, many men across Europe seeking good fortune came to join Duke William's cause. Given William's fierce reputation as a successful warlord combined with England's great wealth, it makes sense that mercenaries would be interested in joining his force. In the middle of the eleventh century, Europe certainly had many such men to spare, and earlier in the year, when Tostig had conducted raids on the English coast after his stay in Flanders, he had done so with Flemish soldiers seeking good fortune rather than Anglo-Saxon men. While narrowing down the diversity of the army is relatively straightforward, determining the precise magnitude of the duke's military force poses a considerably greater challenge. The *Carmen* numbers it at 150,000 men, while William of Poitiers argues that it was 50,000 during the gathering in France but increased to 60,000 just prior to the Battle of Hastings. The Poitevin chronicle vaguely states, "they say" that William had 14,000 men. William of Jumièges does not provide a specific army size but notes that it consisted of 3,000 ships. The *Carmen* is most certainly a very opportunistic estimate. Scholars in the last decade of the nineteenth century favored limiting both the Norman and the English armies to a size of fewer than 10,000 men. The German historian Wilhelm Spatz, in his 1896 book entitled Die Schlacht von Hastings ("The Battle of Hastings"), argued that William likely did not lead an army of 14,000 men into battle. Spatz contended that medieval armies were much smaller and noted that William of Poitiers emphasized that when the forces experienced a month's delay in Dives due to contrary winds, they did not plunder the surrounding countryside, which would certainly have limited the army size (Lawson 2003, 175–176). Robert Wace wrote that his father told him the Norman army's ship count was 696, although in his work *Roman de Rou*, he states that it consisted of 776 ships. The monk Hugh of Fleury claimed that the army consisted of 700 ships but also estimated the army at an unrealistic 150,000 (Rex 2012, 31). The number of ships has, therefore, been estimated at around 700 to 3,000, depending on the source. It was most likely on the lower end of this range. If one were to make a rough estimate of the army size based on this information and multiply it by the average number of men per ship indicated by the *Bayeux Tapestry*, where each ship carries approximately seven men (Lawson 2003, 176), then 1,500 ships would produce a total army size of $1,500 \times 7 = 10,500$ men. Conversely, with 1,000 ships, the army size would be around 7,000 men. Additionally, given that the Norman army marched eleven kilometers from Hastings to fight in the early morning of October 14, 1066, it is unlikely that it was as large as the estimate provided by the *Carmen de Hastingae Proelio*. *Domesday Book* further notes that after his conquest, William provided land for about 4,000 Norman warriors in England. This suggests that the rest of the army likely returned to Normandy or died fighting, leading to a rough estimate of about 7,000 to 8,000 men. The English historian Sir James Henry Ramsay, in his work *The Foundations of England*, also suggests that 5,000 would be a satisfactory number for the Norman army (Lawson 2003, 177). The precise size of William's army remains a subject of debate among historians, but the estimates provide valuable insight into the scale and ambition of the Norman Conquest.

Later English kings, such as Henry V, also took only 8,000–10,000 men across the Channel. While Henry V and Edward IV did so once, it can be questioned whether an eleventh-century duke of Normandy could equal the army size of a thirteenth or fourteenth-century king of England. The historian Francis Baring wrote in his 1961 publication *Domesday Tables for the County of Hertford* that the large figures given by historical sources should not be taken literally but are rather simple rhetorical equivalents of "many," endorsing Sir James Henry Ramsay's and Wilhelm Spatz's arguments that the speed at which the Norman army moved across the English countryside would suggest a smaller army size. Baring concludes with an estimate of 5,000–10,000 men. He also added a note tracing Duke William's route to London after the Battle of Hastings based on the supposedly damaged estates recorded in Domesday Book. Based on this, Baring argues that the army size would not be considerable enough to exceed 10,000 men. While these analyses certainly present a more conservative estimate than those from older sources, Baring's examination of the Domesday estates has since been shown to contain flaws regarding the line of Duke William's march, and thus also the size of his army. Likewise, Spatz's use of the number of Domesday landholders of Norman origin provides little evidence, as those who received land did so over a twenty-year period. Because land was granted gradually over a longer period spanning two decades, it's highly likely that many regular folks never received any land at all, and they might not have even expected to. Additionally, in terms of the speed at which the army moved, one could compare it to Julius Caesar's army in 54 BC which is noted to have landed on the British coast with five legions (likely around 25,000 men) and 2,000 cavalry in over 800 ships around midday without opposition, just like Duke William. Following this, Caesar camped for the night and marched into battle against the Britons before midnight (Lawson 2003, 179). Despite various estimates and interpretations, the true size of Duke William's forces remains elusive.

The seemingly never-ending historical quest to ascertain the precise size of Duke William's army prior to and during the Battle of Hastings has sparked endless debates among historians. Despite meticulous analysis and scholarly scrutiny, deciding upon a definitive number is an elusive task. Arguments favoring specific army sizes can often be contradicted when juxtaposed with alternative historical estimates or assessments based on logistical factors such as food supply, speed of movement, and the impact on the surrounding landscape. While mathematical calculations based on the destruction of landmarks, the pace of the army, or other contextual elements may appear compelling, they intermingle with differing viewpoints, thus creating a tapestry of interpretations rather than a concrete answer. In reality, the limitations and complexities of medieval records, as well as the multifaceted nature of historical analysis, underscore the difficulty in reaching an accurate and conclusive figure for the size of Duke William's army. With this in mind, most commonly read sources on the subject that try to pin down the Norman army size seem to place it within a range of 8,000–14,000 men. With stability and support ensured from his own vassals and troops, William would just need to ensure the safety of his duchy before he began his perilous journey across the English Channel. Despite the fact that Duke William had gotten rid of his two fiercest nemeses, the Count of Anjou, Geoffrey Martel, and the French King Henry I, it would be unreasonable to consider his duchy secure if he were to leave it for an extended period. Therefore, Duke William chose to ride out to the neighboring dukes and counts, as well as the King of France, and formally request that they not attack Normandy while he was away on his expedition. He also urged them to refrain from dissuading knights and soldiers within their own territories from seeking opportunities to join him in his quest for fortune. Most of the neighboring dukes and counts gave William a somewhat chilly reception and preferred to wait and see what happened, as they wanted to avoid the potential error of backing a loser. The only count who decided to join William in person was Count Eustace of Boulogne, who ironically also had a legitimate claim to the English throne through his marriage to Edward the Confessor's sister. Duke William, likely aware of this, requested that the count leave his son as a hostage in Normandy while the invasion took place. The only count who responded in direct negative terms was Count Conan of Brittany, whom Duke William had fought against one to two years prior. He assured William that he would have no hesitation in attempting an invasion of Normandy once William left for England. Unsurprisingly, Count Conan was dead a few days later; supporters of William had smeared poison on Conan's gloves, hunting horn, and bridle (Howarth 1977, 98). This event underscored the dangerous game of political alliances and rivalries in which William was engaged as he prepared for his momentous campaign.

Around the beginning of August 1066, the final ship had been prepared, and Duke William's army was ready to set sail. Unlike their rival Norwegian contenders, led by King Harald Hardrada, the Norman fleet was unseamanlike and improvised. Most of the Norsemen had been raised as seamen since childhood, growing up in the sheltered, tideless waterways of Scandinavia, from which they had traveled by boat. In contrast, the Norman coast offered little sheltered water, an open sea, and five-knot tidal streams, with an interval between high and low water reaching up to twelve meters. Normandy also had far fewer harbors, most of which were at the mouths of rivers like the Dives, where William would assemble his army. Such harbors experienced tides pouring in and out, which meant that small ships could go out on the ebb and return upon the flood (Howarth 1977, 117). In the approximately one hundred and fifty years since their Viking ancestors had landed under the leadership of Rollo, the Normans had largely diminished their proficiency in seafaring. The Norman nobility must have desperately rounded up all the woodsmen and carpenters they could find and ordered them to build a fleet as rapidly as possible. This is illustrated in the Bayeux Tapestry, where men with axes cut down tree branches and build ships loaded with weapons, equipment, and wine. These ships were of the old Norse type, double-ended with sternposts and high curved stems, ornamented with dragon tails and heads at each end. Whether these boats were rowed is difficult to determine. In the Bayeux Tapestry, the only ship shown to be rowed is the one that took Harold Godwinson to Normandy in 1064. William's fleet is depicted with masts and sails, but none of them are being rowed. Around half of the ships do have oar-holes, but no oarsmen are shown (Howarth 1975, 118–119). Such preparations highlight the challenges Duke William may have faced as he sought to reclaim the English throne and solidify his legacy.

Despite the fleet being ready, the army was stuck in the River Dives until a southern wind came along, and on the tenth of August, it was blowing from the north. Ironically, the delayed Norman invasion due to the lack of a southern wind may have been a blessing in disguise for Duke William. In England, King Harold, who was preparing for the imminent Norman invasion, was stationed in the southern part of England with his army of around ten thousand men. They likely stripped the countryside bare, and food would have to be brought in from further away. This led to inflation in the surrounding villages, and the newly coronated king was likely not growing in popularity. The Anglo-Saxon fyrd, a militia composed of conscripted men, had already completed their two months of service for the year 1066, and they were likely growing restless. Nevertheless, the northerly wind persisted throughout August (Howarth 1977, 122–123). As the days passed, the tension mounted, and the impending clash would soon determine the fate of England.

The Norman encampment in the harbor of Dives-sur-Mer on the coast of northwestern France was facing supply shortages after less than two months. If supplies were not maintained at a steady pace, Duke William could face issues with his mercenaries, who naturally held little loyalty beyond the coinage they were being paid. When the weather changed in the second week of September, around the twelfth day of the month, the trumpets quickly sounded in the Norman encampment. The supplies, horses, and soldiers were hurried aboard the ships, and Duke William sounded his trumpets aboard the Mora as the fleet set out for the open sea. Unfortunately for Duke William, he could not have known that no less than a day or two prior, the Anglo-Saxon naval forces had also received their sailing orders. Their orders were simple: they were to return to London to refit (Butler 1966, 167–168). The Norman fleet quickly pushed northeast into the narrow ocean, and at some point between Cap d'Antifer and Beachy Head, the two fleets engaged in battle. While little is known about the exact date, time, and location of this naval battle, it seems that the engagement was brought to an abrupt end by the sudden onset of a storm. According to Butler (1966), this may have been fortuitous for the Normans. While both sides faced severe losses, the invaders' losses would have been greater in the end. The Norman losses were not detailed but were significant. As the storm rose, the Anglo-Saxon commander broke off the fighting, and the Norman fleet escaped southeast past Upper Normandy until it reached the haven of St. Valery in Ponthieu at the broad estuary of the Somme (Butler 1966, 168–189). Some of the ships were wrecked on the shore or lost at sea, and the survivors who made it to St. Valery were understandably exhausted and furious. This unfortunate attempt at a sea voyage led to numerous soldiers choosing to desert, and the Norman expedition was on the brink of collapse.

If one is to believe William of Poitiers, this was the moment when Duke William showed true leadership as he instilled new courage and motivation in his men. The duke cautiously concealed his lack of supplies by increasing the daily rations and ordered that those who had perished in the storm be secretly buried. Additionally, Duke William tried to portray the storm as a blessing rather than a curse. Ironically, it turned out that the storm may indeed have been a blessing in disguise for him, as a large portion of the English fyrd serving in King Harold Godwinson's army was allowed to return to their homes. It was by no means unreasonable for King Harold to permit the fyrd to return home, as signs of any upcoming Norman invasion had significantly diminished at this point, and no one would expect any rational seaman to attempt a crossing of the Channel with an entire army at this time of year. Unfortunately for the Anglo-Saxons, they were gravely mistaken. Furthermore, many of the Anglo-Saxons who decided to leave the southern coast chose to sail to the Thames and up the river to London. Along this journey, many perished due to the same storm that had hit Duke William's fleet. The fyrd returned home, and King Harold left the coastal city of Bosham between September 13 and 16, heading towards London. It was no more than two or three days later that he would receive word of King Harald Hardrada's arrival in England, about two hundred and thirty miles away in Northumbria, where the Norwegian king announced his arrival by burning the city of Scarborough to the ground (Howarth 1977, 124–129).

We have little knowledge of any relationship between Harald Hardrada and Duke William. While they were united by a common cause in their wish to defeat the Anglo-Saxons led by Harold Godwinson, they were also rivals for the kingdom of England. They were likely aware that whichever one decided to attack first would be at a disadvantage, as an early attack could potentially tire their forces, diminish supplies, and expose them to unforeseen challenges. This would allow the other invader to strategically plan and take advantage of the weakened position of the aggressor. Duke William ended up having a crucial advantage, as the climate of Normandy forced his fleet to wait longer than his Norwegian competitor. As it turned out, luck would favor the Norman duke once more, as the Norwegians were defeated, leaving the Anglo-Saxons weakened and requiring them to travel another 250 miles back to Hastings to fend off the Normans after their success against the Norwegian invaders (Neveux 2006, 134–135).

Shortly after this, Duke William's luck would bless him once more, as the southerly wind he had long hoped for returned in an almost symbolic gesture on September 26, one day after the Battle of Stamford Bridge on September 25, where King Harold had defeated Harald Hardrada. The Norman duke gathered his fleet and prepared for the one-hundred-mile journey to Beachy Head in England. He spent one day preparing his fleet on the 26th and set sail on the 27th of September (Howarth 1977, 93, 142). The Norman fleet was led across the English Channel by Duke William, who issued his sailing orders from the Mora. The signal to proceed was given to the remaining fleet by lighting a beacon at the masthead of the Mora, alongside the sounding of a trumpet. Every vassal was to mount a lantern on the mast of their ships and follow the Mora's lead across the ocean. Following Duke William's command, the bugles were blown, and the Mora sailed out into the center of the roadstead. Due to the losses of the earlier voyage, the fleet had decreased somewhat. According to Butler (1966), the fleet still totaled around seven hundred larger transport-type ships, with the remainder consisting of smaller boats typically used for river and coastal traffic. These ships carried an army of approximately five thousand horses and twelve thousand men (Butler 1966, 196). Following a much more peaceful voyage than the one the fleet had experienced on September 12, the Norman invasion force landed in England on the 28th of September (Howarth 1977, 93, 142). Thus, with their preparations complete, Duke William and his forces were finally poised to embark on their long-awaited conquest of England.

8

THE INVASION UNFOLDS

DUKE WILLIAM'S PERSONAL SHIP, the *Mora*, ended up around 12 miles ahead of the rest of the Norman invasion fleet. The ship traveled much lighter, carrying only Duke William, his personal entourage, and their horses. The Norman fleet eventually reached the area in East Sussex known as Pevensey Bay, characterized by a shallow lagoon spanning approximately four miles in width and extending six miles inland. Over time, coastal changes since 1066 have caused significant shifts in sea levels, drastically altering the coastline. During Duke William's era, the coast stretched from Beachy Head to Rye. It is plausible that the Norman fleet navigated across what is now the vicinity of Eastbourne and Bexhill. Hastings, along with its harbor, lay further along the road leading to Eastbourne and Bexhill. From there, the coastline turned northward toward the Brede Estuary, reaching inland as far as Sedlescombe (Rex 2011, 12–13). These geographic details played a crucial role in shaping the logistical strategy of the Norman landing and their subsequent march inland, setting the stage for the decisive confrontations that would follow.

On the 28th of September, around the third hour, at 9 a.m., the Norman fleet successfully landed on the English coast. With the Anglo-Saxon army far away and its fleet having moved to London shortly after the 8th of September, the Normans faced no opposition. Duke William disembarked alongside his army, glorifying God's mercy "from the depths of his heart" (Rex 2011, 13–14). Wace, a Norman poet of the twelfth century, composed the *Roman de Rou*, a chronicle that narrates the history of the Norman people and the events culminating in the Norman Conquest of England. This work offers a significant perspective on the conquest from a Norman viewpoint. The 2004 translation by Glyn S. Burgess has rendered Wace's account accessible to modern readers; references to Wace's work in this chapter are based on Burgess's translation. Rex (2011) argues that as William ascended the beach of Pevensey, he tripped and fell. Though this initially alarmed his men, he rose to his feet holding handfuls of earth. William FitzOsbern, who witnessed this closely, cried out,

"You have England in your grasp, Duke, you shall be king!" (Rex 2011, 13–14). This is supported by the account of Wace, although he attributes the symbolic conclusion to William's fall to the duke himself, noting that Duke William, ever quick to turn an ill omen into a blessing, responded by declaring: "My lords, by the splendour of God! I have taken possession of the land in my two hands. It will never be abandoned without a challenge. Whatever is here is ours. Now I will see who is bold." A soldier nearby swiftly seized a piece of thatch from a nearby cottage and handed it to Duke William, who graciously accepted it, proclaiming, "I accept it, and may God be with us!" (Burgess 2004, 163–164). This symbolic gesture, while simple, left a lasting impression on those present, marking the beginning of the campaign that would soon unfold.

While the overall timeline and major events of William the Conqueror's 1066 invasion of England face minimal criticism, ongoing discussions focus on the specific characteristics of the Norman army's landing site. Most authors argue, as noted earlier, that William landed at Pevensey, and that the landing site was reached by open water, resulting in a rather uneventful landing. This is also recorded in the Worcester Manuscript of the *Anglo-Saxon Chronicle*, where it is stated that Duke William came from Normandy into Pevensey on the eve of the Feast of St. Michael, after which he camped at Hastings market-town (Swanton 2000, 199). Some of the ships in Duke William's fleet were also noted to have strayed off course, landing about thirty miles away from Pevensey at Romney in Kent, where the Norman soldiers aboard these ships were attacked and killed before they made it back to the Norman camp (D. Bates 2016, 234). Other authors, such as Wace, are less specific, simply noting that the duke arrived "near Hastings and first found land there" (Burgess 2004, 163).

Roger of Howden, writing in the twelfth century, describes the English coast in the region as follows: "[t]hen comes Penresse [Pevensey], a town, castle, and good port, which is eight miles from Hastinges [Hastings]." This perspective is supported by Williamson, who, in 1959, conducted a study of the English Channel (Hewitt 2018, 76). Williamson suggests that the Pevensey area was a bay open to the sea during Duke William's invasion. M.K. Lawson (2003) and Peter Brandon (1974) also argue that the Pevensey area was an open bay, or at least a large marsh, measuring 6.437 km in width at the mouth and 9.656 km in depth (Brandon 1974, 111). King's (1962) chapter on Domesday Sussex in *Domesday Book* also notes how the salt works received a deposition of alluvium (surface geological material), strongly indicating that a significant part of Pevensey was likely either an exposed bay or extensively flooded (King 1962, 454–457). While these interpretations are popular among contemporary scholars, evidence exists to contradict them, naturally calling into question the landing site of Duke William and the ease with which it occurred. Stephen Rippon's (2000) research on Pevensey reveals the presence of salt works in the area. However, these tend to be situated near drainage systems, suggesting that the area might not have been predominantly an open bay or significantly flooded (Rippon 2000, 188). Furthermore, King suggests that the Pevensey area had no fisheries at the time of the Conquest in 1066, which further supports the idea of an absence of open water (King 1962, 454). Hewitt (2018) argues that most interpretations favoring the "open bay" hypothesis in Pevensey are based on misinterpretations of articles written by medieval historians on the Sussex coast in the early twentieth century. In these articles, the focus on land reclamation and local tides in historical documents did not fully take into account all the environmental evidence, such as maps (Hewitt 2018, 76). Jennings and Smyth (1990) argue that sea levels in Pevensey have not changed since the Battle of Hastings in 1066 (Jennings & Smyth 1990, 215–221). With this in mind, exceptional floods, such as the one in 1909, may have ensured that the Pevensey area could have supported Duke William's fleet at some point during the day of September 28, 1066 (Hewitt 2018, 76). Moreover, there is a scarcity of historical maps from the era of the Norman Conquest within the available historical sources. One exception may be M.K. Lawson (2003), who throughout his analysis presents numerous illustrative maps, including one from 1724 and a mid-nineteenth-century tithe map (Lawson 2003, 52–58), alongside some topographic maps of the landscape at the time of the Battle of Hastings (Lawson 2003, 139–145). While these are certainly interesting, they unfortunately provide little assistance in mapping the Pevensey area. The oldest cartographic representation of Pevensey available today is the Gough Map, the oldest surviving map of Britain, where the island is represented in a geographically recognizable form. Scholars believe it was developed in the fourteenth century, though some argue it may have been created even earlier, in the late thirteenth century. In this map, the area of East Sussex is presented with the towns of Hastings, Pevensey, Battle, Rye, and Winchelsea. Rye is emphasized as a bay, but no bay is shown around Pevensey (Hewitt 2018, 79). Hewitt (2018) argues that while it is not out of the question that Pevensey may have existed as an open-water bay in 1066, it seems unlikely that the region would have transformed so rapidly into what is depicted in the Gough Map a couple of centuries later (Hewitt 2018, 79–80). Rex (2011) further notes that the monks of Fécamp, who accompanied Duke William on his journey, would have been well-versed in the geography of the area and could have advised the Norman duke on how to find a suitable landing site there. Pevensey may additionally have been chosen to avoid the defended Channel ports, such as Sandwich, Dover, and Romney (Rex 2011, 14). In conclusion, as with many details surrounding the Norman Invasion of 1066, the popular assertion that the Pevensey area was an open bay serving as a landing site for Duke William's Norman fleet may be called into question. There is credible evidence highlighting Pevensey as being home to an extensive marsh, and while this would have made a landing possible for the Norman duke, it would likely have required using a bridge of smaller ships and would have been much more time-consuming and logistically difficult, which contradicts the literature arguing in favor of the ease of the Norman fleet's landing (Hewitt 2018, 83). This complexity underscores the challenges faced by the Normans and invites a reevaluation of the traditional narratives surrounding their invasion.

Despite the discussions surrounding Duke William's landing site, there is little doubt that he and his army eventually found themselves in the Pevensey area, approximately twenty-five kilometers from the town of Hastings. Upon his arrival, Duke William made an unusual decision that one would not expect from a man whose intent was to conquer the Anglo-Saxon nation. Rather than initiating an advance into the countryside as Harald Hardrada had done with his immediate advance on York, Duke William decided to build defenses and sit patiently, waiting for Harold Godwinson to attack him (Lawson 2003, 194). It is likely that William estimated there would be no point in marching inland until he had dealt a resounding defeat to the Anglo-Saxon army under Harold Godwinson. Upon their arrival, the Norman army quickly concluded that Pevensey would be a vulnerable spot to build their fortifications. Beach entrenchments would be exposed to threats from both sea and land. The nearby ancient Roman coastal fort of Anderitum could have been taken into consideration, but it would leave the landing place susceptible to an Anglo-Saxon onslaught, which would make the loss of the ships inevitable. However, a few miles east of Pevensey, there was a small port named Hastings. The peninsula that hosted it could offer good defense, and from such a position, the Norman army would be able to afford indirect protection to the fleet, as an Anglo-Saxon force choosing to strike from the forested area of Andredsweald against the lagoon would be open to flank attacks from the peninsula. The main bulk of the Norman army thus began their relocation from Pevensey to Hastings on the morning of Friday, the twenty-ninth of September, with a small detachment of soldiers left behind to guard the fleet. Facing a massive Norman onslaught, the city of Hastings was quick to surrender without resistance (Butler 1966, 199–200). As for the settlement context of the town of Hastings itself, Jeremy Haslam (2021) provides a comprehensive model for the development of Hastings immediately prior to the battle in 1066. Most scholars cover the events leading up to the engagement and how the battle progressed, but few discuss the character of the battlefield itself at the time and how its landscape helped determine that Duke William of Normandy would be victorious and go on to conquer England from the Anglo-Saxons. Most historical researchers assume that Hæstingaceastre (the Anglo-Saxon name for Hastings) was located at modern Hastings. However, in 1995, Malcolm Lyne and Pamela Combes argued that it may have been situated approximately nineteen kilometers to the west, within the Roman fort at Pevensey. While most scholars, including many cited in the previous chapter, tend to disagree with this, the argument is not as flawed as one might think. Duke William did have his battle command headquarters at Pevensey, and Chronicle D of the Anglo-Saxon Chronicle from 1052 might well refer to Pevensey as Hastings, with the transference of the name-form Hæstingaceastre from Pevensey to the later town of modern Hastings happening later (Haslam 2021, 126–128). Regardless of the exact location of where the battle took place, we know that the Hastings that existed prior to the Conquest was rather simple. It could be described as a quasi-urban settlement containing a marketplace, as well as three churches (St Margaret's, St Peter's, and St Michael's), with a fourth (St Andrew's) located just west of the castle (Haslam 2021, 143). This simplicity highlights the town's modest development, providing important context for the events that would soon shape its future.

Wace argues in his *Roman de Rou* that Harold felt a sense of arrogant superiority after his victory over his brother Tostig and his Norwegian allies. He follows this with a sharp critique: "But the man who gloats is a fool; one joy soon comes to an end. Bad news soon comes; he who kills another can soon die." This remark reflects Wace's likely disdain for Harold, whom he viewed as an illegitimate usurper to the English throne. Yet, Wace also attributes the following words to Harold, revealing the intense pressure he faced during his coronation year. Harold reportedly lamented, "I am very distressed that I was not there when they [the Normans] arrived. Things have gone very badly for me in this respect. It would have been better for me to have lost whatever Tostig asked for than not to be at the port when William came to the shore. I would have protected this point of entry properly. I would have caused so many of them to dive into the water and so many of them to drown that they would never have come ashore and never taken anything of ours. They would have had no escape from death unless they had drunk the entire sea. But this is what pleased the Celestial King; I cannot be everywhere" (Burgess 2004, 166). This expression of regret, as presented by Wace, underscores Harold's sense of helplessness in the face of the Norman invasion—a sentiment Wace portrays as a fitting counterpoint to Harold's earlier arrogance, marking the beginning of his downfall.

According to William of Poitiers and other contemporary sources, Harold began to prepare a fleet of upwards of 700 ships after William's landing. While this was taking place, Duke William allowed his soldiers to ravage the surrounding countryside. This is also depicted in the Bayeux Tapestry, where a house is shown being burned down. According to the *Carmen de Hastingae Proelio*, the Norman army took all the cattle in the surrounding land. Duke William had a massive army to feed, and this strategy would assist in conserving resources while simultaneously provoking the English into an engagement. William of Poitiers supports this argument and suggests that King Harold hastened his march after hearing of the Norman ravaging taking place within his kingdom. The extensive damage inflicted by the Normans on the countryside was recorded by the commissioners of *Domesday Book* about twenty years later. According to early French sources, an exchange of ambassadors took place shortly after. The *Carmen* states that Harold sent an articulate monk to scout the Norman camp and inform them that they must leave immediately.

Naturally, Duke William dismissed this appeal and instead sent one of his monks in return to Harold. The monk implored the Anglo-Saxon king to yield the throne to Duke William, asserting that William arrived with a justifiable claim. According to Wace, the monk that Duke William sent was one named Hugh Margot, who was "very learned, knowledgeable and highly esteemed." Margot met with Harold in London and reportedly told him, "I am a messenger, hear in what respect. The duke sends you word, and I say this to you, that you have very soon forgotten the oath you made him in Normandy some time ago. You have been untrue to your oath. Put things right and give him back the crown and the lordship which is not yours by right of inheritance. You are not king through inheritance nor through the men in your lineage. King Edward, when he was well and had full legal power of disposition, gave his land and his kingdom to his finest relative, William, giving him the best gift he could, as the finest man he had. While in good health, before his death, he gave it to him, and you do him wrong, for you heard this and accepted it. You did not oppose it, rather you swore an oath to him. Give him back his land, do right by him before any more harm comes of it. Such great armies as you and he can muster cannot fight without great harm and great loss; this will be entirely your responsibility. I am well aware that some people will pay for this without being in any way at fault. Give him back his kingdom, which you have; if you keep it from him, you will be doing so wrongly."

Supposedly, this angered Harold so much that he almost could not keep himself from harming the monk, had it not been for his brother Gyrth jumping in between the king and the monk (Burgess 2004, 166–167). Margot was then sent back to Duke William with King Harold's refusal to comply with the request. William of Poitiers slightly disagrees with the *Carmen* and the *Roman de Rou* and argues that Duke William pretended to be his steward when he met with King Harold's messenger, then decided to receive it formally as part of an assembly of his soldiers the following morning. In return to the message by Margot, Wace notes that a messenger from Harold told Duke William that Harold would be willing to grant him safe passage back to Normandy, alongside gold and silver, but William would have to relinquish his claim to the English throne. Duke William supposedly responded courteously by saying, "My thanks to him for these fine words. But I have not come to the country with so many shields in order to obtain his sterlings, but to take possession of the entire land, just as he swore it to me and as Edward gave it to me, handing over to me as hostages two young men of noble lineage, one the son and the other the nephew of Godwin. I still have them in my possession. I took possession of them and will hold on to them, if I can, until I have what is rightfully mine." The messenger counters William's demands by arguing that it would disgrace Harold, who is still capable of defending his kingdom. He warns that if William doesn't accept Harold's offer, they will meet on the battlefield on Saturday, to which William agrees, sending the messenger back with gifts as a show of respect. Wace continues by noting that upon the messenger's return, Harold regrets not having treated William's prior emissary, Hugh Margot, with similar courtesy. Meanwhile, Harold's brother Gyrth proposes a plan for Harold to stay back and let Gyrth lead the troops, arguing that Harold's previous oath to William could bring divine consequences in battle. Gyrth suggests scorched-earth tactics to starve William's forces, but Harold refuses, insisting that he cannot harm his own people by destroying their lands and livelihoods (Burgess 2004, 167–168).

Alongside the message brought by the Anglo-Saxon monk from Duke William, a monk from Fécamp had joined the Anglo-Saxon envoy and, following Duke William's instructions, reiterated the arguments supporting William's claim to the throne. Additionally, the monk proposed a trial by single combat between Duke William and Harold, aiming to prevent the loss of innocent lives due to their conflict over the crown. Supposedly, Harold received this message during his advance and reacted by lifting his face to the sky and asking God to decide that day what was just between himself and William (Lawson 2003, 196). Around the same time that King Harold's emissary reached Duke William at the Hastings camp, the Anglo-Saxon army entered London. King Harold and his cavalry had managed to cover one hundred and forty miles in no less than four days, averaging around forty miles a day. Along the way, and within the city of London, Anglo-Saxon men from around the country began to rally for battle once again under their king. Unexpectedly, King Harold also found a fleet of Danish ships that had arrived in the anchorage below London Bridge. King Sweyn of Denmark, a fierce rival of Harald Hardrada, was probably unaware of the Norman invasion when his ships left the harbor in Denmark. The fleet was likely intended as a supporting force for Harold Godwinson's engagement with Hardrada instead. Nevertheless, the Danes decided to remain to help the man who had bested Hardrada in the upcoming battle against the Norman invaders. Despite this, the English reinforcements were still many days away, and even with the Danish support, King Harold's forces were severely diminished compared to the massive enclave he had marched north with a fortnight earlier when he went to York (Butler 1966, 210). King Harold, however, was restless and wished to punish the Norman pillagers immediately. He ordered his men to prepare themselves as rapidly as they could so that they could engage the Norman invaders alongside their leader, Duke William, before he could flee the country. Unfortunately, the previously commissioned fyrd would be needed once again, along with new supplies. King Harold immediately met with the witan at Westminster and started organizing how they could destroy the invaders. The warships in the port of London were hastily prepared for engagement, and within a week, around three hundred of these vessels would be ready to set out to sea. Butler (1966) estimates that it was likely on Monday, the ninth of October, that the Norman ambassador from Fécamp crossed the Thames, where the English envoy brought him to King Harold (Butler 1966, 211). While Duke William probably did not have a decisively stronger army than King Harold, he was most likely a superior army commander. His willingness to wait patiently for his enemy to reach him and to encourage him to do so as rapidly as possible, without all of his reinforcements, is a clear indicator of his shrewdness. He had everything to gain by staying put and establishing a bridgehead on the English coast.

In the final days before his departure south to engage the Norman invaders, King Harold left Westminster and entered Essex, where he made his plea for victory in the church. Likely leaving Thorney on Tuesday afternoon, the tenth of October, King Harold made it to the Minster of the Holy Cross early the next day, where he knelt in prayer in the chapel. He promised wealth beyond measurement, along with many estates and the service of numerous clerics, if God granted success to the Anglo-Saxon defenders. The king was determined to engage with the invaders before the end of the week and set a deadline of Thursday, the twelfth of October, for his army to leave London (Butler 1966, 214–216). Wace describes how Harold, on his march south to face the Normans, quickly recruited as many Anglo-Saxons as possible, accepting "no excuses other than for ill-health" (Burgess 2004, 166). Although Harold likely succeeded in gathering a substantial number of recruits along the way, his army at Hastings was considerably smaller than the force he had led at Stamford Bridge. By the time he faced William, Harold's forces may have been reduced to as little as half the size of the army with which he had defeated his brother Tostig and King Harald Hardrada.

In his *Roman de Rou*, Wace notes that the Anglo-Saxons considered a wide array of strategies to address the Norman threat. Harold's brother Gyrth suggested that the king should remain behind and allow him to engage in battle on his behalf. Gyrth reasoned that even if he were to lose, Harold would still be alive, able to gather more troops, and confront Duke William at a later date. Additionally, Gyrth proposed a scorched earth tactic, arguing that while he fought the Normans, Harold could "go through this land setting fire to everything, destroying houses and towns, capturing booty and food, swine, sheep and cattle, so that the Normans cannot find any food or anything off which they can live." Although such a tactic might have been effective—and would ironically be employed by Duke William half a decade later in his infamous Harrying of the North—Harold was quick to refuse, stating that he would not allow his brother to battle without him, nor would he set fire to towns or rob his vassals of their possessions. He countered, "How could I harm the people it is my duty to govern? I must not destroy or harm the people to whom I owe protection." In response to Gyrth's suggestion, Harold had his men swear an oath that they would never enter battle without him (Burgess 2004, 168–169). Despite his pro–Norman bias, Wace highlights Harold's sense of responsibility towards his people and his desire to lead by example, emphasizing the moral principles that guided his leadership despite the dire circumstances.

The *Carmen* and William of Poitiers, writing in his work *The Gesta Guillelmi*, both agree that King Harold attempted to take Duke William by surprise prior to their engagement. This sentiment is also shared by William of Jumièges in his work *Gesta Normannorum Ducum*, and the Anglo-Saxon Chronicle E's text statement that he fought before all his army had come may also hint at the possibility of a stealthy assault. With this in mind, many modern scholars, including M.K. Lawson, agree with British historian John Horace Round's 1893 assertion that the events leading up to the battle at Hastings are "doubtful and difficult to determine" (Lawson 2003, 196). This uncertainty underscores the complexities of reconstructing the historical narrative surrounding one of England's most pivotal battles.

Duke William's scouts soon reported the enemy's close approach and William of Poitiers further states that this caused Duke William to hastily assemble the men in his camps, likely meaning the camps of Pevensey and Hastings, and make a speech urging his men to advance for victory into battle with him immediately (Lawson 2003, 194–196). William of Jumièges contradicts William of Poitiers and argues that Duke William ordered his men to stand to arms from dusk to dawn out of fear that a nocturnal ambush might occur. At the break of dawn, he supposedly drew up his soldiers and advanced against the Anglo-Saxon army. If one is to believe this version of events, it would seem that the Norman army had reached Senlac Hill (also known as Battle Hill) prior to the engagement. Senlac Hill is the traditional site where the Battle of Hastings took place and is situated close to the town of Battle in East Sussex, about ten kilometers northwest of Hastings. The area that William's army occupied prior to the Battle of Hastings likely formed a peninsula, protected by the estuary of the Brede to the east and marshland to the north. This would have made the high ground that runs south through Battle and Telham the only viable route to reach Hastings for the Anglo-Saxon army. Harold could undoubtedly have reached Pevensey by making a large sweep to the west around Pevensey Bay through the South Downs, but by that point in time, Duke William must have known that Harold would take the expected route through Battle (Lawson 2003, 197).

On the eleventh of October 1066, King Harold made his return and made the crucial decision not to wait for the reinforcements arriving from the North, confident that the reinforcements that had arrived from around the country to join him in London, in combination with the reinforced fleet under his command, would enable him to best the Norman duke. Despite ill weather forecasts and a lack of reinforcements, King Harold seemed willing to risk it all as he made his journey south on the eleventh of October. The ships made their way across the estuary of the Thames, and as Harold neared the Normans on Friday, October 13, he supposedly told the Norman envoy that Duke William had sent to his camp that on the following day, his just share of the kingdom would be made apparent. With this knowledge in hand, the envoy returned to the Norman duke, who now knew that within a day, he would be fighting the Anglo-Saxon host, eliminating any hopes King Harold may have had of catching the Norman invaders off guard.

In the meantime, the Anglo-Saxon numbers grew as Kentish levies came to join them. Some of these levies had adequate equipment consisting of swords and armor, while others had nothing more than simple clubs and stones lashed to handles of wood. Thanks to the roads built by the ancient Romans, the Anglo-Saxons were able to advance about fifteen miles through the woodland quite rapidly, and in the late morning or early afternoon, the Anglo-Saxon vanguard emerged from the forest a mile north of Bodiam. They continued by passing the Rother, moving toward Sedlescombe and eventually Hastings. Eventually reaching Caldbec Hill, about eight miles from Hastings, the Anglo-Saxon army had a brief halt. Once the main body of the army had gathered, the army commanders led their men from Caldbec Hill along the route through Battle (Butler 1966, 217–225). This allowed the Anglo-Saxon army to take up a fixed defensive position on the ridge of Senlac Hill.

Luckily for King Harold, the area around Hastings was well known to him. He owned estates both to the north and south of the battlefield, and his parents, Gyrtha and Earl Godwin, had held estates all over Sussex. While the Norman sources repeatedly mention how impressive their victory was, given the massive size of the Anglo-Saxon army, they contradict the English chroniclers who stressed King Harold's lack of reinforcements and state of unreadiness. A retreat would likely not have been possible either way. Essentially stuck between the coast, where their ships would face harsh weather conditions as winter approached, and a rumor that King Harold's fleet had been sent to block any retreat, the Normans would eventually be forced to engage (Rex 2011, 60–61). Around nightfall between the 13th and 14th of October, King Harold had his troops drawn up on the ridge of the hill, keeping the housecarls in the center to protect their king, while the fyrd were positioned on either side (Neveux 2006, 137).

On the morning of Saturday, October 14, Duke William moved his army up to the crest of Telham Hill, where he could observe the Anglo-Saxon movements on Caldbec Hill. Unfortunately for the Norman duke, the hill was covered by trees and boggy ground, which would likely create great difficulties for the mobility of his cavalry (Rex 2011, 60–61). As he prepared for battle, Duke William was quick to divide his army into three separate bodies that corresponded to their differing contingents. The center was occupied by the Normans, who would directly face the Anglo-Saxon housecarls, while the two wings were held by allies consisting of the French and Flemish supporters on the right and the Bretons on the left, both facing the fyrd (Neveux 2006, 136–137). As the two armies gathered opposite each other, everything was now at stake. In this crucial moment, it was simply a question of how much patience both sides would exert before hostilities broke out.

9

THE BATTLE OF HASTINGS

AT LONG LAST, THE FATEFUL confrontation with his archnemesis materialized for Duke William. He would finally encounter the adversary he had long awaited, eager to conquer in order to secure his coveted prize: the throne of England. Conversely, should King Harold emerge victorious, he would confront the ultimate trial of the year, affirming his worthiness to succeed Edward the Confessor. The impending battle would unfold in the historical coastal town of Hastings, situated in East Sussex. Contrary to urban warfare, Duke William and King Harold would face each other just beyond the town limits. The Normans assumed the role of aggressors, while the Anglo-Saxons strategically positioned themselves defensively on Caldbec Hill. The armies about to face each other most likely consisted of somewhat equal sizes. The consensus has typically been that they both numbered around 7,000 men each. However, in recent times, scholars tend to place this figure in the lower estimates and instead range the numbers at around 10,000 to 12,000 men. Peter Rex (2011) states that the possible source of this suggestion, Viscount Aimeri de Thours, in his *Chronicle of St. Maixent*, puts the estimate of Duke William at 14,000 (Rex 2011, 63). However, as we know from the previous chapter, some sources, such as the *Carmen*, put the estimate as high as 150,000 men. The English chroniclers tended to disagree with the notion of equal army size, attributing the defeat to a lack of numbers and God not being on their side. Notwithstanding, the protracted duration of the battle suggests that the Norman army size, in contrast to what some historical sources argue, might not have been as overwhelming compared to the Anglo-Saxons (Rex 2011, 63). Ultimately, this complexity surrounding the size and composition of both armies highlights the multifaceted nature of the conflict, suggesting that factors beyond mere numbers played a crucial role in determining the battle's outcome.

While the Norman and Anglo-Saxon armies were surprisingly similar in many regards, they did have some key distinctions, both in how they were created and in the types of troops they contained and the equipment they wore. The Norman army was led by troops referred to as magnates. These magnates were typically members of the ducal family and were also the primary source of soldiers. Most of the land prior to 1066 was held by powerful nobles who had inherited their estates and sent knights into the service of Duke William as a duty. The length of service was likely around forty days a year. Many of these knights may have lived at their lord's hall as household knights, while others may have been settled across his estates in their own holdings. Wealthy knights may even have been expected to supply their lord with a number of troops who lived under them as household men or had, in turn, been given land by them. The noble lords would often have more knights in their service than the duke required (Gravett 1992, 15). The Normans formed their cavalrymen into contingents known as "conrois," organized by multiples of five into groups of around twenty-five to fifty. The more affluent knights would also be expected to bring their assistants, often men of lower birth, along as infantrymen or less well-equipped cavalry. The knights would ride on expensive warhorses and would often require their followers to look after their equipment and assist them in the field. Young men of free birth were often recruited and trained in mounted warfare but were not expected to wear full armor or carry swords in battle prior to their knighthood. The Norman army was primarily made up of infantrymen summoned for the invasion, while others were mercenaries serving Duke William for pay. This bulk of the army often consisted of spearmen and a large number of crossbowmen and archers. The Norman soldiers were equipped with a coat of mail referred to as a "hauberk" as their primary piece of defensive equipment. These were made out of metal, horn, leather, and perhaps cloth or hide in some instances, and were fastened to an undergarment. Most coats had elbow-length sleeves with skirts that reached the knees and split front and rear to ease riding. Some of these were extended and formed a mail hood as well (Graves 1992, 15–19). Together, these elements contributed to the formidable and versatile nature of the Norman military.

Some of the Normans, most notably Duke William himself, have been portrayed wearing mail sleeves extending beyond the hauberk's sleeve. Leggings of mail were also used occasionally, and ordinary leather shoes were preferred for footwear. The horsemen would wear iron pick spurs terminating in small points. As for the helmets, these were usually fitted with a nasal guard and occasionally with reinforcing bands. Most soldiers in the Norman army would use a shield. Some infantrymen would carry a circular wooden shield, which was likely faced with leather and possibly backed with it as well. An iron boss would be riveted in the center of the surface to cover a hole through which the soldier could grasp the shield by an iron strip riveting inside with his hand. Furthermore, a considerable number of these soldiers likely utilized a second strap to secure the forearm, while a "guige" strap facilitated the slinging or hanging of the shield on the back. This strap also served to prevent the shield from being lost or accidentally dropped. The edges of the shield may have been protected by applied bands of leather or metal. At the Battle of Hastings, a significant number of both horsemen and infantrymen adopted kite-shaped shields, featuring a rounded top that extended to a pointed bottom. For cavalrymen, its long shape offered protection as well as the ability to hold it horizontally to protect the horse's flank. All of the Normans depicted in the Bayeux Tapestry also carry this type of shield, which would often be adorned with designs of dragons, lions, or other ferocious beasts.

The Norman warrior would often favor a straight double-edged slashing sword, while the knight would be equipped with a lance consisting of a plain ash shaft that was around eight feet in length and tipped with a socketed triangular iron head. This lance could also be thrown like a javelin if necessary. At Hastings, however, with the terrain being unfavorable to an open-field cavalry charge, the knights would charge in groups, each contingent following the pennon on the lance of their lord. It was more likely that they utilized slim, socketed javelins while the infantry carried broad stabbing spears (Graves 19–22). Some of the knights may have carried a mace as well. Three types are depicted in the Bayeux Tapestry, with one of them featuring a flanged iron head and others with knobbed heads. The third type was carried by Duke William and Odo and can be described as a rough baton of command.

The Norman army also carried two banners with them. The first is depicted in the Bayeux Tapestry on a half-moon-shaped flag with flies and features a raven. The raven banner was one that had commonly been used by the Vikings, including Harald Hardrada, and showed that despite their conversion to Christianity and mingling with the native French populace, the Normans had still clung to their Viking ancestry. The other banner was likely the papal banner, which was carried by Eustace of Boulogne and depicted a golden cross on a white background.

The archers all wore armor, except for a single figure depicted wearing mail. These archers most likely used wooden self-bows, which were around six feet in length. The power of the longbow would not yet be felt, and the self-bows had less draw weight and could be drawn at a shorter distance, perhaps closer to the chest. The effective range against a mailed opponent was likely around one hundred yards. While no crossbowmen are visible in the Bayeux Tapestry, William of Poitiers states that Duke William did in fact use them. The Carmen de Hastingae Proelio also mentions this.

Crossbowmen would have looked very similar to the archers, except for the weapons they carried. The crossbow was likely more powerful than the self-bow and could be loaded by bracing the bow against the feet and pulling back the cord by hand. Small wooden bolts equipped with iron heads and parchment vanes were stored in belt quivers. The Norman army likely included slingers, who were probably unarmored and carried a pouch containing slingshots with an effective range of approximately thirty yards. If these projectiles landed a blow to an unprotected face at close range, they could prove highly lethal (Graves 1992, 22–25). Overall, the diverse array of weaponry and tactics employed by the Norman forces demonstrated their adaptability and strategic acumen on the battlefield.

The Anglo-Saxon army was constructed in a very specific way. Like many other medieval kingdoms, eleventh-century England was defined by a seigniorial structure (Abels 2013, 196). A seigneurial system is similar to a feudal system but differs in certain key aspects. In a seigniorial system, it is the lord of the manor who owns the land, with peasants listed in his service. These peasants would work the land and pay rent to their lords in exchange for protection and the ability to live off the land. The lord of the manor had the right to administer justice and collect taxes and other payments from the peasants, exerting significant influence over any crucial decisions affecting his peasantry. In contrast, in a feudal system, the king grants land (fiefs) to lords (vassals) in exchange for their military service and loyalty. These lords would then grant land to their own peasants, who would provide labor and services in return. The vassals were also able to administer justice over their peasantry and collect taxes from them; however, the king held ultimate authority over all the land and people in the kingdom. The owners of the fiefs were required to conduct mandatory military service as part of the fyrd, as well as maintain bridges and fortresses. These three requirements were known as trinoda necessitas, or the three common burdens. Eligibility for military service was determined based on "hides," a unit supposedly assessed based on the economic worth of land. Around the eleventh century, a five-hide unit marked a thegn, indicating a man of some elite status. A peasant might have held a mail coat and gold sword, but if he owned no land, he would still be designated as a "ceorl." Ceorls were defined as free men of the lowest status rank in Anglo-Saxon England. The king's thegns who owned large tracts of land would bring one man for each five-hide unit they possessed when called to war. During times of conflict, fyrds could be called in for a period of two months, with emergencies allowing this request to be repeated. Such an emergency occurred five times in 1016. Deserting could result in the death penalty as punishment. When national emergencies arose, such as in the case of 1066, the king could call upon the services of every able-bodied freeman (Gravett 1992, 28–29). Thegns had their fiefs measured in hides, and according to Domesday Book, the critical threshold for fyrd service was five hides or more. Anyone possessing more than three hundred hides would additionally be required to provision a ship (Abels 1988; Bradbury 1998, 76). This structured military organization played a crucial role in the defense and governance of Anglo-Saxon England.

The Anglo-Saxon army present at the Battle of Hastings was composed of King Harold's supporters. In the D version of the Anglo-Saxon Chronicle for 1066, it is stated that King Harold "gathered a great raiding army, and came against him at the grey apple tree. And William came upon him by surprise before his people were marshalled. Nevertheless, the king fought very hard against him with those men who wanted to support him" (Swanton 2000, 199). Emphasizing the last part clearly indicates that not everybody supported King Harold. Nevertheless, little empirical testing has been done on these claims. Hewitt (2021) conducted a study in which he used data recorded in Domesday Book to investigate the features of manors related to identified participants in comparison to all recorded manors. DeVries (2003) argues that Anglo-Saxon England had three different types of soldiers. The core soldiers were the housecarls, who were landowners or professional bodyguards serving the king or the aristocracy. The second group was the select fyrd, while the third group was known as the great fyrd, which combined the professional fighters of the select fyrd with supporting troops (DeVries 2003, 210–213). Barlow (2002) argues in his biography of the Godwine family that the Anglo-Saxon army that fought during the Battle of Hastings was primarily comprised of housecarls and thegns under King Harold and his brothers (Barlow 2002, 142). Hewitt (2021) conducted a comprehensive map analysis of the recorded participants, as well as the contributing monastic lordships and estates in 1066, based on data from Domesday Book. He finds that the largest participant manors came from Middlesex in first place and Huntingdonshire in second place. This also indicates where King Harold enjoyed the most popularity in his attempts to gather an army (Hewitt 2021, 745). It should be noted that Domesday Book makes very few direct references to the Battle of Hastings, and therefore only a small sample of the manors that actually participated in the battle has been recorded. Additionally, not every thegn may have been recorded in Domesday Book, but rather just their name, without any title, or neither name nor title. Hewitt's (2021) study shows that most thegns did not participate in the battle; however, it is acknowledged that this may not have been the case, given that many of them were not recorded in Domesday Book for the manors that were investigated. Hewitt's investigation adds some support to the theory that King Harold fought with an incomplete army at Hastings, which, in large part, lacked the support of his thegns, who did not participate in the battle (751). Morillo (1996) argues that the notion of fyrd service has been misinterpreted time and again. Some argue that it was the duty of peasants, with the thegn's obligation being different due to his higher status. Others argue that the late Anglo-Saxon fyrd was composed of a feudal host of landed aristocrats and their commended thegns, who were obligated to serve them due to the fiefs they had been granted (Morillo 1996, 58). Despite disagreements over the role of land, there seems to be universal scholarly agreement that land, and thus the fyrd, played a crucial role in the recruitment of the Anglo-Saxon army. Morillo (1996) argues that fyrd service at the beginning of the eleventh century was intimately connected with bookland. King Cnut the Great stipulated that if a landowner defended his land either by land or sea, he would hold the land undisturbed by litigation and have the right to dispose of it in any way he pleased upon his death. From this notion, it could be asserted that a landholder's title to land possessed in book-right would oblige him to defend said land in person on the king's campaigns. The royal charters and laws of the time also inform us that if one were to desert the royal army or break the king's peace while in the field, they would forfeit their land (Morillo 1996, 59). The Anglo-Saxon army was thus, in large part, a conscripted army. However, it should be noted that King Harold's natural horse soldiers consisted of his heavily equipped housecarls.

In terms of equipment, some scholars believe that the Normans were vastly better equipped. However, if one takes a visual glance at the Bayeux Tapestry, this superiority of equipment does not seem to manifest itself. Here, the weapons and equipment are presented almost symmetrically on both sides of the battlefield. Specifically, both Normans and Anglo-Saxons are shown wearing the same knee-length byrnie, helmets with nosepieces, swords, and long pointed shields. The Anglo-Saxon archers also do not seem to differ from those shown on the Norman side, and the two-handed axe wielded by the Anglo-Saxons is depicted in the hands of Count Guy earlier in the tapestry. In terms of armaments, little uniformity is shown as well. Some of the Norman soldiers are presented wielding spears, while others carry swords or maces. The housecarls and thegns of the Anglo-Saxon army were equipped with hauberks similar to those of the Normans. These hauberks were referred to as "byrnies," and, like the Normans, the Anglo-Saxons were also depicted wearing both kite shields and round shields. The primary difference between Anglo-Saxon and Norman weaponry was most likely found in the popularity of using an axe as a weapon. The Tapestry shows two different kinds of fighting axes, with the first being the Danish axe, which had a cutting edge of around four inches and was mounted on a light haft that could be swung with a single hand.

The broadaxe, on the other hand, was by far the most popular weapon of choice when picking between the two. This axe had a cutting edge of about ten inches and was mounted on a thick haft that was around three feet long, usually wielded as a two-handed weapon (Gravett 1992, 31–34).

The Anglo-Saxons are also, like their Norman counterparts, depicted with their own banners in the Bayeux Tapestry. Harold's headquarters is shown with two representations of the Dragon Banner of Wessex, while Harold is said to have had his own personal flag referred to as "the Fighting Man," which depicted a warrior and was covered in gold threads and gemstones. The Anglo-Saxon army had few archers, and the Bayeux Tapestry depicts only one on their side. Likewise, there is little evidence that crossbowmen were present among the Anglo-Saxons, and it is unknown if the crossbowman was even a military unit that the Anglo-Saxon army utilized at all. Slingers, on the other hand, were probably used as part of the army that the fyrd composed (Gravett 1992, 34). Anglo-Saxon kings had, for a long time prior to King Harold, always surrounded themselves with housecarls who would protect them when battle commenced and die for them if necessary. The common men of the fyrd, who carried out military duties as part of the three common burdens, would fight alongside the household troops. The fyrdmen were expected to serve beyond their regional borders and even across the sea if it became necessary (Gravett 1992, 27–28). Housecarls and wealthy thegns would usually ride to war but dismount and fight on foot once the battle commenced. There has been little evidence to suggest that the Anglo-Saxons used cavalry in battle, and one of the closest sources to suggest this is seen in Snorri Sturluson's work Heimskringla, where he writes that Harold's army "rode" against the Norwegian line of shields during the Battle of Stamford Bridge. However, as discussed earlier, while the grand feat of Sturluson's coverage of the outcome of the Norwegian invasion is likely accurate, most of his specific assertions can be criticized, and many scholars argue that he seems to have mixed up accounts of the Battle of Stamford Bridge with those describing the Norman tactics used at the later Battle of Hastings (Gravett 1992, 28–30). Nevertheless, it is not unlikely that Anglo-Saxon soldiers did use horses as tools of war when battles commenced, but it was certainly not the cavalry that they were famous for in terms of the legacy of Anglo-Saxon military tactics.

On the morning of October 14, 1066, the Norman and English armies came into full view of each other near Senlac Hill. According to the *Battle Abbey Chronicle*, a late and somewhat unreliable source, William paused his march at a location known as Hedgland (or Hecheland) to allow his troops to don their armor. This precaution would have helped ensure his men weren't fatigued from marching in heavy gear. The *Battle Abbey*

Chronicle, a twelfth-century account commissioned by William's successors, provides insight into the battle's events, though it is often criticized for its notable pro–Norman bias. While the *Carmen de Hastingae Proelio* and the *Battle Abbey Chronicle* both describe the armies being in full view of each other, the latter further suggests that Harold's forces had taken up a strong defensive position on the ridge, with Harold positioned on higher ground. This location effectively blocked William's path to London (Wood 2008, 174–179). With limited options and a dwindling supply line, William had little choice but to engage, as delaying further would allow Harold's troops time to recuperate and possibly invite reinforcements from other Anglo-Saxon regions. As the Norman forces finalized their formations, hostilities were about to begin.

The battle that was about to unfold would last for almost the entirety of a day. The engagement itself began in the morning at around 9 a.m. and ended by nightfall, which, in view of the October date, suggests it may have ended at around 6 p.m. Duke William was a cautious strategist who often avoided direct confrontations. The only time he had truly been involved directly in a battle was during the Battle of Val-ès-Dunes in 1047. Now, almost twenty years later, as he neared the age of forty, he would once again risk it all in a violent engagement between two powerful European armies. Battles as crucial as the one soon to transpire were often believed to depend on "God's judgment," since only God was thought to be able to grant victory in clashes with such high stakes at play (Neveux 2006, 137). The hostilities began when the Normans started shooting arrows toward the Anglo-Saxons, who had grouped together and raised their shields into a shield wall. The Bayeux Tapestry highlights this clearly, showing the arrows coming down and hitting the Anglo-Saxon shields with minimal damage. A shield wall accurately reflects its name, as soldiers gather closely, raising their shields in a manner that avoids overlapping. This arrangement ensures that the soldiers within can effectively defend themselves without hindering their ability to strike at the enemy (Rex 2011, 65). After their ineffective ranged assault, the Normans attempted a standard melee engagement against the Anglo-Saxon forces. King Harold positioned himself at the center of the Anglo-Saxon forces, standing on a small mound slightly to the left of the center and a couple of ranks behind the front line. His younger brother, Earl Gyrth, commanded the right wing, leading the engagement against the Breton forces of the Norman army. On the opposite flank, King Harold's other brother, Earl Leofwine, directed the left flank of the Anglo-Saxon army (Rex 2011, 65). The Norman army made a strategic withdrawal, allowing their principal force, which was composed of heavy infantry, a chance to advance. Their objective was to ascend the slope with shields interlocked in a cohesive formation. However, the challenging terrain impeded their attempts to engage the Anglo-Saxon frontline, requiring them to surmount the hill. Despite persistent efforts to breach the Anglo-Saxon shield wall and pave the way for the Norman cavalry, the rough landscape proved to be an obstacle. The housecarls, armed with their notorious Scandinavian two-handed battle axes, stood prepared for the onslaught. According to Wace, the Anglo-Saxons unleashed battle cries, echoing "Out!" and "Holy Cross!" and "God Almighty!" during their engagement with the Normans. In response, the Normans shouted their rallying cry, "Dex Aie!" ("God Helps!").

The consensus among scholars supports the notion that the protracted battle endured for the better part of a day. The melee between Anglo-Saxon warriors and Norman infantry likely persisted for an hour or more. The progression depicted in the Bayeux Tapestry elucidates the phases of the battle. Archers advanced, discharged their weapons, and then tactically retreated, allowing the Norman infantry to ascend the hill, a process that likely consumed a considerable amount of time (Rex 2011, 68–69). Peter Rex (2011) argues that while the Anglo-Saxon line is presented as a static formation of soldiers mostly waiting for the Normans to engage with them, there is no reason to believe that they were not capable or willing to engage in counterattacks through a column of assaults, where two columns of soldiers would converge to form a blunt wedge that could drive back the enemy infantrymen. This tactic had been seen at Fulford when the earls Morcar and Edwin had, albeit unsuccessfully, employed it against King Harald Hardrada of Norway, who, in turn, outflanked them. The shield wall of Anglo-Saxon soldiers, armed with thrusting spears and javelins, would have been able to mount a strategic tactic of fire and shock, consisting of a barrage of missiles of every description, followed by a forward move in which they would hack away with their melee weapons (Rex 2011, 69). The Bayeux Tapestry vividly portrays the stages of combat that took place during the battle, featuring advancing archers and fallen soldiers, some succumbing to dismemberment or decapitation.

After seeing the impossibility of breaking the English forces through sheer melee force, Duke William sent messengers to his cavalry squadrons, who quickly began a charge towards the Anglo-Saxon frontline (Neveux 2006, 137–138). Unfortunately, the difficult terrain left little possibility for maneuver. The Norman cavalry initiated their charge by throwing spears into the Anglo-Saxon defenders, after which they charged with swords in hand in an attempt to break the enemy frontline. After an extended period of fighting, with many soldiers falling on both sides and the surrounding landscape covered in blood, the Anglo-Saxon force still held its ground. The Anglo-Saxons defended their position so fiercely that, after three hours of struggle, the Breton footmen and cavalry, who composed the left flank of the Norman army, were seized by panic and broke into flight. With no leadership or order, the Bretons and their allies fled down the ridge into the swampy bottom of the valley. Seeing this, their Norman neighbors to the right also retreated, leaving their flank exposed. Amidst the chaos of battle, many concluded that Duke William must have been killed, crying out in despair at the loss of their leader. As the cry of defeat spread, the French and Flemings, who comprised the right side of the Norman army, also fell back, leaving the entire Norman army in a chaotic state. Unfortunately for King Harold, who was observing the collapse of the Norman line, his fyrd forgot their orders while focusing on the flight of their Norman foes and stormed forward, ahead of the housecarls who had guarded them, in order to hunt down the escaping enemy soldiers (Butler 1966, 242–243). Butler (1966) estimates that Harold likely sent a force of housecarls, led by his brothers Gyrth and Leofwine, to quickly recall the pursuing fyrd back to their stations. Unfortunately, whether this was the case or not, it was too late. Duke William, who was still very much alive, made a swift response to the structure of the battlefield. He rode down into the valley to confront his fleeing forces, accompanied by the Norman knight Turstin FitzRolf, who carried the papal banner.

As depicted in the Bayeux Tapestry, Duke William famously lifted his helmet to reveal his face and roared at his troops, "Look at me! I am alive and will conquer, with God's help! What madness has taken hold of you, that you flee in this way? What path will lie open before your retreat? Those whom you have it in your power to sacrifice, like a herd of cattle, drive you back and kill you. You abandon victory and undying glory and rush headlong to your own destruction and everlasting dishonor. By flight, not one of you will escape death" (Butler 1966, 244). Despite pleas from Eustace II, the Count of Boulogne, to retreat from the front line, Duke William chose to rally his troops and lead a charge against the Anglo-Saxons gathered at the bottom of the valley. The Anglo-Saxons fought back fiercely, even managing to unhorse Duke William himself with a spear on a couple of occasions. However, the Normans held a significant advantage, and the Anglo-Saxons could no longer benefit from the elevated defensive position they had utilized earlier. The tide of battle began to turn, and King Harold's brothers, Gyrth and Leofwine, fell alongside the fyrd, who had advanced recklessly with little armor and inadequate weaponry (Butler 1966, 244–245). It is said that Gyrth fell victim to Duke William himself, who challenged him to single combat on the battlefield. The Anglo-Saxon earl initiated the engagement by throwing a javelin at Duke William, but he ended up striking the duke's horse instead, causing the Norman warrior to dismount. Seemingly unfazed, Duke William charged at Earl Gyrth, roaring, "Receive from me the only crown you deserve; if my horse is slain,

I will fight on foot." Some believe the duke may have thought he was facing King Harold himself. According to William of Poitiers, Earl Gyrth would not be the only life Duke William would claim in the valley; Poitiers noted that the Norman noble sent "countless souls into the darkness of death" (Rex 1066, 73). While the Normans found the comeback they desperately needed, Duke William still had to regain control over an army that had become disorganized by retreat and had suffered heavy losses during their earlier failed advances (Butler 1966, 244–245). William of Poitiers denotes this as the turning point in the battle, where the Normans achieved a clear victory in the valley while the Anglo-Saxon soldiers who had advanced fell, as their fellow countrymen stayed put, defending their position.

According to the *Carmen*, the same events unfolded but in a different way. In this depiction, the Norman soldiers were not fleeing but merely feigning it, and once the Anglo-Saxons reached the bottom of the valley, they revealed their trickery and turned around to fight back. Ironically, the *Carmen* states that the Anglo-Saxon horde attacked so ferociously that the Norman soldiers ended up conducting an actual retreat after their feigned retreat, but this was halted by Duke William, who rode down to bolster his forces; whereupon they once again turned heel and managed a successful counterattack (Morris 2013, 181–182). Given that both sources agree on the events that unfolded and their outcome, but differ in opinions on how they transpired, it is quite likely that the battle developed in such a way, with a retreating Norman force turning around to gain victory over a reckless Anglo-Saxon advance. In the *Carmen*, the Duke is also depicted as removing his helmet to contradict the rumors of his demise, just as it is depicted in the Bayeux Tapestry. The primary difference between the two accounts is that the *Carmen* depicts the events as a tactical ruse on the Norman side that leads to disaster but then victory, whereas Poitiers portrays it as starting in disaster and ending in success. Poitiers can be criticized for his very pro–Norman stance, as seen when he describes the retreat as honorable, given that Norman knights would only flee if their leader had fallen, which was also the case for ancient Roman forces in similar circumstances. Poitiers claims that the initial retreat must have been due to non–Norman soldiers, such as the Breton knights and other auxiliaries on the left wing of the army. Despite Poitiers' clear bias, there is some truth to his claim that a Norman retreat may not be a sign of cowardice. Norman forces had indeed used such tactics before, successfully, as seen in the Battle of Arques against the invading French forces in 1053 (Morris 2013, 182–183). This complexity highlights the unpredictable nature of warfare, where tactics and survival often intertwine.

After the Norman army had finished slaughtering their foes in the bottom of the valley, both armies took a temporary break from hostilities to catch their breath and replenish themselves with whatever rations they had brought along. Butler (1966) estimates that the Anglo-Saxons had lost about two thousand soldiers. About two hours after the earlier failed assault on the Anglo-Saxon frontline, the Norman cavalry squadrons prepared for yet another charge. Galloping up the slopes of the ridge, the Norman cavalry met a resistant but considerably weaker defense compared to earlier. At this point, the Anglo-Saxons found themselves backed into a corner. William of Poitiers described the early stages of the battle as an endless onslaught, with the Normans "vigorously attacking," while the Anglo-Saxons resisted "as if rooted to the ground" (Rex 2012, 71). However, as the canonical hour of Vespers (approximately 6 p.m.) passed, the Anglo-Saxons had been weakened by multiple feigned retreats by the Norman knights, who would wheel around and slaughter their pursuers. When the knights were not relentlessly keeping the Anglo-Saxons vigilant, the Norman archers and crossbowmen unleashed volleys of arrows, which were quickly followed by infantry assaults. Wounded men were unable to retreat due to the density of their defensive position and found themselves crushed by the press of their comrades (Rex 1066, 74).

As twilight approached, the battle was still raging, with bodies piling up on both sides of the battlefield. Without a definitive break in the Anglo-Saxon shield wall and with night nearing, the Normans were starting to run out of time. Duke William quickly strategized and decided to order his archers to advance as close as possible to the Anglo-Saxon shield wall and fire their arrows over the heads and shoulders of the Norman knights and infantry in a vertical line. This maneuver would place the Anglo-Saxon defenders in an impossible position, forcing them to use their shields to defend against a rain of arrows falling down from above while simultaneously repelling the continuous charges from Norman infantrymen and knights (Rex 2012, 75). With a much weaker defensive formation, the Anglo-Saxon wall of shields was no longer impregnable, and in multiple places, the cavalry successfully pierced through the Anglo-Saxon frontline, striking at the weaker rear, which consisted of lightly armored fyrd (Butler 1966, 245). During the skirmish that followed, Duke William was reportedly struck on the head by an Anglo-Saxon captain but was saved by his helmet. The captain was then slain by the Norman baron Roger of Montgomery. Another Norman baron, Robert fitzErneis, attempted to capture the Anglo-Saxon standard but lost his life in the effort. A group of twenty Norman knights quickly charged into the fray afterward and managed to capture the standard. As the battle neared its end, King Harold was still standing and fighting, seeking to rally the remainder of his men. In a final desperate attempt, he moved forward into the front rank of the shield wall. This advance was quickly spotted by a

Norman soldier, who reported it to Duke William. While fighting vigorously and heroically, the Anglo-Saxon king faced a charge from four determined Norman knights, who ultimately slew him. This was followed by an outcry of "Harold is dead!" among the Anglo-Saxon soldiers, who quickly broke rank and fled. No reports mention any taking of prisoners, and it would be fair to assume that the Normans treated the fleeing Anglo-Saxon soldiers as ruthlessly as they had during the battle (Rex 2012, 75). With Harold's death signaling the collapse of resistance, the battlefield became a scene of chaos as the remaining Anglo-Saxon soldiers attempted to escape the onslaught.

It should be noted that the details surrounding King Harold's death are disputed. William of Poitiers makes no mention of it, while William of Jumièges simply reports that Harold fell "pierced with lethal wounds," mistakenly believing he was slain in the first Norman attack. Rex (2012) argues that this omission may stem from the shameful nature of Harold's death. The *Carmen de Hastinge Proelio* merely states that once news of Harold's death broke, the Anglo-Saxons refused to continue the fight (Rex 2012, 76). While it should be examined critically, the Bayeux Tapestry serves as an important contemporary source for the events of 1066. The famous scene with the text description *"Harold Rex Interfectus Est"* ("Here Harold is slain") depicts an Anglo-Saxon soldier with three arrows piercing his shield and one in his eye. To the right, a Norman soldier is seen cutting down an Anglo-Saxon axeman. Most historians arrive at three conclusions regarding this scene and the demise of King Harold Godwinson: first, that he is the soldier who was struck by an arrow in the eye; second, that he is the soldier who was slain by the Norman knight. A third proposition, first raised by Charles Stothard in the early nineteenth century, is that both men represent King Harold, who was first hit in the eye with an arrow, after which a Norman knight cut him down. This coincides with the medieval historian William of Malmesbury, who argued that Harold was first wounded, and upon this being spotted by a Norman knight, the cavalryman gored him in the thigh, after which Duke William supposedly banished the knight for treating an opponent so shamefully. Other medieval accounts even argue that it was Duke William himself who slew King Harold on the battlefield, although this is extremely unlikely and would most certainly have been depicted in the Bayeux Tapestry if this were the case. It should be noted that the current Bayeux Tapestry, as it exists today, was heavily restored in the nineteenth century. The scene denoting King Harold's demise was so heavily restored during this time that the only original wool remains from the head and shoulders of the soldier with an arrow in his eye. Luckily, sketches were made in the eighteenth century, and one of these sketches from around 1729, commissioned by the French historian Bernard de Montfaucon and sketched by Antoine Benoît, does not depict the soldier receiving an arrow in the eye. Instead, the soldier is shown as a spearman, with the arrow replaced by a spear that is not piercing his eye but is held high in his right arm instead. Likewise, the sketch also shows three arrows in the soldier's spear with very obvious fletchings, whereas the spear has none of these, further supporting the hypothesis that the soldier is holding a spear in his hand and not an arrow. As interest in the embroidery arose in the nineteenth century, a new color copy of the Bayeux Tapestry was commissioned by the London Archaeological Society and produced by Charles Stothard, published between 1819 and 1823. It is in this reproduction that the arrow first appears. Unlike Benoît, Stothard was adamant in his belief that the man who now had an arrow in his eye was King Harold. Unfortunately, it is unknown whether the arrow was Stothard's own invention or whether he accurately restored the Bayeux Tapestry from the latest damage it had faced during the Napoleonic period, where it may have been added between Montfaucon and Stothard (Livingston 2024). This divergence in representations highlights the uncertainty surrounding the true events of King Harold's death and the challenges historians face in interpreting the Bayeux Tapestry.

The circumstances surrounding King Harold's death are just one example of historical events with differing interpretations of the details. It is essential to recognize that the depiction of the Battle of Hastings represents an interpretation based on the works of contemporary scholars such as Wace, William of Poitiers, the Bishop of Amiens, and Guy in his renowned piece, the *Carmen*, among others. However, it is crucial not to regard this portrayal as an unquestionably precise historical narrative. M.K. Lawson (2003) emphasizes that any scholar attempting to delineate the battle's stages is likely to unintentionally underscore certain inaccuracies due to the considerable variation in the historical accounts detailing how the battle unfolded. Some of the stories written following the battle were certainly fabricated, perhaps arising from popular demand to celebrate the Norman victory. An example of this is seen in the *Carmen*, which boldly claims that a juggler on horseback named Taillefer rode up to the front lines, threw his sword into the air, and killed an Anglo-Saxon soldier who charged forward to engage him; after this, Taillefer decapitated the corpse and displayed the head to his comrades, who rejoiced at having gotten the first kill in the battle (Lawson 2003, 211–212). Other sources, such as the one written by the Anglo-Norman chronicler Geoffrey Gaimar about one hundred years later, claim that Taillefer had been riding ahead of the Norman army while singing the song of the legendary Frankish hero Roland. Hoping to achieve great fame through feats of strength on the battlefield, he began a performance of juggling his lance into the air and catching it by the blade. After repeating this performance three times, Taillefer advanced on the Anglo-Saxon army, where he wounded one of their soldiers with his lance. Following this, he rode back into the open space between the two armies, drew his sword, and began to juggle it as well. Unfortunately, after Taillefer juggled his sword thrice, his horse misunderstood the situation and charged aggressively right into the Anglo-Saxon force, where Taillefer supposedly managed to strike at two enemy foes before he and his mount fell victim to an onslaught of spear attacks (Butler 1966, 239–240). While the tale of Taillefer's heroic feat on the battlefield may very well have happened, it is very unlikely that a sword-throwing juggler inflicted the first casualty in such a fantastical occurrence that the entire Norman army stopped to celebrate him rather than focus on the ensuing engagement with their Anglo-Saxon foes.

Another example of historical inaccuracy is found in the writings of the prior, and later abbot, Baudri of Bourgueil, who wrote that the Anglo-Saxons were shocked when the Normans started their initial volley of arrows and some of their comrades fell to them, as the Anglo-Saxons had never faced or been aware of the bow and arrow as a weapon beforehand. Naturally, this is a ridiculous notion, given that even ancient cavemen hunted with bows and arrows. Most scholars assume that Baudri must have been referring to crossbows, which were arguably still a novelty in 1066, but this nevertheless requires one to jump to conclusions based on interpretations and assumptions. Morris (2012) argues that Baudri likely reached this conclusion after reading earlier accounts of the battle, such as the *Carmen* and the writings of William of Poitiers, both of which fail to mention Anglo-Saxon archers while simultaneously insisting that the Anglo-Saxons severely lacked expertise in military matters. Henry of Huntingdon, writing in the twelfth century, came to similar conclusions, arguing that the Anglo-Saxons facing Duke William in the Battle of Hastings were "a people accustomed to defeat, a people devoid of military knowledge, a people that does not even possess arrows" (Morris 2013, 179). Ironically, if these scholars had taken a closer look at the Bayeux Tapestry's depiction of the battle, a single archer is actually presented alongside the soldiers forming the Anglo-Saxon shield wall. A reasonable conclusion would be that the Anglo-Saxons were aware of archery and did indeed have archers in their ranks, but in fewer numbers compared to their Norman foes, which led to the volley fire landing disproportionately on the Anglo-Saxon side of the battle.

While it would be fair to assume a Norman slaughter in the aftermath of the battle, the accounts differ. Some make a contrarian argument that groups of housecarls and thegns made a desperate last stand, where they almost mortally wounded Count Eustace of Boulogne, who managed to flee at the last moment alongside the Duke, after which they rallied their men and returned to the battlefield (Rex 2012, 77–78). A report that has since gone down in legend as the "Malfosse" incident also arose in the aftermath of the battle. This incident involved a devastating fall into a chasm, followed by a massive death toll. The incident was vividly described by Wace's *Roman de Rou* and the anonymously written Latin *Chronicle of Battle Abbey*. The *Chronicle of Battle Abbey* focuses so intently on the incident that it is covered more than the remainder of the entire Battle of Hastings. Wace argues that while many Anglo-Saxons died in the pit, the Normans suffered heavily too, stating that the ditch was "behind the Normans, who had passed round the side of it; they had taken no notice of it. The English pressed the Normans so much, and shoved and pushed them so hard that they forced them back into the ditch, causing men and horses to kick helplessly. You would have seen many men falling, some tumbling on top of others, stumbling and falling flat on their faces, unable to get up. A good number of the English, whom the Normans pulled down with them, died." Similarly, the *Chronicle of Battle Abbey* describes the pit in vivid detail and how it managed to catch the unsuspecting soldiers who fell victim to it: "Lamentably, just where the fighting was going on, and stretching for a considerable distance, an immense ditch yawned. It may have been a natural cleft in the earth, or perhaps it had been hollowed out by storms. But in this waste ground, it was overgrown with brambles and thistles, and could scarcely be presented to the eyes in time; and it engulfed great numbers, especially of the Normans pursuing the English. For when they, unknowing, came galloping on, their terrific impetus carried them headlong down into it, and they died tragically, pounded to pieces. This deep pit has been named for the accident, and today it is called Malfosse" (Winkler 2020, 3–5). The Malfosse incident serves as a poignant reminder of the chaotic nature of battle, where the terrain itself could turn into a deadly adversary.

But what exactly was the Malfosse incident? The term "Malfosse" refers to a ditch into which a great number of soldiers seemingly fell to their deaths as the Battle of Hastings was ongoing. The casualties were supposedly mostly comprised of Norman fighters, but a significant number of Anglo-Saxon warriors also fell victim to the incident. William of Poitiers, the Bayeux Tapestry, Orderic Vitalis, and many other contemporaries writing about the incident decades later describe the episode as a massive tumble in complex terrain, occurring either during the confusion that followed King Harold Godwinson's death, during one of the Norman soldiers' feigned retreats, or during a Norman advance near the closing stages of the battle. The Malfosse incident is an interesting case study due to how much it has been debated by both medieval and modern historians.

Contemporary historians such as Michael K. Lawson argue that it is difficult to discern if Wace's remarks reflect "authentic tradition" or instead a "muddled reflection of statements about ditches" in his earlier sources, while R. Allen Brown argues that the incident is puzzling but clearly a literary construct that had no influence on the outcome of the battle. On the other hand, Edward Augustus Freeman contends that the Malfosse incident had a significant impact, as it was supposedly the last scene of the battle and left a grim mark on the minds of the descendants of the victorious Normans (Winkler 2020, 4). While the Malfosse incident has arguably gone down as one of the greatest moments of fatal danger during the legendary Battle of Hastings, it was not the only disaster that occurred; other medieval reports mention additional incidents of Norman soldiers falling into ditches elsewhere and being trapped by Anglo-Saxon soldiers in unfavorable terrain. Rex (2012) notes that even in modern times, it would be hazardous to ride around the fields of Hastings in October, and in the evening, it becomes almost impossible (Rex 2012, 78). This serves as a reminder of the treacherous landscape that played a crucial role in shaping the battle's outcome.

As night descended upon the battlefield, the conflict that had raged for hours finally came to a close. The sun dipped below the horizon at 4:54 p.m., casting long shadows over the fallen, while twilight lingered until 6:25 p.m., marking the somber end of a day that would forever alter the course of history.

10

THE AFTERMATH

DUKE WILLIAM OF NORMANDY had finally achieved the primary objective of his mission by defeating his arch-nemesis, Harold Godwinson, on the battlefield. However, before he could earn the epithet "The Conqueror," he still needed to subdue the English nation and establish himself as its new ruler. With its main defending army gone, and a large Norman force at his side, William had little difficulty in forcing his way through the country. In the five days following the battle, William returned to his camp in Hastings, partly to allow his weary troops some well-deserved rest and partly to await a deputation from the Anglo-Saxon leaders. When none came, he marched from the camp with his remaining forces. He began by moving to Dover, where he punished the town of Old Romney, whose inhabitants had killed the crew of one of his invasion ships that had strayed off course. Dover quickly submitted, and the Duke continued to Canterbury, where representatives of the city came out to offer their submission before he even reached the gates. The city of Kent soon followed suit, and panic quickly arose in London. Archbishop Stigand of Canterbury and Archbishop Ealdred of York elected to support the young Edgar Ætheling as king, possibly with the backing of Earls Edwin and Morcar (Gravett 1992, 82–83). Edgar Ætheling, the grandson of King Edmund "Ironside," who had ruled in 1016 before being defeated by King Cnut the Great of Denmark, had a legitimate claim to the throne of England through his royal blood (Daniell 2003, 2, 10).

By November, however, the Norman duke grew impatient as the earls and bishops of London debated whether to support Edgar Ætheling or submit to William's claim. The duke responded by leading his army around London and menacing the city from the south, where he burned down Southwark and drove off any English soldiers who tried to resist him. This strategy worked to some extent, as at least one leading Anglo-Saxon noble, Ansgar, a court official, stood out and openly advocated for the city's submission to Duke William. In the meantime, Duke William moved up the Thames and allowed his army to pillage as much as they wanted before circling back through the Chilterns toward the city. By mid-December, he was residing at the estate of Berkhamsted, which had belonged to one of King Harold's fallen thegns. It was here that the leaders of the Anglo-Saxons finally reached him to inform him that the earls of Mercia and Northumbria, Edwin and Morcar, alongside Edgar Ætheling (who had renounced his claim to the throne), as well as a number of bishops, nobles, and other significant representatives of London, had all agreed to submit to his authority. They handed over their hostages and swore loyalty to him, after which arrangements were made for his coronation at Westminster on Monday, December 25 (Christmas Day) (Crouch 2007, 96). Ironically, King William likely did not see himself as "The Conqueror." He viewed himself as the rightful successor to the Anglo-Saxon King Edward the Confessor, with the conquest of England by force being necessary but not ideal. William aspired to govern as the Danish King Cnut the Great had done—with the acceptance of the Anglo-Saxons—but Norman customs were far more foreign to them. Within two years, what began as an occupation would evolve into a full-scale conquest. Over time, the offices held by Anglo-Saxon individuals gradually transitioned to Norman hands. The dispossessed Anglo-Saxons often faced execution, exile, imprisonment, or simply faded into obscurity (Butler 1966, 291). These changes, though gradual, would lay the groundwork for the complete transformation of English governance and society in the years that followed.

According to William of Poitiers, Duke William was hesitant to accept the crown of England and proclaim himself king. Given that the entire purpose of the conquest had been to succeed Edward the Confessor as king instead of Harold Godwinson, it would not be unreasonable to assume that this scene may be Poitiers' own invention, designed to portray his Norman overlord as thoughtful and modest. However, it is noted that Duke William hesitated to crown himself due to the rebellious state of the country and his desire to be crowned alongside his wife Matilda, who was still in Normandy. These points seem more plausible, as only the southeastern part of the country was under his control at this time (Morris 2013, 197–198). Despite his hesitation, Duke William eventually agreed to be crowned king, at the behest of both his Norman supporters and the Anglo-Saxon nobility, who wanted their nation to return to stability and security under a strong ruler. Poitiers argues that Duke William hoped that once he began to reign, any rebels would be discouraged from challenging him. When William reached London some days later, his reception was lukewarm at best. Poitiers notes that the advance guard had been ordered to build a fortress within the city to defend against "the inconstancy of the numerous and hostile inhabitants" (Morris 2013, 198). The fortress would serve as a clear symbol of

Norman authority, solidifying William's presence in the heart of the kingdom.

The coronation turned out to be a tense affair, with the crowded abbey precincts heavily policed by Norman soldiers. The English nobility and the populace came out in large numbers to witness the event, which was presided over by the Archbishop of York, Ealdred, rather than Stigand of Canterbury. This choice was likely due to Stigand's close association with the late King Harold, although Stigand was still present to witness the coronation. Geoffrey, the Bishop of Coutances, stood alongside Archbishop Ealdred, ensuring that William's coronation could be presented in both French and English. When William was proclaimed king by "hereditary right," panic broke out among the English crowd, prompting the guards to engage with the throng, which inadvertently led to several houses in the abbey precinct catching fire. Nevertheless, despite the screams and shouts outside, the coronation continued with various anointings, benedictions, and investitures. Orderic Vitalis, who wrote of these events many decades later, noted that William became visibly tense and nervous on his throne as some members of the congregation began slipping out through the doors to assist with firefighting efforts. Ultimately, the coronation concluded, and the Duke of Normandy became the King of England. The newly crowned King William solidified his status in his great round seal, which depicted him on one side in the traditional image of a king sitting on his throne with orb and scepter. This seal also displayed an image of the king riding as a mailed warrior, complete with banner and shield; it appears that the goldsmiths of London had been given his old ducal seal to expand and replicate. This presented a message of dual authority. William was now both a king and a duke, though historians argue that he considered himself very much a king even during his visits to Normandy, not just when he was in England (Crouch 2007, 96–99). His wife Matilda would later follow suit when she visited England in the spring of 1068 to be crowned at Westminster (Gravett 1992, 88). This moment marked the beginning of a new era in English history, as the Normans began to weave their influence into the very fabric of the kingdom.

Despite the coronation and support from Anglo-Saxon nobles and religious leaders, resistance to the perceived military occupation of the country by a foreign power would be a recurring theme during King William's reign. The Normans and their French allies composed a tiny minority of the English population at the time, and to ensure their authority, King William embarked on a castle-building spree. This involved constructing motte-and-bailey castles throughout the land, as they had done back in Normandy. These fortified structures were easy to build and effectively defended against rebel attacks, as demonstrated in York in 1069. As rebellions persisted, the Normans continued to build castles, with London ultimately housing three, including the famous Tower of London (Neveux 2006, 140). These strongholds not only served as military bases but also symbolized Norman dominance, asserting their control over the landscape and the people.

King William also treated his collaborators quite well. According to William of Poitiers, shortly after his coronation, King William decided to "liberally distribute" whatever King Harold had "avariciously shut up in the Royal treasury" to those who "had helped him in the battle." While some of these funds were given to soldiers and mercenaries, most were used to enrich Norman monasteries, with a tribute extracted from the English added to it. However, the Anglo-Saxon Chronicle counters Poitiers's account, arguing that King William had robbed the monasteries and that in all the areas the Normans overran, "they caused to be ravaged" (Rex 2011, 98). For the Anglo-Saxons, particularly those who had supported King Harold, times would only grow tougher. King William quickly made it clear that he did not recognize King Harold Godwinson's nine-month rule as legitimate, presenting himself as the direct heir and successor of King Edward the Confessor. Bishops and magnates sought confirmation of any land grants made during Harold's brief reign (Rex 2011, 98). With King William not acknowledging Harold's rule as legitimate, any grants made during that time were called into question. Bishops and magnates needed to confirm these grants, which would likely face significant scrutiny under the new Norman ruler. Without valid confirmation, King William could revoke these grants or redistribute them to his Norman supporters. This process also symbolized power: for the bishops and magnates, it was a way to affirm their loyalty to King William; for the new ruling Norman elite, it was a means to consolidate their authority.

A profound way in which England changed following the Norman Conquest was in terms of linguistics. Before 1066, the dialect known as "Old English" or "Anglo-Saxon English" was spoken in England. This language was heavily influenced by the Germanic tribes (Angles, Saxons, Jutes, and others) who settled in England during the early Middle Ages. Notable works such as *Beowulf* and the *Anglo-Saxon Chronicle* were written in this language. However, as the Normans came into power, the ruling class and the legal system soon began to speak Norman French. This infusion of Norman linguistics into the pre-existing Anglo-Saxon culture led to the creation of the language now known as "Middle English," a dialect of English spoken from approximately 1066 to 1485, when Henry VII, the first Tudor monarch, ascended to the English throne. After this period, Middle English was replaced by Early Modern English. This is why the language is referred to as "Middle" English—it falls between Old English and Modern English. Most people familiar with the English language would likely find Middle English more comprehensible than Anglo-Saxon English due to its notable literary works that are still read today, such as *The Canterbury Tales* by Geoffrey Chaucer (Blake 1992, 1–2). While Middle English was developing, England experienced a linguistically multicultural phase in which three languages were spoken: French, Latin, and English. French, spoken and written in the variety known today as Anglo-Norman, was used for literary works, religious writings, and official documents. Anglo-Norman eventually gave way to what became known as Anglo-French in the early thirteenth century. Anglo-French was essentially an administrative language that the English had to acquire as a foreign language, and it never posed serious competition to English. Latin remained the language of administration and religion throughout the Middle English period, while English was primarily used for specific religious purposes. Although English was the spoken language of most citizens, it was regarded less favorably than both Latin and French in court circles. Initially, English appeared in written texts sporadically, but over time, it increasingly supplanted French and eventually Latin.

A major influence on the English language due to the Norman Conquest came from the influx of monks trained in France. These monks were accustomed to French spelling conventions, and while these did not yet represent a standardized French spelling system, they gradually transferred some of their spelling habits to English, altering its appearance (Blake 1992, 5–10). Notable changes included the abandonment of Old English letters such as æ ("Ash"), þ ("Thorn"), and ð ("Eth"). In Middle English, æ and ð were quickly dropped, while þ was used very seldomly. New letters, which were rarely used in Old English, such as k, q, x, and z, were gradually introduced. This shift contributed to the decline of the West Saxon standard of Old English, which had been used by the educated elite. By the twelfth century, the influence of Latin and French resulted in the abandonment of the rigid Old English spelling system, giving rise to a more fragmented and diverse spelling system in Early Middle English. This change allowed scribes to adapt their spelling to better reflect the spoken language of the time (Blake 1992, 10–11). Thus, the Norman Invasion profoundly reshaped English linguistics by introducing Norman French, which enriched vocabulary and altered syntax. This blending of languages not only transformed the English lexicon but also set the stage for the evolution from Old English to Middle English, marking a pivotal shift in the language's development.

The Normans also changed England from a legal standpoint. Regulatorily, lordship and kingship in eleventh-century England were as integral to the legal setting as local communities. Kings often dealt with regions through resident local officials rather than relying on a multitude of individuals dispatched from the central government. Despite this, England was heavily governed compared to the rest of contemporary Europe, through a combination of lordship, royal administration, and local self-government (Hudson 2018, 1). Before 1066, the king's court could be ruled without his presence, likely by a politically significant individual such as Earl Thorkell or the Archbishop of Canterbury. After the Norman takeover, it was often left in the hands of family members instead; if this was not possible, one or several royal officials would serve (Hudson 2018, 23). Prior to 1100, evidence of justices residing in the localities was sparse, but the Norman period saw an increase in innovation within the royal provision of justice in these areas, although details are somewhat obscure due to historians of the time referring to different types of individuals as "justices." Hudson (2018) defines four main categories here. The first is the resident justices, who had certain jurisdiction throughout one or multiple shires. The second consists of minor local officials responsible for attending to the king's pleas. The third includes individuals appointed to hear specific cases as royal justices. The fourth and final category encompasses "itinerant justices," who were sent on a circuit of counties to hear a broad variety of cases (Hudson 2018, 24).

Before the conquest, Anglo-Saxon writs were typically addressed to the thegns (local noblemen) of the various shires. A writ is a formal written order issued by a governing authority, typically a court, commanding someone to do or refrain from doing a specific act. Writs are used in legal contexts to enforce rights, address grievances, or ensure the proper administration of justice. They serve as authoritative legal documents that direct actions or decisions. Writs were important in eleventh-century England as they enabled the king to exercise centralized authority and enforce legal decisions across the kingdom. They provided a standardized method for managing land and property disputes, which were crucial for maintaining social and economic stability. Additionally, writs served as official records, ensuring accountability and consistency in governance and administration. After 1066, writs were generally addressed based on the recipient's status, determined by the amount of land they held (Hudson 2018, 27).

When the Normans conquered England, rather than scrapping the entire English legal system and replacing it with a replica of the one in Normandy, they opted for coexistence. The existing English courts in late Anglo-Saxon England coexisted with those established after the conquest. Cases could be transferred from one court to another, and overlords could hear complaints from sub-tenants about justice defaults by intermediate lords. It should be noted that the capacity to transfer cases was primarily a royal prerogative. The failure of the hundred court (local courts dealing with minor legal matters) to deliver justice could lead to a hearing in the shire court (a regional court). Cases heard in seignorial courts (courts run by lords over their own estates) could be transferred to the shire court once a default of justice was proven, and from there, they could be transferred to the king's own court (Hudson 2018, 39). Governing would not be easy for the Normans. Many historical sources argue that the Normans were viewed as an oppressive and malign foreign power by most of the Anglo-Saxon populace. This perception likely explains the nervousness with which the Normans interacted shortly after the conquest. The Normans took steps to defend themselves through various measures, such as their campaign of building castles and fortresses around the English countryside. This is noted in the Anglo-Saxon Chronicle, which states that the Norman regents Odo of Bayeux and William FitzOsbern "built castles far and wide throughout the land, oppressing the wretched people, and things went continually from bad to worse." The eleventh-century churchman and bureaucrat Richard FitzNigel wrote that "what was left of the conquered English lay in ambush for the suspected and hated race of Normans and murdered them secretly in woods and unfrequented places as opportunity offered." This led to the creation of many folk legends, such as Hereward the Wake, an Anglo-Saxon resistance leader who fought against the Norman occupation. Such traditions would later merge into the legendary tale of Robin Hood. The Normans did not sit idly by; they made sure to crush any attempts at resistance either by force or through sanctions. One example of this was the implementation of a "murder fine" on entire districts when one of their men was killed there (Clanchy 2014, 29). This climate of fear and repression would shape the dynamics of Anglo-Norman relations for years to come.

In post-conquest England, land and reputation became two of the most significant assets one could own. It was through land, lordship, and "honors" that the new nobility obtained their wealth and prestige. A man could obtain land by marrying into the aristocracy. An aristocratic woman could inherit land, but she would not hold it herself; this honor would fall to her husband. If she were unmarried, the land would rest with her lord, who could, in turn, marry her off to a man from whom he might seek favor. But what happened to all the wealthy properties and large landholdings in Anglo-Saxon England following King William's conquest? According to William of Poitiers, King William restored the possessions of many of his former opponents, such as Earl Eadwine and Earl Morcar, while other sources argue that he demanded hefty tributes in return. Domesday Book makes numerous references to "the time when the English redeemed their lands." Englishmen would thus, in many cases, have to buy back their estates from King William. Many of these English had, of course, perished during the Battle of Hastings and were no longer in a position to bargain for their land and properties. The Conquest had essentially annihilated the ruling class of England, both physically and genetically. Around four to five thousand thegns had been eliminated either through battle, exile, or direct dispossession, in what might be the biggest transfer of property in English history. An English chronicler notes that "some were slain by iron, others placed in prisons ... many were driven from their native land and the rest oppressed." Many of these Anglo-Saxon nobles fled to Scotland or Denmark, and some even became mercenaries in faraway lands such as Byzantium, where a small English colony was supposedly established near Nicaea. Harold Godwinson's daughter also fled and married a Slavic prince, while the last Anglo-Saxon earl, Waltheof, would face decapitation in 1076 (Tombs 2016, 46–47). This upheaval led to a significant power vacuum that reshaped the dynamics of land ownership and governance in post-conquest England.

An interesting account of what happened to many of the Anglo-Saxon exiles is explored in the source *Chronicon universale anonymi Laudunensis* ("The Universal Chronicle of the Anonymous of Laon"). This chronicle was written by an anonymous English monk of the Premonstratensian order at Laon in France and concludes in the year 1219. It has survived in two thirteenth-century manuscripts located in the Bibliothèque nationale de France in Paris and in the Deutsche Staatsbibliothek in Berlin. What makes this source particularly intriguing is that it is one of the very few to mention the Anglo-Saxon emigration to the Byzantine Empire following the Norman Conquest. Historians generally agree that this event took place, supported by Byzantine documentation and the accounts of Ordric Vitalis and the hagiographer Goscelin, who also reference it. However, it is mentioned very little, and medieval chroniclers in England make no reference to it. The fourteenth-century saga on Edward the Confessor, entitled the *Játvörðar saga* (with Játvörðar being the Old Norse version of "Edward"), was most likely based on the information provided by the *Chronicon* and alleges that the English chieftains hated King William so thoroughly that, following a failed attempt to gain assistance from the Danish King Sweyn, a number of Englishmen, led by Sigurðr, Earl of Gloucester, sold their land and left England. Eventually, the refugees arrived in Sicily, where they learned that the Byzantine Emperor Alexius had just come to power and was under attack. Recognizing how revered Scandinavians in service to Byzantium were, they saw this as an advantageous opportunity and decided to go to Constantinople, where they won Alexius' favor by engaging in a triumphant battle on his behalf. After this, the refugees stayed in Constantinople, with some accepting Emperor Alexius' offer to join the ranks of his bodyguards. However, some of the Anglo-Saxon exiles sought land of their own, which Alexius refused, as he did not want to relinquish territory that was already owned by his own people. Nevertheless, he informed them that some land across the Black Sea, which had formerly been under Byzantine rule and was now occupied by heathens, would be available to them should they wish to go there. Some of the English refugees chose to sail there, naming their settlements after English towns and recruiting bishops and clergy from Hungary to form a religious community. The *Játvörðar saga* and the *Chronicon* both describe these events and share many similarities. Both specify the ranks of the leaders involved, the number of barons and earls who emigrated, as well as how many ships they took with them. They also delve into the journey across the Mediterranean and highlight key stops along the way, such as Septem on the coast of northern Africa and the islands of Minorca and Majorca. The arrival in Constantinople and the honor that Alexius bestows upon the emigrants is further confirmed by Orderic Vitalis. However, the most significant aspect—the six-day journey the English emigrants undertook as they sailed across the Black Sea to a land they named Nova Anglia ("New England"), where they also named the towns after English locations—is mentioned only in the chronicle and the saga. Both texts also mention how the Greek Orthodoxy found in the Byzantine Empire was rejected by the emigrants in favor of the Latin rites of the Hungarian church. With this in mind, it should be noted that the Icelandic author of the saga has significantly shortened his material. The Latin content in the saga is also condensed, with longer Latin sentences often summarized into more succinct phrases. However, the Icelandic version occasionally provides more detail than the Latin chronicle, such as additional information about the route from England and specific promises made by Alexius regarding New England, including the naming of some settlements after English cities, such as London and York (Fell 1974, 179–182). Jonathan Shepard, a historian and scholar specializing in Byzantine Studies, has found evidence in Crimea of names indicating potential English settlements, including one that may have been named "London," which persisted into the late Middle Ages. However, it is unrealistic to expect that linguistic and racial identities could be preserved for an extended period, so it is not surprising that the records are sparse and often unreliable. The British writer Robert Byron highlighted some challenges in documenting the presence of English exiles in Byzantium, noting that until 1865, Varangian tombstones were still visible near Bogdan Serai. When the British ambassador requested their transfer to the British cemetery at Scutari, the Turks repurposed them for construction, and copies of the inscriptions were accidentally destroyed in 1870. While the *Chronicon* and the saga offer intriguing insights into the impressive journey across Europe undertaken by some English exiles following King William's consolidation of power in England, it should be noted that the *Chronicon Laudunensis* may not be entirely accurate. Nevertheless, it provides one of the few comprehensive accounts of the Anglo-Saxon emigration, especially in comparison to the brief and often unreliable narratives of Orderic Vitalis and Goscelin (Fell 1974, 194–196). Although the *Chronicon* and the saga may contain distortions, they are worth considering, as they could be based on genuine information about the Anglo-Saxon exiles. In contrast, the *Játvörðar saga* stands out for its clarity and coherence. Whether this is due to the original work or the compiler's skill, it deserves greater attention and less dismissal than it has previously received.

The fate of the lands owned by the English nobility is revealed in a writ, most likely written during the early days of King William's reign, in which the Norman king insists that the abbot of Bury St. Edmunds must surrender to him "all the land which those men held ... who stood in battle against me and there were slain." This list indirectly names some of the greatest landowners in the kingdom, such as King Harold himself and his brothers Gyrth and Leofwine. King William kept much of this land for himself but was also quick to redistribute it to many of his closest followers. King William's half-brother Odo was given all of Kent, which had belonged to Leofwine, alongside the castle of Dover. William FitzOsbern received the Isle of Wight and lands in adjacent Hampshire (Morris 2013, 202). This extensive redistribution of land helped to establish a new class of Norman nobility in England, significantly elevating the status and influence of many newly arrived Normans.

In Anglo-Norman society, land ownership was closely tied to the concept of lordship. When a lord granted land "in fee" to someone, it meant that the land was given in exchange for a service, typically military service, thus creating a feudal relationship. The person receiving the land would perform an act of homage to the lord, acknowledging their obligation and loyalty. If there was no prior relationship between the lord and the recipient, the ceremonies of "seising" (taking possession of the land) and doing homage were often closely linked. This practice was influenced by traditions brought from Normandy, as well as the effects of the Norman Conquest, which reinforced these feudal ties and practices. The king would distribute land to his followers, who, in turn, distributed lands to their own men (Hudson 2018, 98). This intricate web of land ownership and loyalty not only shaped the political landscape of England but also laid the foundation for social hierarchies that would endure for centuries.

Feudalism is a term frequently mentioned in discussions of the medieval ages; however, it is often used carelessly, without a clear definition of its context or what it entails. The word may evoke a vague sense of familiarity, but few people can provide an accurate definition on the spot. In this book, feudalism is defined as the hierarchical structure of landholding and military obligations established by the Normans in England. In such a structure, a vassal would receive land (a fief) from a lord, perform homage, pledge loyalty, and provide military service, often by supplying the lord with knights. This system was rooted in Norman practices and allowed tenants to sub-grant land, creating a multi-tiered network of obligations and loyalties. Historically, it was accepted that the Normans introduced feudalism into eleventh-century England. However, since the 1960s, many historians, including John Gillingham, have argued that this is a myth; the idea that the Normans were able to introduce an entirely new system of landholding and military organization almost overnight has faced considerable criticism. With this in mind, sources such as Domesday Book contain records such as "Berengar de Tosny holds of the king twenty hides in Broughton, and Robert and Reginald and Gilbert hold of him" (Huscroft 2013, 255). For clarity, this meant that Berengar de Tosny was a tenant of the king who held twenty hides of land in the area of Broughton. The second part indicates that Robert, Gilbert and Reginald were all sub-tenants of Berengar, thus indicating the feudal hierarchical structure that many historians argue in favor of in Anglo-Norman England.

The 1066 Conquest brought profound changes to England, blending Anglo-Saxon and Norman practices to shape the foundations of common law. While continuity was maintained in local justice systems, lower-level landholding, and the treatment of offenses, the Normans introduced significant innovations in higher-level landholding and seignorial courts. This integration led to a notable degree of legal standardization and uniformity, enhanced by the authoritative role of the Norman kings. Religious policies in England were also dictated by the Normans. King William's greatest supporter, Pope Alexander, received enormous amounts of gold and silver, as well as the trophy of King Harold Godwinson's own banner, featuring an image of an armed man embroidered in gold (Morris 2013, 201). On the Anglo-Saxon side, King William initially attempted to allow Archbishop Stigand to continue occupying the See of Canterbury, perhaps as a gesture of solidarity with the citizens of the nation he had conquered. However, this symbolic alliance between the old Anglo-Saxon church leaders and their Norman conquerors would not last long. In 1070, Stigand was replaced by the new Archbishop, Lanfranc, and imprisoned. Many other significant Anglo-Saxon religious figures faced a similar fate, as seen in the example of the priest Regenbald, who was replaced by the Norman Herfast, later granted the title of Chancellor (Rex 2011, 99). When Lanfranc—who was Lombard by origin but Norman by adoption—took over the church, the English language was superseded by Latin as the written language of government. This shift was likely exacerbated by the fact that Lanfranc and many other foreign clerics did not speak Old English and were unwilling to learn it (Clanchy 2014, 30). Many argue that Lanfranc even despised the English language, a claim supported by the actions of Norman abbots at St. Albans, who demolished shrines and burned relics in England. When the monks of Glastonbury attempted to resist the imposition of Norman liturgy in 1083, they were slain or wounded by government soldiers, who shot arrows from the choir loft. According to the Anglo-Saxon Chronicle, "blood came down from the altar onto the steps and from the steps to the floor." English libraries quickly began to disappear, and the now pro-Norman Church of England, ruled by Lanfranc, rose as a cultural power leading a new order. While the attempted cultural annihilation brought significant changes to pre-existing Anglo-Saxon society, certain fundamental elements of the past survived. Many of the old English saints did not fall out of favor for long, and figures such as St. Edward the Confessor rose to become national and royal patrons (Tombs 2016, 47–48). The Conquest fundamentally altered the landscape of England; it also set the stage for a complex cultural interplay that would define English identity for centuries to come.

An interesting field of examination is the personal naming patterns that emerged after the Norman Conquest of 1066. Before King William's successful invasion, names such as Alfred, Æthelred, and Edward were among the most popular choices for boys in England. However, within two decades of the invasion, names like Geoffrey, Richard, and, most notably, William became some of the most favored, even among families of Anglo-Saxon descent. By 1170, these names had become so prevalent that King Henry II was able to hold a special session at court during Christmas where only men named William were allowed to enter (Vincent 2011, 73). In the more remote parts of England and among the lower classes of society, Old English personal names remained favored. A century after the invasion, areas such as Cumberland had numerous individuals with Old English names like Uthred, Orm, or Gamel. One such individual, a priest named Orm from the East Midlands, wrote the earliest surviving book composed in the new Middle English language—the form of English influenced by Anglo-Norman vocabulary that emerged after the Norman Conquest. Orm's work, a collection of rhyming homilies, is known as the "*Ormulum.*" The most famous literary work written in Middle English, *The Canterbury Tales*, would emerge in the fourteenth century. Among the royals at court, Norman names continued to dominate the naming tradition; however, this began to change in the 1230s. A combination of patriotism and piety led King Henry III, the great-great-great-grandson of William the Conqueror, to name his eldest sons Edward and Edmund in commemoration of King Edward the Confessor and St. Edmund, two of the greatest Anglo-Saxon saints and historical figures (Vincent 2011, 74–75). This shift in naming practices reflects not only the blending of cultures but also the enduring legacy of Anglo-Saxon heritage within the evolving English identity.

In the end, the Norman invasion changed England permanently. The aggressive construction of castles, bureaucratic and regulatory changes, foreign influence among the ruling class, monastic reforms, and alterations to the English language brought significant transformations to the England once ruled by the Anglo-Saxon kings. However, the Normans did not demolish Anglo-Saxon society to build an Anglo-Norman society from scratch; instead, they merged existing Anglo-Saxon structures with Norman innovations, creating a uniquely hybrid culture and governance system. The invasion was not the sole determinant of the structural changes in England in the following decades. Some historians argue that earlier changes brought by foreign rulers such as Cnut and his Danes, or later rulers like Henry I, were equally, if not more, significant in shaping the transformations that England underwent.

11

THE BAYEUX TAPESTRY

THE BAYEUX TAPESTRY IS A MAGNIFICENT piece of contemporary history from the time of the conquest. Today, it commands its own museum and has undergone over 200 years of examination. Technically, the tapestry is an embroidery on linen cloth measuring approximately 70 meters in length and 50 centimeters in height. The level of detail in the tapestry is, relatively speaking, positively unique; it contains 626 people, 757 animals (of which 202 are horses), 37 buildings, and 41 ships. Despite its impressive nature today, the Anglo-Saxons would have found it quite ordinary, given that it lacked the use of gold thread, which they regarded as a hallmark of excellence. Art historians mostly agree that it was made in Canterbury under the auspices of William the Conqueror's half-brother, Odo, who was the Bishop of Bayeux. In terms of its themes and depictions, the tapestry illustrates the political and military events that led up to the Norman invasion of England in 1066, the detailed preparations prior to the launch of the invasion, the naval journey to Hastings, and the battle itself. The final scene shows the Anglo-Saxon army in flight as the Normans claim their victory on the battlefield (Daniell 2003, 12). As such, the Bayeux Tapestry offers invaluable insights into the cultural context and perspectives of the people involved in this transformative period.

The Oxford English Dictionary defines propaganda as "the systematic dissemination of information, esp. in a biased or misleading way, to promote a particular cause or point of view, often a political agenda" (Oxford English Dictionary 2024). While there is no definitive proof that the Bayeux Tapestry presents a falsified story, it is told from the victor's perspective. Authoritarian figures seeking to exert power through propaganda, such as Adolf Hitler and Napoleon Bonaparte, were immensely impressed by the tapestry's instructional value in illustrating the last successful invasion of England (Szabo & Kuefler 2015, ix). With the Bayeux Tapestry, the Normans effectively conveyed their view on the invasion through vibrant artwork. This extensive embroidery visually narrates the events leading to the Norman Conquest of England in 1066. It serves as Norman propaganda, depicting Harold Godwinson as a betrayer who broke his oath to Duke William and usurped the throne. The tapestry emphasizes William's legitimate claim to the crown and portrays his invasion as a justified response to Harold's treachery. By highlighting Harold's betrayal and William's conquest, the tapestry reinforces the Normans' view of their actions as righteous and necessary, while legitimizing William's rule in both English and European eyes. Thus, the Bayeux Tapestry is not only an artistic achievement but also a significant piece of political propaganda.

The following three pages highlight pivotal scenes from the Bayeux Tapestry. These scenes depict Harold's supposed betrayal, his coronation as King of England, the Norman resurgence during the Battle of Hastings, and culminate with the death of Harold Godwinson, marking the end of Anglo-Saxon rule and securing William's victory.

The scene depicts the infamous death of the last Anglo-Saxon King, Harold Godwinson, as he is allegedly hit in the eye with an arrow. The description *HIC HAROLD REX INTERFECTUS EST* ("Here King Harold was slain") immortalizes his death as the Bayeux Tapestry comes to a closure with the flight of the English army. As explored in the ninth chapter of this book, this scene has sparked considerable debate among historians, particularly due to the restoration of the Bayeux Tapestry. Many argue that Harold was struck down by the knight to his right in the scene, and that the extensive restoration the tapestry underwent in the nineteenth century mistakenly added the arrow as the cause of his death. This theory is supported by Bernard de Montfaucon's 1729 sketch. While Harold's death is indisputable, the exact manner of his demise remains a subject of speculation.

Artistically, the Bayeux Tapestry narrates the events leading to the Norman Conquest of England. It begins with King Edward the Confessor commanding Harold Godwinson to go to Normandy, possibly to confirm William of Normandy as his successor. Harold and his men are depicted embarking on this journey, wading bare-legged to the boat, accompanied by their prized hunting dogs and a hawk carried by one of the men. Below this scene is a depiction of Aesop's fable "The Wolf and the Lamb," likely included to add moral commentary or resonate with medieval audiences familiar with Aesop's tales. Harold is captured by Guy of Ponthieu and commanded to disarm before their meeting. The next scene shows William's messengers riding swiftly to demand Harold's release, their speed illustrated by their wind-blown hair. Harold is shown heroically saving two soldiers from the quicksand near Mont-Saint-Michel, a tense scene as men and horses are engulfed by rising waters. Harold's bravery is evident as he carries one soldier on his shoulder while dragging another to safety. After this, Harold returns to England, and the upper border of

DETAIL OF THE BAYEUX TAPESTRY, 11TH CENTURY. Harold Godwinson is shown swearing a pledge of fealty to Duke William with the text description *HIE WILLELMO VENIT BAGIAS UBI HAROLD SACRAMENTUM FECIT WILLEMO DUCI* ("Here William came to Bayeux, where Harold swore an oath to Duke William"). Harold Godwinson would notoriously later break this supposed oath by crowning himself King of England, leading to the Norman Invasion.

11. The Bayeux Tapestry

DETAIL OF THE BAYEUX TAPESTRY, 11TH CENTURY. Harold Godwinson is seen wearing the English crown, with the description *HIC DEDERUNT HAROLDO CORONAM REGIS* HIC RESIDET HAROLD REX ANGLORUM STIGANT ARCHIEP[ISCOPU]S ("Here they gave Harold the king's crown. Here sits Harold, King of the English, with Archbishop Stigand").

DETAIL OF THE BAYEUX TAPESTRY, 11TH CENTURY. Bishop Odo and Duke William are shown rallying their troops during the Battle of Hastings: HIC ODO EP[ISCOPU]S BACULU[M] TENENS CONFORTAT PUEROS HIC EST WILLEL[MUS] DUX ("Here Bishop Odo, holding a staff, comforts the boys. Here is Duke William"). Duke William is shown lifting his helmet to show that he is still alive in an act of inspiration and reassurance to his troops.

this scene features the fable "The Crane and the Wolf," which may reflect themes of cunning and survival relevant to the narrative. Harold is then shown, possibly in a defensive posture, delivering news to King Edward. King Edward dies shortly afterward, depicted on his deathbed, and Harold is crowned King of England. Halley's Comet appears in the sky, witnessed on April 24, 1066, and interpreted as an ominous sign. The tapestry matches this image with a fleet of ghost-like ships in the border below, ethereal because they are only stitched in outline without colored infill. This fleet likely hints at the future seaborne invasion that Harold Godwinson will face from either King Harald of Norway or Duke William of Normandy. This is shown through the messenger informing King Harold of impending danger, likely referring to the anticipated invasions by the Norwegians and Normans. William's fleet of approximately 800 ships is depicted being built and crossing the English Channel. The scene shifts to the Normans launching their naval invasion, after which Duke William and his men are shown dining, where Bishop Odo, William's half-brother, blesses the food and wine—a scene compared to Leonardo da Vinci's "The Last Supper" (though the tapestry predates Leonardo by several centuries). William orders fortifications to be dug at Hastings.

The final part of the tapestry focuses on October 14, 1066—the Battle of Hastings. The designer captures scenes of dramatic bravery and violence, with depictions of arrows raining down and the challenging terrain of the battlefield. Harold's brothers, Gyrth and Leofwine, are killed, but the English, holding the high ground, continue to resist fiercely. A caption notes, "HIC CECIDERUNT SIMUL ANGLI ET FRANCI IN PR[O] ELIO" ("Here English and French fell at the same time in battle"). The lower border beneath this scene graphically depicts the battle's brutality, with images of butchered men, horses, dismembered limbs, and looted corpses. The battle culminates in the infamous scene of King Harold's death, shown in the tapestry as either being struck by an arrow in the eye or cut down by a Norman sword. Scholars continue to debate the exact cause of his death as depicted in this scene. The Bayeux Tapestry is an epic visual narrative that combines historical storytelling with rich symbolism. The central story of the Norman Conquest is framed by intricate borders featuring animals and scenes that may allude to the events depicted or make the narrative more engaging for contemporary audiences. The Latin inscriptions help identify key figures and places, but their placement suggests they may have been added after the primary images were completed, raising questions about their role in the overall design.

In the eighteenth century, a popular myth emerged that the Bayeux Tapestry was crafted by Queen Matilda, the wife of King William. However, there is no historical evidence to support this claim, and most historians have dismissed it as a legend that gained undue prominence over time. The Tapestry's history is less legendary than the rumors suggest. It may have appeared in the poem *Adelae Comitissae* by the eleventh-century poet Baudri of Bourgeuil (d. 1130), which was written for Adela, William the Conqueror's daughter and Countess of Blois. Baudri describes a pictorial wall hanging and adds details about its appearance, as seen in the passage describing the conscription of ships: "The ash, the oak and the ilex fall, the pine is uprooted by the trunk. The aged fir is hauled down from the steep mountains; labour gives value to all trees." While this seems to describe the scenes in the Bayeux Tapestry where William's army gathers resources to construct their invasion fleet, many historians argue that the first certain mention of the Tapestry is in a 1476 inventory of the treasury of Bayeux Cathedral, alongside altar cloths, banners, and curtains. The tapestry is referenced as "Item 262" (Daniell 2003, 12–13). Its description reads: "Item, a very long and narrow hanging, embroidered with images and writing depicting the conquest of England, which is hung around the nave of the church on the day and through the octaves of the relics." Matching this description with the tapestry is straightforward. A century later, Bayeux was sacked by the Huguenots in 1562, a group of French Protestants known for their conflicts with the Catholic majority during the French Wars of Religion. Almost two hundred years later, the Intendant of Caen, New Jersey. Foucault, noted the Tapestry's existence, after which it came to the attention of Antoine Lancelot in 1724, who submitted a preliminary report to the Academy of Inscriptions and Literature. A couple of years later, the Tapestry received proper identification and description from Dom Bernard de Montfaucon in 1729–1730 in the first two volumes of his *Les Monuments de la Monarchie Françoise* ("The Monuments of the French Monarchy") (Musset 2002, 14–15).

Unfortunately, it is currently unknown what the Bayeux Tapestry looked like in its original state. It was most likely very similar to the version preserved at the museum today, but as covered in Chapter 9 of this book, several modifications have been made to the embroidery, including the depiction of Harold Godwinson's death and how it occurred. Montfaucon published contemporary drawings of the Tapestry, completed by Nicolas-Joseph Foucault (d. 1721), an administrator from Normandy, in the first volume of his book on the French monarchy. After commissioning Antoine Benoît to copy the rest of the embroidery for reproduction, Montfaucon went on to publish this copy in the second volume of his *Les Monuments de la Monarchie Françoise*. Montfaucon notoriously requested that Benoît record the style of the Tapestry as accurately and faithfully as possible, regardless of how "vulgar and barbarous" it might appear. As a result, Benoît's drawing ended up being notably different from Foucault's.

While Foucault's drawing was more refined, Benoît's was more faithful to the original medieval style, capturing its "vulgar and barbarous" characteristics as Montfaucon had instructed. Interestingly, both the Foucault and Benoît drawings clearly show that the ends of the Tapestry—likely the areas most exposed when it was hung, folded, or rolled up during its approximately seven hundred years of existence—were already in poor condition when Montfaucon decided to publish them around 1729–1730 (Pastan et al. 2014, 24–26). Even in Foucault's drawing, which presents an idealized version of the Tapestry, the vertical border on the left edge of the textile is awkwardly connected to the rest of the decoration. Additionally, disruption is visible to the right of the word "Rex" in the inscription, where an oddly placed tower and a diagonal mending seam correspond to illegible letters in the rest of the inscription. Further evidence of damage appears in the next scene, where only the hindquarters of a horse are depicted. Recent analysis of the embroidery, where less effort has been made to conceal restorations or additions, has confirmed the poor preservation of the first scene of the Tapestry, particularly in the borders and the left vertical edge. These findings show that Foucault's drawing captured the first scene at a time when a portion of the second scene had been folded over and tacked down to hide a significant tear in the fabric. At the end of the textile, the seemingly final scene, depicting the Anglo-Saxons fleeing the Battle of Hastings, is also in poor condition, as revealed by rectangular patches or gaps visible in Benoît's drawing. Benoît did not include the inscription *"ET FUGA VERTURUNT ANGLI"* ("And the English have turned to flight"), likely due to the Tapestry's compromised state. Due to the condition of the fabric, many historians have argued that the embroidery was either never completed or that scenes are missing from it. However, given that there are reasonable and practical explanations for the condition of the opening and closing scenes in the Tapestry, this may not necessarily be the case (Pastan et al. 2014, 24–26). The Bayeux Tapestry sparked a heated dispute among British historians in the 1890s over how much the Norman invasion had affected the English constitution. The catalyst for this discussion was Edward Freeman, whose *History of the Norman Conquest* had cited the Bayeux Tapestry as a key document. Freeman, an independent scholar with a private income, was not attached to any academic institution and had failed to achieve academic recognition until 1884, when, at the age of 61, he was appointed Regius Professor of Modern History at Oxford. Freeman's view was patriotic—he argued that the Conquest had little impact on the British Isles. In his view, the hero of 1066 was Harold, not William. While this may seem odd, given that the Normans had blended into English society for almost a millennium, it reflected the self-confident Britain of the 1860s and 1870s, which had learned to celebrate its ancient roots. Perhaps with this in mind, the anniversary of the Battle of Hastings was also ignored in 1866.

However, times changed in the 1880s, when scholars began to recognize and appreciate the Norman achievement. One of Edward Freeman's chief detractors was John Horace Round, who argued that the Norman Conquest fundamentally altered English society through the introduction of feudalism, which swept away the old Anglo-Saxon structures irreversibly and immediately. Round continued to challenge Freeman, accusing him of deliberately twisting the Tapestry's evidence, leading to a renewed dispute. After the First World War ended in 1918, the Germanic contribution to Anglo-Saxon culture took a lower profile, and France was no longer seen as a threat but rather as an ally. Tapestry studies of the time also reflected these shifts in attitude, with a greater emphasis placed on Duke William's role, rather than Harold Godwinson's. This anti–Germanic sentiment only worsened a little over twenty years later, when Nazi historians commandeered the Tapestry and argued that the Normans were, in fact, Germans, and that Duke William was a prototype Führer (Hicks 2007, 199–201). The first demand to see the Tapestry came from a member of the local Propagandastaffel, the network of Nazi Propaganda Offices that Joseph Goebbels had established as an integral part of the Occupation structure in France. The custodian had little choice, and on the 22nd of September, the Bayeux Tapestry was unveiled to its first Nazi viewers. News of this spread quickly, and in October, another Nazi officer, who claimed to be an archaeologist, was given permission to take photographs of the Tapestry, even though this meant exposing the fragile fabric to flash bulbs in an underground room. This trend continued over the following months. The Nazi officers were particularly intrigued by the scene where William's fleet crossed the English Channel, the moment in which the invasion unfolded. Despite Hitler abandoning "Operation Sea-Lion," the planned naval invasion of Britain in September 1940, many of these officers likely saw it as a miraculous prophecy of their campaign against England. Heinrich Himmler, the leader of the SS, also took a personal interest in the Bayeux Tapestry and famously wrote a "thank-you letter" on the 7th of January 1943, where he stressed the importance of the Tapestry for the "glorious and cultured Germanic history." The Nazis notoriously referred to the Bayeux Tapestry as the "Norman Tapestry" to emphasize the Normans' supposed Aryan ancestry.

Despite the influence of the war, scholars of other nationalities were also permitted to investigate and take photographs of the Tapestry. The historian André Lejard took photographs in July 1943 for a book he eventually published in 1946. In England, the Tapestry became the subject of a book by Eric Maclagan, director of the Victoria and Albert Museum, who published it as part of the King Penguin series in 1944 (Hicks 2007, 209–231). Visitor numbers began to soar during the 1960s and 1970s, prompting the Bayeux authorities to create a more modern exhibition space for the Tapestry to accommodate its growing popularity. Controversially, the Tapestry was moved from its home at Hôtel du Doyen, where it had been housed (except during the war years) since 1913. However, this move allowed for a thorough examination, cleaning, and photography of both the front and back of the Tapestry. Ultimately, the building chosen to house the Tapestry was the Grand Seminary, built by the Bishop of Bayeux in the late seventeenth century. Construction began in 1980, and early in 1981, the Historical Monuments section of the Ministry of Culture invited a group of textile restoration experts to inspect the hanging and provide advice on any necessary repairs or cleaning before the Tapestry was installed in its new location. These experts were shocked to find signs of decaying fabric and threads, dust, traces of mold, and even the smell of vinegar, alongside suspicious evidence of decomposition. However, full testing and analysis had to wait until the Tapestry was finally removed from display, which could not happen until the new building was ready. Georges Duval, a local architect and the chief architect for Historical Monuments, who had restored Matilda's foundation, the Abbaye-aux-Dames in Caen, was chosen to design the new exhibition space. Duval, however, was not a textile specialist, which led to differing priorities between him and the textile experts. This caused significant disagreements regarding how the Tapestry should be cleaned and displayed. Duval clashed with the restorers from the Swiss Abegg Foundation, who had been considered for the cleaning project and had even offered to do it for free. The Historical Monuments section decided to keep the project under French control, and malicious gossip soon began to circulate. Someone allegedly suggested that the Tapestry be cleaned by immersing it in water, which, given the Tapestry's size, would require a gigantic pool and around two hundred people to hold it up. The French later claimed that this proposal came from the Abegg Foundation, which the foundation denied. The English also joined the debate, with some English conservators, who believed the Tapestry should belong to England, jokingly threatening to throw valuable French furniture from the Wallace Collection into a pool as well. A rumor even spread that the Olympic swimming pool in Paris had been chosen for the dunking, and in January 1983, art critic Brian Sewell described the stalemate in these terms: "Under no circumstances would the fabric be removed anywhere, least of all to the hated capital, as even an Olympic pool was too short (by 22 yards). It could not matter that their own pool was shorter still—a hundred local women would be put into training to support the Tapestry for the five days and five nights that it would be immersed over the New Year holiday of 1983. No one considered the problem of how to fill a swimming pool with pure distilled water, and no one thought of the additional issues that would arise from the presence of a hundred human bodies in that water with the Tapestry, as they might discharge oils, acids, and fluids that have no place in the conservation of ancient fabrics" (Hicks 2007, 298–99). The pool story was most likely nothing more than a joke, and the Tapestry was undoubtedly never immersed. The restorers who undertook a second, more detailed inspection following its removal from exhibition concluded that it was in fairly good condition after all and that it only needed a gentle cleaning. Subsequently, the Tapestry was installed in the new state-of-the-art display that opened on the sixth of February 1983, although the results of the examination were not published until July 2004 (Hicks 2007, 299–300). This renewed focus on the Tapestry's preservation not only alleviated concerns over its condition but also underscored the importance of careful conservation practices in maintaining such a significant historical artifact.

As of today, the Bayeux Tapestry continues to be housed in the Bayeux Museum, where it remains one of the most important and popular cultural artifacts in France. The Bayeux Tapestry stands as an extraordinary historical artifact and a remarkable piece of art that has captivated audiences for centuries. Its intricate depictions of the events leading up to and including the Norman Conquest offer invaluable insights into the political landscape of eleventh-century Europe, a time when power was often asserted through military might. Despite being shrouded in myths—such as the legend of Queen Matilda's involvement—and undergoing significant restoration, the Tapestry remarkably preserves the Norman perspective with striking clarity. Its evolution from a potentially modest, celebratory wall hanging to a revered historical treasure underscores its enduring significance. While inherently biased, the Tapestry serves as an exceptional primary source for understanding the Norman Conquest and its aftermath, solidifying its place as a dynamic and invaluable piece of history.

12

THE HARRYING OF THE NORTH

KING WILLIAM DID NOT HAVE AN EASY time ruling England. His early reign was constantly threatened by sporadic native rebellions and threats from the Scots, the Welsh, and the Danes. Adding fuel to the fire, back in Normandy, King William faced challenges from neighboring duchies, the French monarchy, and even some of his own family members. After 1073, William spent most of his time in Normandy, primarily engaged in conflicts with the men of Maine in 1073, the Bretons in 1076, the Angevins in 1077–1078 and again in 1081, and the French in 1087. Although William spent most of his time in England from 1067 to 1072, this was primarily to suppress rebellions. The most notorious of these rebellions occurred in 1069–1070 when the Northumbrians joined forces with a Danish fleet to support the English claimant to the throne, Edgar Ætheling. They managed to capture York, and according to the Anglo-Saxon Chronicle, killed "many hundreds of Frenchmen." The Norman response to this rebellion has since been branded as the "Harrying of the North," during which King William systematically burned the countryside in the winter of 1069–1070 and destroyed villages, ensuring that neither Danish invaders nor Northumbrian rebels could find anything to sustain themselves in the future (Clanchy 2014, 30). This brutal campaign not only instilled fear among the English populace but also highlighted the lengths to which William would go to consolidate his power in the face of ongoing resistance.

A "harrying" refers to a sustained, aggressive, and destructive military campaign aimed at causing widespread devastation and demoralization among the enemy. Such a campaign is often conducted to weaken the enemy's resources, disrupt their ability to resist, and instill fear. The tactics employed during a harrying typically include burning crops, destroying homes, and killing livestock, leaving the affected area economically and socially devastated. The events leading up to the "Harrying" of the

North began almost immediately after the conquest. King William faced numerous rebellions, threats, and invasion scares during his early reign. There was widespread fear among the new Norman elite that the English would rise up against them or that Flemish, Irish, or Danish war bands would seek to repeat William's invasion against England's new overlord. Despite this, none of the attempted rebellions or invasions amounted to much, primarily due to a lack of coordination and division among the English rebels (Vincent 2011, 69–70). Not only did King William have to be on constant lookout for foreign threats and challenges from the people he now ruled over, but he also had to deal with dissatisfied former allies, such as Eustace II, Count of Boulogne. Count Eustace had fought alongside William during the Battle of Hastings, but due to presumed dissatisfaction with his share of the spoils and perhaps some ambition stemming from his marriage to Edward the Confessor's deceased sister, he chose to accept the invitation of local English rebels to launch an attack on the Norman castle at Dover in Kent (Lawson 2003, 244). This complex web of threats and discontent set the stage for the drastic measures William would soon employ in the North.

The alliance between Count Eustace and the rebels might seem unusual to an outside observer, given Eustace's history as a foreign adversary. He had previously attacked Dover in 1051 and fought alongside King William at Hastings, where some sources, such as the *Carmen de Hastingae Proelio*, even suggest that he was the one who personally slew King Harold on the battlefield. However, the rebels were likely driven by their deep-seated animosity toward their new Norman overlords. Additionally, Eustace had participated in a rebellion against William in 1053 that aimed to overthrow the young Duke. In the first half of 1067, another rift occurred between King William and Count Eustace. Orderic Vitalis attributes this to jealousy on the count's part, while William of Poitiers, though less specific, suggests that King William was justified in his actions (Morris 2013, 209–210). The insurgents coordinated with the count to bring a fleet full of armed men to Dover and then make himself master of the castle. The insurgency was timed to coincide with the absence of Bishop Odo and Hugh de Montfort, the greatest lay Norman landowner in the shire, who were preoccupied with issues north of the Thames. Eustace made a successful landing and was quickly joined by the Kentishmen. The insurgency likely hoped their actions would attract spontaneous reinforcements and support from neighboring areas, but contrary to their expectations, the garrison put up a tougher fight than anticipated, and even the citizens of Dover, who likely had no love for Count Eustace, joined in aiding the garrison against the attackers. Faced with imminent defeat, Count Eustace decided to withdraw toward his ships, but the garrison counterattacked,

12. The Harrying of the North

and Eustace jumped to the early conclusion that either Bishop Odo or de Montfort must have returned unexpectedly. The count fled with his army, which faced heavy losses as many of them fell from the cliffs. While the count managed to escape, a "nepos" (either an actual nephew or a male relative) was captured. Almost simultaneously with Count Eustace's retreat, Bishop Odo and Hugh de Montfort returned and completed the mopping up of the unsuccessful rebellion, causing the remaining English insurgents to scatter. Meanwhile, the English exiles who had fled the country were desperately seeking assistance from abroad, with many prominent Englishmen going to Denmark to seek support in recovering their lands. However, the Danish King, Sweyn Estrithson, preferred to watch events develop from afar and missed any hopes of overturning the conquest (Rex 2011, 112–113). King Sweyn's initial reluctance to engage actively with the situation reflected the cautious approach he took in dealing with the complexities of English affairs during this tumultuous period.

In 1067, trouble began brewing in Northumbria. Theoretically, the north of England was still under the rule of Earl Morcar, who had been elected by the northerners themselves following their successful rebellion against Tostig Godwinson in 1065. However, from the onset of his rule, Morcar had been obliged to share power. The 1065 rebellion had been triggered by the murder of Gospatric, head of the house of Bamburgh. Mindful of this and seeking to solidify his authority through pragmatic measures, Morcar immediately ceded control above the Tyne to Gospatric's nephew, Oswulf. While peace in the North seemed to have been achieved, at least temporarily, the Norman Conquest quickly disrupted this arrangement. At the beginning of 1067, just before King William returned from Normandy, he upset the delicate balance between Morcar and Oswulf by granting the earldom of Northumbria—or at least its northern half—to a Yorkshire thegn named Copsig. This appointment was surprising, as Copsig had previously been Tostig's lieutenant and was just as hated in the north as his former master. However, Copsig had been quick to submit to King William, in a way that Oswulf evidently had not, and had somehow managed to convince the king that he should rule the north as well. William of Poitiers described Copsig as being "entirely favorable to the king and supportive of his cause." Unfortunately for both Copsig and King William, this confidence in Copsig's appointment was gravely misplaced. Just a few weeks after Copsig's arrival in Northumbria, he fell victim to an ambush in which Oswulf personally hacked off his head. One might imagine that Oswulf would prepare for a future clash with King William for this act of defiance, but during the autumn of 1067, Oswulf himself was ambushed and killed by a robber's lance (Morris 2013, 210–211). Despite all the turmoil in his new kingdom, it was none of these insurgencies or rebellions that caused King William to return to England in 1067. Instead, reports of a wider conspiracy had drawn him to hasten his return. The details of this conspiracy are sketchy at best, but the general conclusion seems to be that during the final weeks of 1067, King William learned of a conspiracy against him organized by the surviving members of the Godwine family. According to Orderic Vitalis, King William received intelligence while in Normandy indicating that the troops he had left behind in England were about to be massacred as part of an English plot against him. William of Jumièges argues that the plotters intended to attack the Normans on Ash Wednesday, when they would be walking barefoot to church. In 1068, this date would have been February 6. William therefore hurried across the Channel, sailing from Dieppe on the sixth of December 1067 and arriving safely at Winchelsea the next morning. He then made his way straight to London, where he would celebrate Christmas while trying to sniff out any conspirators. According to Orderic Vitalis, King William was said to have gone to great pains to appease everyone; he was especially gracious toward the English lords and bishops who attended him, granting them favors and offering them the kiss of peace while simultaneously instructing his Norman followers not to let their guard down (Morris 2013, 211–212). King William went on to hold a mid-winter council where numerous rebels were put on trial, including the absent Count Eustace, who managed to regain his favor with King William later in 1068 through "beneficia" (gifts intended to appease King William) (Rex 2011, 113). The various trials and discussions during this council revealed the complexity of loyalty and dissent among the remaining English nobility in the aftermath of the conquest.

At the beginning of 1068, King William received the intelligence he had been seeking. His scouting knights confirmed that the city of Exeter had sent messages—messages that William intercepted—to other cities, encouraging them to join a rebellion against their new Norman ruler. With the plot uncovered, King William sent a message of his own to Exeter, demanding that its citizens swear fealty to him. The identity of the plotters remains unclear, as both William of Poitiers and Orderic Vitalis do not address this important detail in any capacity. However, thanks to terse accounts from English sources, it is known that the ringleaders of the conspiracy were surviving members of the Godwine family, with Harold Godwinson's mother, Gytha, playing a key role. The last time Gytha made a significant historical appearance was when she bargained with King William over Harold's body. Afterward, she had gone west to begin her plans for revenge. It is unsurprising that Gytha had not forgiven the Normans for their invasion in 1066, given that she had lost four of her sons (Harold, Tostig, Leofwine, and Gyrth) during that fateful year, with the fifth, Wulfnoth, withering away in a Norman prison. Gytha seemingly worked in conjunction with Harold Godwinson's sons from his first wife, Edith Swan-Neck. Harold had been married to Ealdgyth for a short time before his death, a marriage that produced no children. However, before this marriage, Harold had been married to Edith Swan-Neck according to Danish custom, and they had at least five children together, of whom at least three were boys. These sons, likely in their late teens or early twenties by the time of the Norman Conquest, had also fled west after their father's death at the Battle of Hastings and crossed the sea to Ireland. Together with Gytha, they planned to restage the successful Godwine comeback of 1052 by utilizing a mercenary fleet from Ireland, perhaps with an allied invasion fleet from Scandinavia. According to William of Poitiers, the plotters sent multiple envoys to the Danes "or some other people from whom they might hope for help." Orderic Vitalis supports this by stating that the plot was "supported by the Danes and other barbarous peoples."

Naturally, King William was adamant about stopping this plan before it could manifest. When Exeter refused his demand for fealty, he quickly raised an army and marched westward. According to Orderic Vitalis, this was the first time King William demanded military service from his new English subjects. William still relied on his many Norman soldiers, but combining them with an English force turned the rebellion in the West Country into a loyalty test, with those refusing to aid the king seen as supporters of the rebels. At first, William seemed poised to repeat his past successes. As his army drew close to Exeter, a delegation of leading citizens rode out to meet him and negotiate for peace, similar to what other urban leaders had done in 1066. These delegates promised to open their gates to the king and obey his commands, and they handed over hostages as a sign of good faith. However, according to Orderic Vitalis, these men immediately resumed "their hostile preparations, encouraging each other to fight for many reasons" upon returning to the city. The rebels may have been trying to buy time until their allies from overseas arrived. Or a difference of opinion may have existed among the rebels, with some hoping to use the rebellion as leverage for better treatment from King William, who had recently imposed what John of Worcester referred to as "an unbearable tax," inspiring many citizens of Exeter to rebel. Regardless, the failed negotiations led to an escalation of force. Upon King William's arrival, he found the city of Exeter's walls manned on its ramparts.

In a final attempt to induce surrender, he ordered one of the hostages to be blinded in front of the walls, hoping to instill fear in the rebels. Unfortunately, as Orderic Vitalis notes, this merely strengthened the defenders' determination. William of Malmesbury even mentions a vulgar reaction from one of the rebels, who dropped his trousers and farted loudly in the king's general direction in response to the violent incident. Orderic describes the siege that followed as a hard-fought encounter, where William attempted to storm the city for several days, during which the Anglo-Saxon Chronicle notes that "a large part of his army perished." However, after eighteen long days of fighting, the citizens agreed to surrender. Orderic Vitalis and William of Poitiers argue that they had no choice, as the Normans had been relentless in their assault, while William of Malmesbury adds that a portion of King William's forces managed to gain entry into the city after a section of its wall collapsed. The English chronicles, in contrast, argue that the surrender came about due to the desertion of the Godwine family. John of Worcester supports this, noting that Gytha "escaped with many in flight from the city," with the D Chronicle of the Anglo-Saxon Chronicle backing this up by noting that the citizens surrendered "because the thegns had betrayed them." Gytha sailed into the Bristol Channel, taking refuge on the small island of Flat Holm. This enabled King William to negotiate with the more moderate faction of the rebels in Exeter. He refrained from seizing their goods and guarded the city gates to prevent looting. The Anglo-Saxon Chronicle offers a more skeptical assessment, arguing that King William "made fair promises to them, and fulfilled them badly." Nonetheless, the citizens seemed to have secured a somewhat favorable outcome in their negotiations with King William, as Domesday Book showed in 1086, when it noted that Exeter paid the same tax as it had "in the time of King Edward." King William followed up his victory by establishing a castle in Exeter, then leading his army into Cornwall, where Orderic notes that he put "down every disturbance that came to his attention." It was probably around this time that King William handed command of this region to a Breton follower named Brian, after which he disbanded his Anglo-Norman army and returned to Winchester to celebrate Easter (Morris 2013, 212–215). William's return for Easter marked a moment of respite after his campaign against the rebels, but the insurgency in Exeter would soon prove to be the beginning of a larger conspiracy against his reign.

While peace seemed assured, King William quickly found that Exeter was merely the spark of a larger rebellion. During the summer of 1068, the sons of Harold Godwinson, together with their cousin Tostig, the son of Harold's brother Sweyn Godwinson, arrived with an armed fleet provided by their father's former ally, King Diarmaid Mac Mael n'Ambo of Dublin and Leinster. Meanwhile, King William celebrated Easter at Winchester and welcomed his wife Matilda, who was crowned Queen at Westminster on May 11, 1068. Shortly after Matilda's coronation, according to The Worcester Chronicle, King William was informed that men of the North had gathered and were preparing to make a stand against the Norman conqueror. Earl Edwin of Mercia had not attended Queen Matilda's coronation, and it soon became apparent that he was allied with the rebels. Edwin had long felt threatened by the many castles the Normans had built within his earldom, especially along the Welsh border, where William FitzOsbern and other Norman nobles were constructing a chain of fortifications. It is fair to assume that Edwin felt slighted by the gradual shift in authority. According to Orderic Vitalis, King William had promised Edwin authority over much of Northern England, along with the hand of one of William's daughters in marriage—neither of which materialized. Thus, Edwin gathered his forces and contemplated open rebellion.

Mercia, however, was the least of William's problems. The real center of the rebellion lay in Northumbria, a region and its nobility that had yet to fully submit to the conquest. The Northumbrians had not yet witnessed any Norman troops on their lands, and it is possible that they believed they could, like Exeter, strike a bargain with the Conqueror, as they had with his predecessor, Edward the Confessor, in 1065. If they harbored any such beliefs, they would soon find them gravely mistaken. King William's fury at the rebels was growing, and he quickly gathered his forces to march from Winchester into Mercia, building castles along the way as he headed north. William began by constructing a motte-and-bailey at Warwick, which still stands within the bailey of Warwick Castle to this day. He may have built a second castle at Leicester next, although the Anglo-Saxon Chronicle does not confirm whether this happened at that time. Once he reached Nottingham, King William built yet another castle there. The Mercians were shocked by the unexpectedly rapid pace of William's advance, and Earl Edwin, alongside his brother Earl Morcar of Northumbria, quickly disbanded their forces and surrendered to the Conqueror (Rex 2011, 120–122).

Simultaneous to William's campaign in the north, the sons of Harold had begun their invasion when they landed in Somerset and began wreaking havoc around the mouth of the River Avon. Failing to take Bristol, they gathered loot and returned to their ships, after which they continued raiding along the Somerset coast. While levies or groups of militia from the local population managed to inflict heavy casualties on the raiders in a battle, John of Worcester credits the sons of Harold as the victors of this skirmish and notes that they continued to raid in Devon and Cornwall before returning to Ireland with their spoils. Nevertheless, if the intention of this attack was to re-establish the Godwinson dynasty in England, it was an abysmal failure. Orderic Vitalis notes that, at the same time, "Certain Norman women, consumed by fierce lust, sent message to their husbands, urging them to return at once, and adding that unless they did so with all speed, they would take other husbands. For they dared not join their men themselves, being unaccustomed to the sea-crossing and afraid of seeking them out in England, where they were engaging in armed forays every day and blood flowed freely on both sides." Whether this was true or not, it seems to explain the apparent exhaustion on the part of many of the Norman soldiers serving King William. Orderic notes that many of the soldiers guarding the castles of Winchester and Hastings began to abandon their posts and return home. These desertions naturally put more stress on the Conqueror, who was putting all of his efforts into dealing with the rebellions. Despite the fact that the English were rebelling against the Norman dominion of their lands, King William's solution seemed only to worsen the situation. The king addressed the issue of the deserters by promising even greater rewards to those knights who stayed by his side, rewards that often manifested through the forceful transfer of English estates. Nonetheless, the sons of Harold had been beaten for now, and King William apparently felt so confident that he decided to return to Normandy at the end of the year (Morris 2013, 220–222). This was a miscalculation, as the unrest in England was far from resolved.

The peace in England would not last long, and William would return within less than a year's time. In the beginning of 1069, King William attempted to tighten his grip on the ever-rebellious northern regions by appointing an outsider, Robert Cumin, as the new Earl of Northumbria. Robert Cumin had supposedly arrived in England alongside a band of Flemish soldiers, and many historians attribute his origin to Flanders. Undoubtedly aware of the brutal end met by his predecessor, Earl Copsig, Cumin came north with a considerable force of around five hundred to nine hundred soldiers. The local chronicler Simeon of Durham provides a full account of what happened next. Supposedly, the new earl advanced and left a trail of destruction in his wake, allowing his men to pillage and rampage through the countryside as much as they wanted along the way. Cumin seemingly sought to manage the territory beyond the River Tyne, and when the locals heard of his coming, they fled their homes to prepare for his arrival. However, Simeon notes that the Northumbrians faced such a harsh winter and heavy snowfall that they had no choice but to fight. Meanwhile, Earl Cumin had reached the city of Durham, where, despite the pleas of the local bishop, he entered the city and allowed his men to continue their looting and slaughter in their quest for quarters. Simeon describes the outcome as equally predictable. "At first light," the Northumbrians burst through all the gates and rushed through town, killing the earl's companions wherever they found them. The earl tried to barricade himself inside the house of the bishop, but the attackers responded by setting the building on fire, and those inside either burned to death or were cut down as they tried to escape the inferno. The earl was just as unlucky, as he was killed alongside his men on the 31st of January 1069. The successful revolt led to an English reawakening, with the men of York shortly thereafter rebelling and killing the new governor of the castle at York. Orderic Vitalis notes that "the English now gained confidence in resisting the Normans, whom they saw as oppressors of their friends and allies." This also inspired foreign exiles, such as Edgar Ætheling, to return to England and join the insurgents, leading an attack on York. The Sheriff of York somehow managed to get a message through to the king, informing him that he and his men were still holding out but were in dire need of support. King William arrived with yet another unprecedented haste, catching the rebels completely by surprise. According to the Anglo-Saxon Chronicle, King William was ruthless, and the entire city of York was ravaged, with York Minster being made "an object of scorn." Edgar Ætheling and many of the most significant rebel leaders managed to escape, with Edgar returning to Scotland. King William decided to remain in York for an additional eight days, during which time he ensured the construction of a second castle. Before leaving to celebrate Easter in Winchester on the thirteenth of April 1069, King William committed the city of York to the custody of William FitzOsbern (Morris 2013, 222–224). This decisive action marked a turning point in the struggle for control over the North, demonstrating William's determination to quell any further dissent.

King William's rest would remain limited, however, as the Danish fleet arrived at some point between the fifteenth of August and the eighth of September. King William was made aware of this arrival while he was out hunting in the Forest of Dean. The Danes were led by Jarl Asbiorn, the brother of Danish King Sweyn, and Jarl Thurkill. They were accompanied by King Sweyn's three sons: Harold, Cnut, and Beorn (also called Leriz). The invaders had also brought a Danish bishop named Christian of Aarhus with them. The Danish invasion fleet consisted of at least 240 ships and began raiding South-East England, starting at Dover, continuing to Sandwich, and then around to East Anglia, where they attacked Ipswich and Norwich. Nevertheless, the invaders were repelled at each of these places. According to Orderic Vitalis, King Sweyn had been motivated to initiate his invasion due to the "death and disaster which had overtaken his men in Harold's war." This claim seems rather dubious, given that there is no real evidence that Danish soldiers were involved in the Battle of Hastings, despite William of Poitiers claiming that this was the case. Peter Rex (2011) argues that the Norman writers may have been confused by the Danish names of many of the thegns from the Danelaw. Additionally, Harold Godwinson did employ some Danish mercenaries in his army, but these had not been sent by King Sweyn himself. Orderic Vitalis believes that King Sweyn's actions arose from his desire to claim the English kingdom through inheritance, given that he was the son of Cnut the Great's sister Estrith. Furthermore, Edward the Confessor and Harthacnut were half-brothers (sons of Queen Emma), which made King Sweyn the cousin of Edward the Confessor by the conventions of the time (Rex 2011, 135–136).

In September 1069, the Danes took up station on the Humber, and the local English began to rally to them. According to Florence of Worcester, more ships from Denmark arrived while the Danes were on the Humber, and a fleet from Scotland carrying Edgar Ætheling may have also arrived to join the Danes. Edgar Ætheling carried out a foraging raid at Lincoln, where the English rebels supporting him were repelled by the garrison of the castle, which captured many of the rebels and took them prisoner, while Edgar Ætheling managed to escape. According to Orderic Vitalis, Edgar Ætheling was supported by Earl Waltheof, a thegn named Siward (perhaps the wealthy northern thegn Siward Barn), and a thegn named Adelinus. Other sources propose that the rebels were also joined by supporters from Northumbria and some of the Yorkshire leaders such as Archil, Karli and his four sons (Cnut, Summarlithr, Thorbrand, and Gamal), and Elnochus, alongside a number of nobles from East Anglia, including Aelfwold, the abbot of St. Benet's at Holme, and Eadric, who had been the Steersman of King Edward the Confessor, as well as the thegn Ringulf of Oby and Abbot Aethelsige of St. Augustine. All of these rebels would eventually go into exile in Denmark. The Northumbrians were led by their earl, Cospatric, and the fact that Karli fought alongside them shows just how hostile the Northumbrians were to King William's rule. Karli had killed Ealdred, the uncle of Cospatric, and Thorbrand the Hold had killed Earl Uhtred, Cospatric's grandfather. Despite this, they were seemingly willing to put their history behind them in the pursuit of an even greater enemy. King William was naturally fully aware of many of these insurgents at this time, including the defection of Earl Waltheof.

By September 19, the Normans in the castle of York began to take preemptive precautions and set fire to the houses surrounding the castle in order to create a "dead zone" of open space. Unfortunately, the fire quickly got out of control and destroyed much of York, including York Minster. On September 21, the Danes arrived at York but made no attempt to remain there, given that there was now no plunder to be had and they had no means of laying siege to a castle. Nevertheless, the fire managed to draw the garrison out, and up to 3,000 Normans were supposedly slain, with Earl Waltheof credited with slaying one hundred—most likely an exaggeration. The Danes showed little mercy to the fallen and left the corpses to be devoured by wolves. According to the Abingdon Chronicle, "men of all classes took part" in the revolt, and all those who had long resented the rule imposed on them by a foreign tyrant began to band together in open rebellion. At the same time, the entire South Western peninsula of England also rose against the Normans, and further north, rebellions arose in Cheshire and Staffordshire. King William refocused his attention from his Northumbrian campaign to deal with the situation in the North West.

Unfortunately for the English rebels, while the rebellions were numerous, they were incredibly uncoordinated and lacked a master hand guiding them. They had no links between them and were loosely arranged; in areas such as the South West, the Norman forces led by Bishop Geoffrey of Coutances, Count Brian of Brittany, and William FitzOsbern easily quelled the rebels. FitzOsbern was ruthless in his victory, ordering the right hands and noses to be cut off from the rebels that the bishop and the Count had captured. The Normans began a rapid counter-advance from London, Winchester, and Salisbury, and at Exeter, the citizens supported the Normans while the garrison of the castle broke out to drive off the besiegers, who were in turn slaughtered by the Normans. Bishop Geoffrey of Coutances advanced to the relief of Montacute Castle (near Yeovil in Somerset), where he also mutilated the captives. King William was primarily concerned about the Northumbrian rising, which posed the greatest danger due to its support from foreign powers such as Denmark and Scotland. The king responded by launching an attack against the Danes in Lindsey, North Lincolnshire, with the purpose of driving them back into Holderness. This move put a wedge between the Danes and the Northumbrians. Orderic Vitalis insists that King William engaged in fierce combat against the Danes but provides no further details. At the same time, despite the castle of York implementing a scorched earth tactic, the Northumbrians were able to storm it, slaughtering the garrison and capturing the High Sheriff of Yorkshire, William Malet, and his family. The rebels were quick to retreat from the devastated city and sought refuge within the marshes of Lindsey, where they hoped to regroup with the Danes. However, the Danes had retreated to the Isle of Axholme, seeking protection from the marshes that surrounded it (Rex 2011, 136–140). With the disorientation of the rebels and their allies, it would seem that King William was satisfied with the deterioration of the insurgency.

Nevertheless, the Normans were in turmoil. King William had been attempting to assert his authority over the English realm for three years while pursuing elusive enemies who resorted to guerrilla hit-and-run tactics. Despite these challenges, King William remained resolute in his pursuit of the Danes, advancing on Axeholme and pushing them further into Holderness. He left Count Robert of Mortain and Count William of Eu to deal with the Danes while he personally attended to an uprising in Staffordshire, then headed to York after hearing rumors that the Danes planned to re-occupy the city. When King William reached York for the third time, he laid waste to the land, sparing no one in his path. By the time he arrived, York was a burnt-out city surrounded by desolate countryside. His first priority was the restoration and fortification of the castles, which were quickly repaired and strengthened. William decided to spend Christmas in York and requested that the royal regalia be sent from Winchester so he could hold a crown-wearing ceremony to solidify his authority over the region. While the Danish army was not merely a band of mercenaries but represented the military might of Denmark—a nation that had previously conquered England—they showed little interest in engaging the Normans in open battle. Their primary objective was to exploit the instability in England through looting and pillaging. However, they moved much more slowly than their predecessors of the ninth and early tenth centuries and lacked the extensive use of horses. This left their raiding parties vulnerable on open terrain, where Norman cavalry devastated them. Additionally, their Northumbrian allies seemed more interested in seeking revenge than in driving out the Normans entirely. When York was captured, the Northumbrian leaders, Cospatric and MaerleSweyn, showed little desire to advance further south, likely hoping to establish a separate kingdom in York, as had been done in the tenth century. As winter approached, the northern rebels withdrew, expecting that King William would not pursue them in the cold weather. They may have been waiting for King Sweyn of Denmark to arrive in person, as he was expected to do in the spring of 1070. However, this never materialized. Sweyn's expeditionary force suffered from the harsh winter, and York, devastated by fires, was unsuitable as a base, offering no shelter for the Danes hoping to winter there. As the Danes retreated to Axeholme with the Normans in pursuit, their leader, Jarl Asbiorn, eventually conceded defeat. The Normans permitted him to forage for supplies on the condition that he leave England the following spring. Asbiorn did not depart empty-handed; King William agreed to pay off the Danish soldiers to ensure their departure, effectively paying a Danegeld. The winter proved hard on the Danes, and many perished due to food shortages.

 With York secured and the Danes no longer a threat, King William turned his attention to the Northumbrian rebels. He surprised them by remaining in York over Christmas. With their prospects dim, many leading Englishmen began seeking peace with William, who was not without mercy. Edgar the Aetheling received no immediate reconciliation, but he was allowed to return to the king's favor in 1074 when he was granted unspecified honors. Earls Waltheof and Cospatric were allowed to retain their earldoms and renew their submission, though their power had likely diminished significantly by then. Cospatric made his submission by proxy rather than in person when William marched as far north as the River Tees. Neither earl remained loyal for long, but William tolerated this for the time being due to the practical limits of his authority in the region. Earls Edwin and Morcar were similarly allowed to retire to Chester after their men were driven out of Stafford (Rex 2011, 142–145). Although some semblance of peace had been achieved, King William's patience had worn thin.

By this point, the Norman king was determined to find a way to effectively counter the Northumbrian guerrilla tactics of attack and retreat. Stationed in York, William remained on high alert, with the ever-present fear of another northern uprising weighing heavily on his mind. As the King of England, William needed to assert his authority over a region that had not fully accepted his rule. His brutal campaign in the North was not only an effort to quash rebellion but also a means of demonstrating the necessity of his central authority. By decisively punishing those who defied him, William aimed to establish the "sword of justice," ensuring that others would recognize the futility of resistance and the advantages of supporting his reign. It was at this point, with the Danes out of the picture, that King William ordered his "harrying" of Northumbria. Quite similar to the ways in which the Romans carried out their destruction of Carthage, William wanted to ensure that any remaining rebels were brutally suppressed and wished to set an example for any future would-be rebels. Orderic Vitalis writes that King William had never before shown such cruelty, as he commanded that the entire region be stripped of any sustenance, which in turn led to around 100,000 people dying of famine. While this figure may be an exaggeration, the devastation that was unleashed was undoubtedly not. Over a decade later, when King William's commissioners visited Northumbria to carry out the Domesday survey in 1086, they noted many of the villages as "waste," and recent evidence suggests that Yorkshire may well have been a desert in 1070 (Lawson 2003, 245). With his patience worn thin, King William was ruthless, and perhaps a tad bit desperate, in his bid to quell the many rebellions that had plagued his reign.

The harrying entailed the burning of houses, the slaughter of animals, and the uprooting and burning of crops. It was, in short, a total annihilation of the livelihood of the denizens living in Northumbria. No spring crops could be planted, and King William's soldiers ensured that even ploughs and other farming tools were destroyed. The twelfth-century English chronicler Roger of Hovedon wrote that the harrying was a horrible spectacle in which bodies were left out in the open to rot as worms ate them because no one remained to cover them with earth. Many people supposedly resorted to eating cats, dogs, horses, and, in some severe occasions, even human flesh. Others became slaves in order to survive, and the city of Durham became a refuge for the poor and sick, who would lie there while dying of hunger and disease. The villages of Northumbria became deserted and, according to some northern sources, the "lurking place of wild beasts and robbers." Banditry ran rampant, and order ceased to exist. Much of the Northumbrian land, especially urban, was seized and used to build castles, abbeys, churches, and cathedrals. Some were also given to Norman traders. King William made sure to favor Norman settlers as well when lands were to be distributed following the harrying. Norman lords extended patronage over many of the surviving English landowners, increasing their own holdings and diminishing the land of any English subject who might dare to rebel. King William kept a keen eye on much of the distribution of land, ensuring that no baron could create a power base mimicking the feudal principalities he had known in France, and that no Norman would ever rise to the power that earlier Anglo-Saxon earls such as Godwin, Siward, Leofric, and Harold had held. Despite this, much land was seized illegally, as Orderic Vitalis references, where Norman knights and barons consistently encroached on lands owned by the Church. While the Church often managed to successfully lobby the King to assist them in restoring their lands, not all of them were returned to their hands. The lands between England and Scotland also suffered greatly as a consequence of King William's harrying. In the spring of 1070, when King William returned south, King Malcolm of Scotland devastated parts of Cleveland and Durham, taking advantage of the weakened state in the north. Earl Cospatric, on his own account, also ravaged Cumbria. Orderic Vitalis, who wrote after King William's death, dared to voice his concerns regarding the harrying as well, noting that "I dare not commend him. He levelled both the bad and the good in one common ruin by a consuming famine ... he was ... guilty of wholesale massacre ... and barbarous homicide" (Rex 2011, 149–156).

Orderic Vitalis had, notably, written his account of these events based on what he himself had read from the extremely pro–Norman William of Poitiers, often content with simply repeating Poitiers' words. However, when it came to Poitiers' account of the Harrying, Orderic ceased copying and said the following: "My narrative has frequently had occasion to praise William, but for this act which condemned the innocent and guilty alike to die by slow starvation I cannot commend him. For when I think of helpless children, young men in the prime of life, and hoary greybeards perishing alike of hunger, I am so moved to pity that I would rather lament the grief and sufferings of the wretched people than make a vain attempt to flatter the perpetrator of such infamy. Moreover, I declare that assuredly such brutal slaughter cannot remain unpunished. For the almighty Judge watches over high and low alike; he will weigh the deeds of all in an even balance, and as a just avenger will punish wrongdoing, as the eternal law makes clear to all men" (Morris 2013, 230–231).

Despite the horrendous consequences of the Harrying for the Northumbrian region and its population, the intent behind the Harrying was clear: to put an end to English opposition. The Harrying of the North largely succeeded in achieving this goal. The Danes returned to Denmark the following spring after receiving what one might refer to as their "danegeld" from King William. In 1071, King William received word that many of the most notable English rebels were ready to surrender. He would go on to campaign the following year in Scotland against King Malcolm, who also submitted to his might. While resistance to Norman rule was not fully suppressed in a single year, the Harrying of the North devastated the region so severely that survival became the primary concern, with rebellion taking a distant second. Over time, Northumbria gradually became more integrated into the English kingdom, and its glory days of successful resistance against southern autocratic rulers would never return.

13

DOMESDAY BOOK

BY THE MID-1080S, KING WILLIAM had largely consolidated his rule over England. Unlike his Anglo-Saxon predecessors, whose authority was often constrained by powerful earls and the Witan—an assembly of nobles and clergy that advised the king—William redefined the English monarchy. Through his redistribution of land to loyal Norman barons and the centralization of power, he transformed the crown into an absolute authority, reducing the influence of the nobility and ensuring that all landholders owed direct loyalty to him. Vast areas of the English realm remained under the direct control of the Crown or newly instated Norman nobles allied with William. The four great earldoms established by Cnut the Great were abolished, and the Witan disappeared. Although assemblies were still summoned, they became known as "concilia" or "parlements," referring to formal meetings between the king and his leading feudal tenants. King William redefined kingship in England, and the legitimacy he imposed on the English crown would shape royal authority for centuries. His successors continued to wield centralized power embedded in the royal institution, much more so than other great monarchs, such as the kings of Francia or the German emperors (Tombs 2016, 49).

A prime example of this power was Domesday Book (1085-1086), a multifaceted document that began production in 1085 and was completed in 1086. According to the *Anglo-Saxon Chronicle*, Domesday Book was initiated at King William's Midwinter court in Gloucester in 1085. At its simplest level, Domesday Book is a nationwide inventory that documented the dominion of England's new ruler, William I (1066-1087). On a deeper and more complex level, it represented a political statement—a symbolic manifestation of King William's power and authority. If King William was to be seen as the "owner" of the English nation through his right of conquest, everyone else would essentially be a landholder who held land from him, whether they were peasants, knights, or earls (Jones 2018). Domesday Book essentially solidified the Norman Conquest of England by providing the king with detailed knowledge of 13,400 named places under his control. However, the far northern areas of Cumberland, Northumberland, Durham, and Westmorland were excluded due to the disputed nature of their possession. According to a royal treasurer, it was named Domesday Book because "its decisions, like those of the Last Judgement, are unalterable," and as a nationwide survey, it is "unrivalled, not only in medieval Europe, but anywhere at any time."

The intention behind Domesday Book was likely to address the chaos arising from the land-grabs that had followed the post–Conquest rebellions, to clarify the value and tenure of the King's possessions, to facilitate taxation, and to bring the English nation under the rule of written law. Sworn juries provided information on their districts, which was recorded by royal commissioners in Latin. The *Anglo-Saxon Chronicle* notes that the king sold his land on "very hard terms—as hard as he could," and this harshness would be felt by the conquered English peasantry (Tombs 2016, 49–50). Domesday Book listed the types of land in England and their uses, including minerals, manufacturers, fisheries, over 6,000 mills, and individuals categorized as "productive people" (primarily adult men in this context) and their status, such as earls and villagers.

Domesday Book also refers to "villeins," of whom it counts 109,000. A "villein" was a type of peasant who was feudally tied to a lord's manor. They held and worked land in exchange for providing labor, services, and dues to the lord, but had limited personal freedom and could not leave the manor without the lord's permission. By 1066, slavery had faded from practice in Normandy, but it was still widespread in England. By 1086, however, there was a marked decline, highlighted in Domesday Book, which shows that slavery had decreased by approximately twenty-five percent. Historians typically attribute this shift to economic factors, suggesting that the Normans preferred serfs, who could hold land and pay rent, over slaves who worked for free but required housing and food. While this was likely the primary reason, it is also probable that a significant portion of Norman society found the concept of slavery morally objectionable. William had banned the slave trade, seemingly at the prompting of Lanfranc, and is said to have freed many hundreds on his expedition to Wales. Slavery was condemned at an ecclesiastical council in 1102, and by the 1130s, it had disappeared from England (Morris 2013, 338–339). In Domesday Book, a count of 28,000 slaves is noted, alongside animals ranging from oxen to beehives. It also recorded the value of these holdings, in part to showcase England as a wealthy and developed agricultural country.

In terms of land ownership, the royal family held twenty percent, the church held twenty-five percent, and a group of prominent aristocrats controlled another twenty-five percent—less than the English aristocracy had controlled under the Godwines. Essentially, around 250 individuals controlled the country, including the king, the great prelates (appointed by the king), and approximately 170 barons with landed incomes over £100 per year—nearly all of whom were new arrivals. The remaining thirty percent of the land was held by about 2,000 foreign knights (followers of King William) and 8,000 other settlers, some of whom were rank and file of the conquering army, while others had followed in the wake of the conquest. The remaining holders were the surviving English free peasantry. Of nearly two million English, only four Englishmen—none with names familiar today—remained major landowners, and only about twenty had annual incomes exceeding £20 (Tombs 2016, 49–50). According to the discontented author of the *Peterborough Chronicle*, often called the E manuscript of the *Anglo-Saxon Chronicle*, the Domesday Survey, completed in August 1086, omitted nothing—not "a single virgate of land ... not even one ox, nor one cow, nor one pig." Domesday Book detailed how England's assets had been redistributed since 1066, revealing a total surveyed value of around £76,000 in 1086. King William was by far the wealthiest individual in England, with estates covering 17 percent of the country (Kay 2020, 23–24). King William became the ultimate lord in England, and with the knowledge provided by the survey, he had precise information on who owned what and where it was located.

The core principle of Domesday Book is that all land tenure originated from and ended with the king. Each recorded county has its own chapter, beginning with a list of lands owned by King William in that shire. Following this, the lands held by others (bishops, abbots, barons, earls) are listed, with each noted as holding land from the king. Should a landowner die or rebel, the king's ministers could quickly identify the estates owned, however scattered, and send sheriffs to seize them, thanks to the survey's details. Domesday Book was thus a charter of confirmation for landowners, securing title to their estates, often acquired through conquest. It also served as a directory for royal administrators, enabling them to track land ownership, make transfers, and levy charges efficiently. It is important to note that Domesday Book, for all its significance, was likely just one outcome of the Domesday Survey. Domesday Book provided William and his successors with an unprecedented means to manage their aristocracy efficiently, while also profiting substantially from this arrangement. However, Domesday Book did not resolve the financial crisis King William faced in 1086. William urgently needed funds on a scale that could only be raised through a national tax. It is probable that another aim of the Domesday Survey was to gather data to reform the geld tax. William's need for revenue is underscored by the fact that, while the extensive Domesday Survey was underway, royal tax collectors toured the country, imposing an additional punitive geld of six shillings per hide. This taxation was so contentious that the Bishop of Hereford remarked on how "the land was vexed with much violence arising from the collection of royal taxes." In many ways, 1086 was both a dire and portentous year, marked by violence, mass assemblies, threats of foreign invasions, and mercenaries prowling through many towns and cities. Many associated King William's great survey with God's day of Judgment. *The Anglo-Saxon Chronicle* reflects this sentiment, stating: "a very vexatious and anxious year throughout England, because of a pestilence among the livestock; and corn and fruits were at a standstill. It is difficult for anyone to realize what great misfortune was caused by the weather; so violent was the thunder and lightning that many were killed. Things steadily went from bad to worse for everybody. May God Almighty remedy it when it shall be His will!" Yet these threats would not persist for long.

In 1086, the Great Assembly at Salisbury was convened—a significant gathering of lords and landholders summoned by King William the Conqueror to swear loyalty, consolidate his authority, and further the implementation of the feudal system in England. This assembly, closely tied to the creation of Domesday Book, established clear records of land ownership and marked a final consolidation of Norman power. By this time, the storm clouds had providentially cleared, and shortly before the August 1 ceremony, news reached England of the death of King Cnut IV of Denmark on July 10, assassinated in a church by rebellious nobles. Cnut IV had long coveted the throne of England, but with his death, the threat of a Danish invasion was finally lifted, leaving England firmly in Norman hands. Meanwhile, the single scribe responsible for compiling Domesday Book began his monumental task, condensing the information from the circuit returns to create the master volume. Experts estimate that this scribe likely persevered for at least a year. As he approached the end of his work, with six of the seven circuits completed, he unexpectedly, for reasons unknown, put down his pen, leaving the final return unredacted. This has provided the modern world with an unfinished version of Great Domesday Book alongside the original circuit return for the eastern counties, known as Little Domesday Book (Morris 2013, 324–326). Despite historians being left with an incomplete record, Domesday Book still offers a fascinating glimpse into the complexities of early Norman governance and the challenges of documenting a newly conquered land.

While Domesday Book is often referred to in terms of the great survey of England that it conducted, it is, in essence, an accounting document. Professor David McCollum-Oldroyd of Newcastle University Business School highlights the significance of Domesday Book as an accounting tool: "Domesday Book of 1086 is regarded as a landmark in accounting history, primarily because it heralded a written system of government accounting in England, notwithstanding that it reflected concepts of accountability, decision-making, and control" (Oldroyd 1997, 14). The accounting significance of Domesday Book has prompted historians to carry out meticulous analyses of the historical records of the old English shires. Jones (2018) notes that these studies have produced major insights into medieval agricultural practices as well as the productivity of medieval agriculture. A series of analyses by John McDonald has demonstrated a relationship between the payment of the Geld (a national tax originally instituted to protect against the Danes, known as Danegeld) and the annual value of the manor. Additionally, it was found that several factors made land more likely to be taxed favorably. These factors included who owned the land (the tenant-in-chief), the administrative area in which the land was located, and its proximity to a town. Furthermore, it was shown that the efficiency of medieval farms in Essex and Wiltshire was roughly comparable, with farms in Essex performing well even when compared to those in modern economies. Finally, an analysis examined how well land was managed across different types of estates, including royal estates (owned by the king), ecclesiastical estates (owned by the church), and lay estates (owned by non-religious individuals). It was found that management and production methods were similar in both Essex and Wiltshire. This indicates that regardless of the type of ownership, land management practices were fairly consistent across these regions.

Domesday Book appears to have been executed in a five-stage process. First, King William required each tenant-in-chief (e.g., barons, abbots, or bishops) and each sheriff in England to provide an initial list of men and manors. This represented a massive and unprecedented government intrusion into the lives of every citizen, serving as the starting point for the survey. Second, a set of investigators visited each county to create an inventory of manors and resources, such as livestock and people, producing a comprehensive stocktake of everything of value throughout England. Third, although it is unclear if this was done universally, Robert, Bishop of Hereford, claimed there was a second visit to verify the accuracy of the first investigation. Fourth, the collected data was compiled into a full and unsummarized document known as Little Domesday, which contained extensive accounting and fiscal data on taxation and inventory. Finally, the data was summarized into Great Domesday. Both Little and Great Domesday Books were written in Latin and organized into shires, with landholdings recorded in manors. The records passed down to posterity include Little Domesday Book, which covers Suffolk, Norfolk, and Essex in greater detail, and Great Domesday, which covers 32 counties but excludes the three eastern counties and the northern counties of Durham, Westmorland, Cumberland, and Northumberland due to the rebellious state of the North. The difficult circumstances in these areas, highlighted by events like the Harrying of the North, likely led to their omission. Additionally, many areas in counties like Cheshire were laid waste due to rebellion and subsequent military repression. For the first time in Western European history, a written administrative document provided a comprehensive overview of a nation's resources, building upon the existing fiscal systems of the Anglo-Saxon state and church and the systematized administrative records such as charters, hidage records, and legal codes. The Anglo-Saxon fiscal administration was probably the most advanced in Europe by 1066, with a significant role for written documentation in assessing income, tax collection, and other obligations. Notably, the Domesday Survey was a public event, unlike modern censuses, which are treated confidentially (Jones 2018).

It should be noted that Domesday Book was not just a fiscal or feudal record but also a reflection of King William's assertion as Edward the Confessor's legitimate successor. It aimed to document land conditions not only in 1066 and 1086 but also during Edward the Confessor's reign. The survey was tied to judicial inquiries, as it settled disputes over ownership that had persisted since the Conquest. Many entries sought to resolve ongoing legal claims by referencing pre–Conquest conditions, highlighting William's desire to formalize the sweeping changes brought about by the Norman Conquest (Douglas 1999, 352–353). Domesday Book's deliberate documentation of land conditions under Edward the Confessor, rather than under Harold Godwinson, underscored William's claim as Edward's rightful successor. By focusing on land tenure as it existed before and after 1066, the survey effectively disregarded Harold's short reign, further undermining his legitimacy as king. This strategy reinforced William's narrative that Harold's kingship was an unlawful interruption, justifying the Norman Conquest and the subsequent redistribution of land.

Despite the impressiveness of Domesday Book, it also gave rise to a shocking number of disputes during the reign of William the Conqueror. Several thousand complaints can be found in the text, where individuals who possessed land or rights are accused of holding them outside the law. Occasionally, these complaints in Domesday Book are both double-sided and specific, including arguments from both litigators and responses from local juries and witnesses. One example can be taken from the survey's Hampshire folios, where a detailed description of a suit is provided between William de Chernet and Picot the Sheriff, who currently holds the land from the king. William de Chernet claims that it belongs to his manor based on inheritance and insists on using pre–Conquest laws until the king decides: "Picot holds two and a half virgates from the King. TRE Vitalis held them as a manor in alod from King Edward.... William de Chernet claims this land, saying that it belongs to the manor of Charford in the fee of Hugh de Port, through the inheritance of his antecessor. He brought his testimony for this from the better and old men from all the county and hundred. Picot contradicted this with his testimony from the villeins, common people, and reeves, who wished to defend this through an oath or the judgment of God, that he who held the land was a free man and could go where he wished with the land. But William's witnesses would not accept any law but the law of King Edward, until it is determined by the King." The quote describes a legal dispute involving land ownership in England during the period following the Norman Conquest. It details how Picot holds two and a half virgates of land from the King, which were previously held by an individual named Vitalis in the time of King Edward (abbreviated as TRE, or *"Tempore Regis Edwardi"*). This phrase signifies the conditions and ownership of the land before the Conquest, emphasizing its historical significance. William de Chernet claims that this land rightfully belongs to his manor of Charford, asserting his inheritance from his ancestor. He presents testimony from respected local men to support his claim, while Picot counters this with evidence from the villeins (common people) and reeves (local officials), arguing that he is a free man entitled to the land. The witnesses supporting William refuse to accept any law other than that of King Edward, illustrating the tensions between pre-Conquest and post-Conquest legal frameworks. The dispute reflects the broader struggles for land and authority that arose after William the Conqueror's invasion.

Such detailed descriptions are uncommon, but they imply that beneath the typically brief Domesday accounts of disputes were heated arguments and passionate opinions. Furthermore, Domesday Book typically presents only one side of a story. For instance, in Northamptonshire, Guy de Raimbeaucourt's estate included land in the village of Isham, recorded under his name. However, the entry ends by mentioning that the Bishop of Coutances claimed "three little gardens" in the area. We don't know how Guy responded to this claim or defended his position, but the inclusion of this note indicates that the issue was discussed during the inquest. Similarly, some entries include detailed histories of estates, suggesting that issues about land ownership were debated during the survey. For example, in the description of Kenchester in Herefordshire, it doesn't explicitly state there was a complaint, but the details provided indicate that a landholder named Hugh the Ass was worried about losing some of his property. The text explains that Hugh had loaned a part of his land to Earl William (William FitzOsbern), who was long dead by then. Earl William had given it to King Maredudd, who had been a ruler in South Wales. It goes on to mention that now Maredudd's son Gruffydd controls two small farms there. Even though the entry doesn't use legal terms like "claimed back" or "seized," it's clear that Hugh was concerned about this situation. The worries and complaints found in Domesday Book make up most of the information that isn't just about land ownership and estates. Furthermore, most of the recognized data—including details about land holdings, values, peasant populations, livestock, and fields—was likely sourced from administrative documents such as tax records, lists of payments from royal estates, and surveys of manors. This information may have come from reports created by tenants-in-chief specifically for the survey. While this data might have been reviewed or refined by the jurors of Domesday, it's unlikely that they originated it or discussed it in depth during the survey itself (Fleming 2009, 1–2). This reliance on pre-existing records emphasizes Domesday Book's role as a consolidation of existing knowledge rather than an entirely new creation of information.

Domesday Book should be viewed not merely as a record of land ownership but as a crucial legal document from England's history. Its intricate details, ranging from the number of livestock to the roles of various individuals, reveal that it is the most comprehensive legal text surviving from the period before Common Law emerged. When we look beyond the statistics, we find a wealth of material derived from the testimonies of jurors and the sworn statements of lords in 1086. This evidence highlights the contentious nature of land ownership at the time, illustrating how the English past and the Norman present intertwined to create complex property claims. Analyzing Domesday Book in this light offers new insights into the Normans that settled in England, the challenges faced during the Conqueror's reign, and the essential role of the inquest. Furthermore, it sheds light on the mechanics of justice during this period, revealing how men protected their holdings, relied on established legal customs, and developed new methods of safeguarding their land. The oral and public nature of law at this time is emphasized, underscoring the significance of communal memory in legal practices. The testimony contained in Domesday Book not only outlines legal practices of the eleventh century but also demonstrates how land law was evolving rapidly under William's rule due to the circumstances of the Conquest.

Viewing the Domesday inquest as a foundational event illustrates how it was instrumental in forging a new, hybrid Anglo-Norman legal system. Thus, the legal information within Domesday Book, when considered in its historical context, provides a vital understanding of the legal landscape of early medieval England and the transformative changes that were taking place. While King William would go on to die just a year after its completion in 1087, Domesday Book enabled the essentials of feudalism and a feudal kingdom to be established in England. Domesday Book reveals a complex transition in landholding after the Norman Conquest.

Between 1066 and 1086, the Old English elite was replaced by William's followers, resulting in significant land redistribution influenced by conquest, private interest and the clash of the Norman culture with that of the Anglo-Saxon. While Norman practices disrupted established norms, older English customs helped maintain continuity in land law. The 1086 inquest was pivotal, as it scrutinized every property in England and began to formalize legal norms around inheritance and property rights. This laid the groundwork for a hybrid legal framework that would govern land tenure, balancing Norman innovations with established English customs. Ultimately, Domesday Book highlights the emerging legal landscape shaped by both conflict and consensus in post–Conquest England.

14

THE DEATH AND LEGACY OF THE CONQUEROR

BY THE LATE 1080S, KING WILLIAM I of England was approaching his sixtieth birthday. Reaching such an age during medieval times was considered impressive, though being the ruler of a powerful nation like England undoubtedly afforded him certain privileges that made life less strenuous. Despite political conflicts and heavy taxation, the English kingdom was prospering, and some of the credit must go to its Norman rulers. Most importantly, they provided greater security against raids and invasions. King William's ambitions for his new kingdom led to the creation of many new buildings, jobs, and trade. The castles built by the Normans became the focal points of trading centers, causing towns to grow and multiply. Exports, especially wool, agricultural products, and minerals, flourished. Trade expanded rapidly, and many products were sent to southern Europe, which enhanced existing ports like London and Ipswich while simultaneously creating new ones in Hull, Lynn, Boston, Newcastle, and Portsmouth. In agriculture, the Normans introduced rabbits and fallow deer into carefully controlled warrens and forests. The feudal system was given a more centralized and stringent form after the Conquest had swept away many existing rights and eliminated most of the Anglo-Saxon thegns. King William granted land or "fiefs" to his barons in return for their military and political services, and they, in turn, granted it to their own followers for similar services. All of the land and its men were not a legal part of this hierarchy.

Unlike other European feudal systems, the English one recognized no powers or rights independent of the king. Barons did not possess large continuous areas of territory but rather scattered holdings instead. This arrangement allowed England to escape the trend that had tormented the European continent, as central authority did not fragment but was strengthened. Great barons would never be able to create autonomous and warring principalities akin to those seen in pre–Conquest Anglo-Saxon

England or France (Tombs 2016, 50–51). To cement his control, William's careful distribution of land ensured that no baron could amass enough power to challenge the crown, thus preserving a centralized monarchy. This structure, along with the economic and military reforms introduced by the Normans, would lay the foundation for how England was to be ruled for many centuries.

Despite the blossoming of his kingdom, the last three years of William's life, from 1085 to 1087, can be described as embodying the final crisis of his dynamic reign, where all of the chief characteristics of his rule were displayed in conjunction. During the twenty-four-month period between the autumn of 1085 and William's death in September 1087, the Conqueror witnessed a revival of a hostile federation against his Anglo-Norman kingdom in a form reminiscent of earlier decades. William spent the final months of his life either at war or in active preparation for it, with a notable administrative achievement occurring through the taking of the Domesday survey as well. *The Anglo-Saxon Chronicle* of 1085 notes the beginning of this crisis in 1085: "In this year people said, and declared for a fact, that Cnut, king of Denmark, son of King Sweyn was setting out towards England, and meant to conquer that land with the aid of Robert, count of Flanders." Cnut IV was the son of Sweyn Estrithson and had attempted to revive the Scandinavian claims on England. In the meantime, King Philip of France was actively supporting William's rebellious son, Robert Curthose, while Odo, Bishop of Bayeux, despite being imprisoned by King William, had enough influence to incite rebellion among many of William's English and Norman subjects. In the north, King Malcolm stood hostile on the Scottish border.

While William had to deal with all of these troubles, he was at the same time aging and did not have the vitality of youth anymore. Queen Matilda had also recently died, which must have put an additional strain on him. His health was deteriorating, and he was becoming notoriously corpulent. Yet William acted with much vigor once he became aware of King Cnut's invasion schemes, deciding to lay waste to the coastal districts of England so that any invading force would find no provisions. For his part, he crossed the Channel "with a larger force of mounted men and foot-soldiers than had ever come into this country," according to Orderic Vitalis. Regardless, many of these men were likely mercenaries, and William's ability to pay them was impressive given his dire financial situation; however, this was likely possible due to the great geld he had levied on England in the previous year (Douglas 1999, 346–347).

The lead-up to all of these consequential events had been long in coming. King William had spent all of 1084 and more than half of 1085 in the northern parts of France. According to the Abingdon Historia,

14. The Death and Legacy of the Conqueror

King William was in Normandy on 9 January 1084 and again on Easter, 31 March, together with his sons Robert and William, while the third son, Henry, was at Abingdon. King William went to Rouen on 19 June, where he appointed his former chaplain Rainald, a monk at Jumièges, as abbot of Abingdon. A Fécamp diploma entirely devoted to Norman business suggests that King William made a visit to Upper Normandy at some point in 1085 as well. According to John of Worcester, King William did not cross to England before the autumn of 1085. William's absence from England in 1084 suggests it may have been one of his more peaceful years, during which he did not have to deal with domestic rebellions while fending off foreign invasions. Conflict began when the vicomte of Maine, Hubert de Sainte-Suzanne, rebelled against King William. This led to the siege of the castle at Sainte-Suzanne. According to Orderic Vitalis, the siege laid by King William lasted a total of three years and ended when Hubert crossed to England to reach a settlement with the king in either late 1085 or early 1086. A charter for the abbey of Saint-Vincent of Le Mans notes places Hubert's Channel crossing between 23 May 1085 and 20 April 1086. Unfortunately, Orderic Vitalis's narrative is the only surviving written account of the siege. While it is exceptionally detailed, it is obscure in terms of why the quarrel between Hubert and William arose. It does indicate that Hubert defied William because the king had offended him, initially in an insignificant way and later in a more serious one. After Hubert's Channel crossing, peace was secured between him and King William, and Orderic notes that no further conflicts arose between the two for the remainder of the Conqueror's life (Bates 2016, 452–455).

At the same time, King William's oldest son, Robert Curthose, had been away from Normandy for around three years, likely due to being sent into exile. A reconciliation was attempted in 1085 when Robert was present at Gloucester during William's Christmas court. Nevertheless, Robert was, according to the twelfth-century Benedictine monk and chronicler Robert of Torigni, still in exile during his father's final illness in 1087. Matilda's death must have further strained relations between King William and his son Robert, as she would no longer be able to serve as a mediator between the two. Odo of Bayeux's support for Robert during the wars that followed King William's death indicates that the bishop's imprisonment had also removed a powerful ally from Robert's cause. At the same time, Robert's younger brother William was being elevated to a more prominent status in England and was knighted in 1086. According to Orderic Vitalis, neither Robert nor William was blameless. Robert may have left his father's lands for trivial reasons out of stubbornness and disobedience, but King William was also guilty of regularly criticizing his son in public and often behaved with great emotion rather than rationality.

King William took his massive army across the Channel in the autumn of 1085 to deal with the threat of the Danish invasion that King Cnut IV of Denmark had planned in alliance with his father-in-law, Count Robert the Frisian of Flanders. King William had good reason to take the threat seriously. Prior invasion armies in 1069 and 1075 had been transported in 300 and 200 ships, respectively. The planned invasion in the mid–1080s had supposedly required over 1,000 ships, with Count Robert of Flanders supporting the Danes with an additional 600. To make matters worse, the king of Norway was supposedly also involved. In his *Vita Wulfstani*, William of Malmesbury states that King William was frightened, which, when translated, may imply a sense of alarm; however, it more accurately reflects his recognition of the significant scale of the impending invasion. In response, the devastation William ordered along the English coasts—intended to prevent invading forces from gathering provisions—was comparatively limited. This is evidence of the difference William enacted when using ravaging as an aspect of warfare compared to using it as a form of political punishment. According to a former monk of St. Augustine's, Ailnoth, who had taken refuge in Denmark and was therefore likely prejudiced against King William, King Cnut IV of Denmark was responding to a desperate appeal from the English to free them from the tyranny to which King William and his followers had subjected them.

Regardless, by early 1086, it must have become clear to King William that the Danish invasion was not going to happen, and he dismissed part of his army, although he still kept other troops stationed with him. According to William of Malmesbury, the invasion failed due to adverse sea conditions and the internal policies of the Danish kingdom. Pope Gregory VII, a significant figure in the eleventh century, was known for his efforts to reform the Church and assert papal authority, which often put him at odds with secular rulers. After his death in 1085, the German anti-king Hermann of Salm, who had been backed by Cnut against Henry IV, sought refuge in Denmark. In the meantime, Henry IV advanced north into Saxony to pursue Hermann. Cnut also faced a rebellion from his brother Olaf and had to manage dissent over the taxes he imposed, likely to fund a planned military expedition. An anti-king is someone who claims kingship without recognition from the legitimate ruler. Furthermore, the coinage reforms of Cnut, alongside his now-lost equestrian seal, suggest an imprudently ambitious set of changes that might have also incited rivalries. Cnut IV was murdered in Odense Cathedral on 10 July 1086 and would later be canonized in 1099 as a martyr and saint. With the rebels of Sainte-Suzanne also having submitted at this time, King William had miraculously escaped unscathed from what may have been the greatest threat he faced in his lifetime (Bates 2016, 456–459).

14. The Death and Legacy of the Conqueror

Following William's success against the Danes and at Sainte-Suzanne, he chose to summon "all the landholders of substance in England, whose vassals soever they were" to the vast and open space of Old Sarum hillfort in Wiltshire, in the town of Salisbury, on 1 August 1086. King William required each of these men to swear a personal oath of loyalty to him. John of Worcester suggests that every earl, baron, sheriff, knight, bishop, and archbishop in the country was there, although this is likely an exaggeration. Regardless, King William must have had a couple of thousand men. This was followed by a ceremony that was unprecedented in both England and Normandy, where each of the men present swore that they would be faithful to King William against all others, with this oath taking precedence over any previously sworn allegiance to an overlord. For reasons unknown, the significance of this sworn oath is omitted by most contemporary writers. *The Anglo-Saxon Chronicle* skips it completely and jumps to King William collecting an additional heavy tax "upon every pretext he could find, whether just or otherwise," before he left England and returned to Normandy. *The Anglo-Saxon Chronicle* then goes into great detail about the terrible weather and the many diseases affecting the men and cattle of England in 1086 and 1087, while ignoring any events occurring during William's return to Normandy.

In the meantime, Robert of Flanders had once again appealed to King Philip of France, who agreed to encourage raids from the Vexin into Normandy. These raids overran the Évreux area and pillaged with little opposition. It was hardly surprising that King Philip opposed King William. William had risen from his status as a ducal vassal in Normandy to Philip's equal as the King of England, although he still remained Philip's vassal in Normandy and Maine. Philip undoubtedly viewed William's unusual rise to power as a grave threat and supported any opposition to his rule. William of Malmesbury claims that King William had fallen ill around this time and notes that King Philip supposedly taunted him by claiming that he was "lying in" and "keeps his bed like a woman after her delivery" (Cole 2016, 213–214). This was likely an insult directed at the king's increasing corpulence, mockingly hinting that he resembled a pregnant woman. According to William of Malmesbury, when King William heard of King Philip's insult, he swore, "When I go to Mass after my lying in.... I will offer a hundred thousand candles on his behalf" (Morris 2013, 328). Offering candles at Mass was a common practice in medieval Christianity, symbolizing prayers for oneself or others. William's vow suggests a grand gesture of goodwill or prayer for Philip yet implies condescension, indicating that King Philip would need more than a hundred thousand prayers to contend with William's wrath.

Eventually, King William had recovered from his illness by the end of

July 1087, when he led an army into the Vexin to pillage and burn the town of Mantes, which had served as a springboard for raids into Normandy. *The Anglo-Saxon Chronicle* accurately notes that King William was not attacking his own overlord and argues that, while doing so, he also destroyed all of the town's churches and killed two anchorites who were burnt to death there. According to Orderic Vitalis, this would also lead to his downfall, as he rode too close to the heat of the burning town and fell seriously ill as a consequence. William of Malmesbury offers an alternative explanation, arguing that when King William's horse leapt over a ditch, the pommel of his saddle was driven into his large belly, inflicting a serious injury upon the aging king. Regardless of whether Orderic Vitalis's or William of Malmesbury's account is accurate, King William's injury would turn out to be a fatal one. The king was taken back to Rouen, where his condition worsened. He was unable to withstand the noise and heat of the city and was moved to the Priory of St. Gervase outside the walls, where his subjects began to realize that no medical intervention would be able to save the king's life. Despite emphasizing the constant state of agony that King William found himself in, Orderic Vitalis gives us multiple pages of purported speeches from him, some of which describe the entirety of his career and confess freely to any accusations that Orderic Vitalis could throw at him, specifically the persecution of the Anglo-Saxons "beyond all reason." A more believable part then follows where King William describes his final decisions before he dies. King William ordered that money be given to the poor and for building churches, specifically to replace those that had recently been burned down in Mantes. Prisoners were to be freed, including such notable ones as as Earl Morcar, Roger de Breteuil, and even the younger brother of King Harold Godwinson, Wulfnoth, whom William had held for over thirty years. Despite King William's seemingly generous mindset on his deathbed, he had little love left for his brother Odo, whom he refused to free from prison. However, upon the persuasion of his half-brother Robert of Mortain and the other powerful magnates who had gathered at his bedside, King William eventually agreed to free Odo of Bayeux, although he supposedly did so while warning them, "You ... are bringing on yourselves a serious calamity."

When the decision came as to who would inherit his mighty kingdoms in Normandy and England, William ruled that Normandy should go to his oldest son, Robert Curthose, despite their hostile history with each other. King William supposedly argued that the land had been granted a long time ago and such a grant could not be annulled, despite his son being a "proud and silly prodigal." According to Orderic Vitalis, King William was more vague when it came to his successor for the English throne, with William supposedly stating, "Having ... made my way to the throne of that kingdom by so many crimes, I dare not leave it to anyone but God alone" (Cole 2016, 213–216). Regardless, King William followed up this statement by immediately indicating that he hoped God would favor his third son, William Rufus, who was the second oldest after Robert Curthose, given the early death of his middle son, Richard. King William then provided a letter for his son William Rufus to take to Lanfranc to confirm his choice and sent his son away immediately. Teresa Cole (2016) argues that despite this claim by Orderic Vitalis, William Rufus was actually at the coast about to sail away when he heard of his father's death. Despite this, William Rufus would go on to inherit his father's kingdom and eventually be coronated as King William II of England. Finally, King William bequeathed his youngest son, Henry, £5,000 in silver, after which he supposedly also sent him away. If this account is true, it would mean that none of King William's sons or immediate family members were present when he drew his final breath in the early morning of 9 September 1087. If Orderic Vitalis is to be believed, the aftermath of the king's death can be described as extremely bizarre. Supposedly, everybody who had been present at the king's bedside "became as men who had lost their wits," with all the magnates quickly rushing off to secure their lands, while all the lower servants stripped the body and the royal apartments of everything of value.

This would only be the beginning of a humiliating affair for the dead king. When everybody had fled, a country knight was the only one left to arrange the preparation of the corpse and its transportation to Caen, where it could be buried (Cole 2016, 214–216). However, on the way there, a fire broke out in the city, and everybody left the hearse to help extinguish it. During the funeral itself in the Abbey of St. Stephen, a crowd of bishops and abbots had gathered to lay the king to rest. This concluded with a bishop of Évreux giving a long and eloquent sermon, where he extolled many of William's virtues. He concluded this sermon by asking the crowd to forgive their former liege if he had ever done them any wrong, at which point a loud protest was initiated by a man who angrily claimed that the church had been built on his father's land and that he had never been compensated. A quick inquiry established that this was indeed true, after which the man was compensated with an immediate cash payment, and the funeral continued (Morris 2013, 331). As a final coup de grâce, the coffin had been made too small for the overweight king, and when his servants attempted to cram his body into the small space, his stomach burst, filling the church with an "intolerable stench" and bringing a rapid conclusion to the proceedings. Orderic Vitalis, perhaps foreshadowing how extreme this turn of events may seem to future historians, noted that he had carefully investigated the details of King William's death and subsequent burial and had given "not ... a well-feigned tragedy ... nor a humorous comedy ... but a true narrative ... for the perusal of serious readers." He then delivers a heartfelt and somewhat sad tribute marking the end of a great king: "A king once potent and warlike ... lay naked on the floor, deserted by those who owed him their birth, and those he had fed and enriched. He needed the money of a stranger for the cost of his funeral. He was carried to the church amidst flaming houses, by trembling crowds, and a spot of freehold land was wanting for the grave of a man whose princely sway had extended over so many cities, towns and villages.... There is but one lot for rich and poor.... Trust not then, O sons of men, in princes who deceive, but in the true and living God who created all things" (Cole 2016, 213–216). Following the ill-fated burial, King William's remains were interred quickly and with little ceremony.

In terms of his physical appearance, several sources have survived with testimonies on this matter. Visually, in the Bayeux Tapestry, King William is shown wearing both military and civilian clothing, but this is simply an image and not a portrait. In civilian attire, William would wear a long tunic and a cloak; he is depicted with a sword in hand and a sort of badge likely resembling his ducal office. His hairstyle is cut short and combed forward like a crew cut, while the back of his neck and head is shaved. When he leads his men toward Brittany, he is depicted wearing a padded tunic and carrying a baton. Later, while enthroned in the scene where King Harold swears an oath to him, William is seen wearing a full-length robe and a large cloak, similar to the one worn by Harold when he is later enthroned as king. Contemporary accounts of King William suggest that he was a man of much majesty, both seated and standing, capable of overawing his audience. An anonymous monk of Caen describes William as "great in body and strong, tall in stature but not ungainly." While Orderic Vitalis makes it clear that the king suffered from obesity at the time of his death, this only applies to the later years of his life. Numerous references highlight his strength and endurance in his earlier years, portraying him as a hardy warrior with no shortage of physical fitness. Instances of this are described in scenes such as one where King William is said to have carried the coat of mail of his companion William FitzOsbern as well as his own at one point. King William seems to have lived a healthy life, with few recorded instances of illness. William of Malmesbury describes the Norman Conqueror as "of proper height, immensely stout, with a ferocious expression and a high bald forehead." William is described as being able to fire arrows from his bow while simultaneously riding his horse at a gallop. Vocally, William has been credited with having a harsh, perhaps guttural voice, which he would soften when being persuasive (Rex 2012, 257–258). According to William of Malmesbury,

14. The Death and Legacy of the Conqueror

William would use his voice to employ colorful oaths "so that the mere roar of his open mouth might somehow strike terror into the minds of his audience" (Morris 2013, 327). He was supposedly temperate in drinking and eating and abhorred drunkenness in others. He was also officially a devoted husband who remained loyal to his wives, with no records of marital infidelity or any illegitimate offspring. Many centuries later, in 1522, the sixteenth-century historian Charles De Bras claims that three clergy from Rome—a cardinal, an archbishop, and a bishop—alongside the Abbot of the Abbaye aux Hommes, Charles de Martigny, permitted King William's tomb to be opened so his body could be inspected. The body had been perfectly preserved, which casts some doubt on Orderic Vitalis's claims of his corpse bursting during burial. The corpse was described as that of a large man with remarkably long arms and legs. A local artist was paid to create a painting of the embalmed corpse, which was exhibited in the abbey's church for many years. Unfortunately, the painting was lost when the tomb was pillaged during the religious wars in 1562, and only a femur survives of King William's body. Nevertheless, the femur allows for an estimate that King William was around five feet ten inches in height, which was fairly tall for an eleventh-century man. This stands in contrast to his wife Matilda, who was notably shorter. When her casket was opened in 1961 and her remains inspected, it was estimated that she was about four feet two inches tall (Rex 2012, 257–258). Altogether, these descriptions of King William paint a portrait of a formidable and imposing figure whose physical presence and disciplined lifestyle undoubtedly contributed to his ability to command loyalty and respect, both on the battlefield and in court.

The contemporary legacy of William the Conqueror was complex. While his Norman allies vigorously promoted his successes and hailed his military triumphs, he also faced considerable criticism. Orderic Vitalis, who often praised William and the Normans for their astonishing conquest of England and establishment of a strong central governing authority, was not shy in condemning the excessive violence that William had inflicted on the native English populace. Orderic began his account by praising William, noting that death deals with rich and poor alike, and while William had been a powerful king, feared by many, the period between his death and funeral left him naked and needing the charity of strangers. Nevertheless, this did not reflect on his character, and Vitalis praised William as a good ruler, a lover of peace who relied on wise counsel, feared God, and protected the Church (Morris 2013, 331–332). Regardless, according to Vitalis, William apparently confessed: "I did not attain that high honour by hereditary right but wrested it from the perjured Harold in a desperate battle with much effusion of human blood … by the slaughter and banishment of his adherents.... I subjugated England to my rule. I have persecuted its native inhabitants beyond all reason ... and ... cruelly oppressed them." Vitalis also laments the fall of the Anglo-Saxon aristocracy and says that his fellow conquerors "grew wealthy on the spoils of England whilst their sons were either shamefully slain or driven as exiles to wander hopelessly through foreign kingdoms." Nevertheless, Vitalis still praises William for his generosity toward the church, claiming that William was never guilty of simony (Rex 2012, 249–250). Simony is the act of selling or buying ecclesiastical privileges, positions, or sacred items, often regarded as a form of corruption within the church. William's innocence in this matter was significant, as it meant that the integrity of the church was maintained during his reign, fostering trust among the clergy and laity and thereby strengthening the relationship between the monarchy and the church. Vitalis also sought to distinguish William, whom he regarded as noble and peace-loving, from the Normans as a whole, whom he viewed less favorably: "They arrogantly abused their authority and mercilessly slaughtered the native people, like the scourge of God smiting them for their sins.... Noble maidens were exposed to the insults of low-born soldiers and lamented their dishonoring by the scum of the earth.... Ignorant parasites, made almost mad with pride, they were astonished that such great power had come to them and imagined that they were a law unto themselves. O fools and sinners! Why did they not ponder contritely in their hearts that they had conquered not by their own strength but by the will of almighty God, and had subdued a people that was greater and wealthier than they were, with a longer history?" (Morris 2013, 332).

 Vitalis shows little love for the Normans but makes it clear that it was the will of God that enabled them to conquer England. As for King William, if the quote that Vitalis attributes to him is accurate, it would suggest that William openly admitted he was not King Edward's true heir, while simultaneously acknowledging himself as a brutal dictator who subjected the English populace to abhorrent cruelty. William of Malmesbury also offers his own criticisms of the Norman ruler, condemning William for his actions during the Harrying of the North. However, William of Malmesbury was less severe in his judgment than Orderic Vitalis, asserting that William was "somewhat too harsh towards the English" because he found them untrustworthy, which led him to "deprive the more powerful of them first of their revenues and then of their lands." Malmesbury notes that William supposedly refused to allow anyone of English nationality to aspire to any position of dignity, although he concludes by remarking, "the Normans ... have my loyalty" (Rex 2012, 250). Despite their harsh judgments, both Vitalis and Malmesbury ultimately recognized William's formidable authority and the stability he imposed. William of Malmesbury conveys little remorse regarding the Conquest of England, portraying the native Anglo-Saxons as a people given over to gluttony and lechery, lax in their Christian faith, and addicted to wassail, an alcoholic beverage. In contrast, he describes the Normans as a cunning and martial people that were well-dressed, skilled in constructing impressive structures, discerning in their cuisine, notably more pious, and leading lives of modesty. The twelfth-century English historian and cleric Henry of Huntington seems to echo this perspective, characterizing the Normans as uncivilized in their "unparalleled savagery" but nonetheless viewing them as God's chosen people in their conquest of England. Huntington notes, "God had chosen the Normans to wipe out the English nation," attributing this to the Anglo-Saxons' deviation from righteousness, thereby deserving punishment by the Norman scourge. This interpretation is mirrored by Orderic, Malmesbury, Eadmer, and the Anglo-Saxon Chronicle (Morris 2013, 337–342). Robert Wace offers a perspective similar to that of Orderic Vitalis, recounting that William supposedly admitted, "I conquered England wrongly; many men died wrongly there ... and I took the kingdom wrongly. What I have wrongly taken, to which I have no right at all, I ought not to give to my sons" (Rex 2012, 250).

While it is possible that William may have expressed some regret for his actions regarding his rule over the English, it is highly unlikely that he would ever shy away from his original claim of being Edward the Confessor's true heir, even if he knew it to be a falsehood. To question or disavow that claim would have undermined his entire rule, leaving his conquest open to challenges from rival claimants. Even if he were privately aware that his claim was dubious, William would have been deeply invested in maintaining this narrative to legitimize his claim to the throne he had conquered, both in the eyes of his Norman supporters and the broader European political landscape. Publicly retracting such a claim would have risked delegitimizing not only his reign but also the legacy he intended to pass on to his descendants. Regardless, there may be some truth to the notion that William regretted his oppressive rule against the English, as multiple contemporary sources seem to agree with this narrative. Meanwhile, writers in France generally took vicarious pride in the Conquest, seeing it as a triumph of Frankish military strength. Elsewhere in Europe, opinions were more mixed. A Bavarian writer named Frutolf of Michelsberg wrote that William had brutally subjugated England to his will, sending its churchmen into exile and its aristocracy to their deaths. Another German writer named Wenric of Trier, who had lambasted Gregory VII in 1080 over his relationships with several rulers, offered even harsher criticism of King William and his conquest. He claimed that some of the pope's "friends" had "usurped kingdoms by the violence of a tyrant, paved the road to the throne with blood, placed a blood-stained crown on their heads, and established their rule with murder, rape, butchery, and torment." No names are mentioned, but the new king of England was clearly the ruler that Wenric intended to reference. Gregory VII wrote a letter to William in the same year, lamenting the criticism he endured due to his earlier support for the Conquest. The Anglo-Saxon Chronicle's account of William, whose obituary was supposedly written before 1100, perhaps around the time of William's death, offers a lengthy and detailed description of the king. It portrays William as a man of wisdom and power, stern but compassionate toward those who loved God, fostering the growth of religion during his reign. This is evidenced by the construction of Battle Abbey and Canterbury Cathedral. In 1066, England had around sixty monasteries, but by 1135 that number increased manifold to approximately 250–300. William is also praised for his achievement with the Domesday Survey and his commanding authority over the British Isles, including Wales and Scotland. The chronicle suggests that had he lived just two more years, Ireland might also have come under his rule. However, after listing his positive attributes, the chronicle swiftly shifts to William's more negative traits. It notes that "assuredly in his time men suffered grievous oppression and manifold injuries." The castles he built are described as a "burden to the poor," and his greed in heavily taxing his subjects is condemned as "most unjustly and for little need." The account concludes by emphasizing William's relentless nature, stating that he was indifferent to the hatred of his subjects. Those who wished to keep their lives and lands had no choice but to submit entirely to his will (Morris 2013, 333–334). This obituary, though largely balanced in its praise and criticism, reflects the complex legacy William left behind—a ruler whose accomplishments were undeniable, yet whose methods often sparked resentment among his subjects. *The Anglo-Saxon Chronicle* provides a rare contemporary perspective on William, combining both admiration for his achievements and a deep awareness of the suffering his rule inflicted on the people of England. Ultimately, *The Anglo-Saxon Chronicle* leaves its readers with a portrait of a king whose ambition reshaped the British Isles, though at great human cost.

Despite the supposed humiliating ending during his unfortunate burial, King William left behind a legacy of unparalleled conquest. He had successfully conquered the English nation on a daring journey from his much smaller duchy across the English Channel, and his invasion of England would also be the last time a foreign invasion successfully managed to conquer the country. With the conquest, England was now tied to the European continent. Brownworth (2014) estimates that approximately

14. The Death and Legacy of the Conqueror

twenty years after the conquest, more than two hundred thousand French and Norman settlers had arrived in England, and one in five of the native Anglo-Saxon population had either been killed or starved to death due to the foreign seizure of livestock or land (Brownworth 2014, 71–72). In the royal court, French replaced English, and nearly all of the powerful Anglo-Saxon figures disappeared from influence. The Anglo-Saxons witnessed their leaders fall victim to poverty, imprisonment, or death. King William imposed heavy taxes on his subjects, and large swaths of the country were depopulated to serve as royal hunting forests, while he filled England with his many castles as a visible symbol of its new overlord. The advancement of William from duke to king also meant that the French king now technically had another king as his vassal, and any future English kings would now have to perform the ceremonial acts of homage for the lands of Normandy. Naturally, British sovereigns had no interest in this, and France and England would engage in centuries of conflict over the English rulers' influence and territory in France. England would, for a time, continue to be ruled by King William's immediate family. Three of William's four sons survived into adulthood, with two eventually becoming Kings of England. His eldest son, Robert, inherited the title of Duke of Normandy, while his younger sons, William Rufus and Henry, ascended to the English throne. Decades later, Henry would face his elder brother Robert Curthose in battle, emerging victorious and reunifying England and Normandy under a single ruler once more.

CONCLUSION

THE NORMANS, A PEOPLE FORGED in the crucible of war, built their duchy in the early tenth century through a blend of sheer martial prowess and opportunistic alliances. Their resilience in maintaining a semi-autonomous status within the Kingdom of France, despite their French suzerain often attempting to undermine them, borders on the surreal. While the kings of France supported Norman rivals and schemed to curb their power, the dukes of Normandy not only survived but flourished. By the eleventh century, they had pushed their dominance beyond the borders of their duchy, successfully conquering foreign lands like Sicily and, most famously, England.

Duke William's conquest of England in 1066 was a testament to both his strategic genius and what at times seemed like supernatural luck. His invasion came at a moment of extraordinary weakness for England. The kingdom was mired in a fratricidal struggle between Harold Godwinson and his rebellious brother Tostig, which left its political and military structures fragile. At the same time, William had neutralized threats at home, defeating one of his most significant adversaries, Geoffrey Martel, while the King of France, Philip, was essentially neutralized in his minority with William's father-in-law serving as his guardian. William's timing was impeccable: just as Harold had repelled a massive Norwegian invasion led by Harald Hardrada, his forces were exhausted from their victory at Stamford Bridge, allowing William to land his army. The English army, weary and diminished, faced a fresh Norman force with little time to recover.

William's extraordinary fortune in discovering the English kingdom so vulnerable, coupled with his decisive victory at the Battle of Hastings, irrevocably transformed the course of English history. His reign marked the beginning of profound changes: the integration of Norman French with Old English gave rise to Middle English, reshaping the linguistic landscape of England for centuries to come. The establishment of an absolute monarchy meant that the king's power became total, erasing the once-significant influence of the Anglo-Saxon aristocracy. Earls like

Godwin, who had previously posed legitimate threats to the throne, found their power diminished and ultimately extinguished in the wake of William's centralized authority. Through a process of sub-infeudation, King William created a list of tenants and under-tenants who all owed him loyalty, reinforced through feudal obligations alongside an oath of loyalty. William's introduction of Norman feudalism fundamentally altered the social structure, while the Domesday Survey, an unparalleled historical record, provided a comprehensive inventory of land and resources, setting a precedent not seen in other European nations of the time. The creation of Domesday Book was an extraordinary accomplishment. Medieval Europe had no parallel in terms of such a detailed, comprehensive survey. The Domesday inquest stands as a testament to William the Conqueror's iron will and unmatched authority. While other rulers of the time would not have dared attempt such a monumental task, William's ambition and need for absolute control over his new kingdom compelled him to gather vast amounts of information on wealth, land ownership, and tax capacity. The result is a statistical record without equal in medieval governance, unmatched in scale and precision. Although the English nation endured significant suffering during this period, its economy not only survived but thrived, leading to rapid growth in infrastructure and urbanization. The convergence of Norman and Anglo-Saxon influences laid the groundwork for a new England, one that would rise from the ashes of conflict to become a pivotal force in European history.

A recurring theme throughout this book, and indeed the events surrounding the Norman Conquest, is the question of legitimacy—both in claiming the right to rule and in consolidating power as an absolute monarch. William and his Norman allies were astute in understanding that military victories alone were not enough; true power rested on a foundation of perceived legitimacy. The Norman invaders excelled in shaping that perception. Through a deft combination of religious endorsement, political alliances, and masterful propaganda, they framed their conquest as not just a triumph of arms but as a divinely sanctioned right. William's claim to the English throne was buttressed by the backing of Pope Alexander II, who granted his invasion the moral authority of a holy cause. This papal support was not merely a one-time moral boost for William's troops or a signal to other European powers that his campaign was a divinely sanctioned crusade to purify England; instead, it served as a crucial tool for consolidating his reign after his coronation. By framing any rebellion or challenge to his authority as an act against God, William effectively deterred dissent. This enduring support was highlighted more than a decade after the conquest when Pope Gregory VII sent a letter reaffirming the endorsement given by his predecessor, Pope Alexander

II. This reaffirmation not only legitimized William's claim to the throne but also secured his continued backing from the powerful medieval Catholic Church. The German philosopher Friedrich Nietzsche famously stated, "There are no facts, only interpretations." Although Nietzsche lived nearly a millennium after the Norman invasion, the Normans undoubtedly grasped the essence of this idea. The claim that Edward the Confessor had explicitly named Harold Godwinson as his successor on his deathbed was overshadowed by William the Conqueror's vehement assertion that he had been wrongfully deprived of his rightful inheritance. Dissent against this narrative was intolerable, and William's portrayal as Edward's true heir was upheld as an undeniable truth. This perspective is vividly illustrated in the Bayeux Tapestry, which reinforces this version of events. With the victors penning history and medieval historians often grappling to maintain objectivity amidst prevailing biases, and sometimes even being constrained from criticizing their rulers, the legitimacy of either claim remains uncertain to this day. While William's assertion that he was robbed of his right to the English throne may indeed have been valid, the truth of his narrative, whether accurate or not, served as a powerful justification for his invasion. Following his military success, this narrative solidified into historical fact. Ultimately, even if Harold Godwinson was the legitimate successor to Edward the Confessor, his claim was eclipsed by William's military prowess. The Normans' keen understanding of the power of narrative, combined with their strategic acumen, allowed them not only to conquer England but also to maintain control over a divided and resentful populace. By intertwining their conquest with notions of divine right and just rule, they crafted a legacy that extended beyond mere military victory, securing their place as both rulers and architects of a new Anglo-Norman order.

On a more personal note, in reviewing the extensive literature on the Norman Invasion of 1066, I have noticed a discernible difference in tone and perspective between authors from the United Kingdom and foreign authors. British historians often appear more sympathetic to the Anglo-Saxon cause under King Harold Godwinson. It should be noted that this tendency reflects a broader generalization and certainly does not apply to every British author. However, in my opinion, it is significant enough to highlight as a trend in modern historical writing on the subject. This divergence in perspective may stem from the cultural and national contexts within which these historians operate. British authors may feel a closer connection to Anglo-Saxon heritage and thus portray their struggle with more empathy, whereas foreign authors may approach the topic with a more detached viewpoint. An example of this can be seen in the monument in Bayeux erected by the United Kingdom in honor of the soldiers who perished while storming Normandy's beaches during World War II. Beneath this statue is a plaque that reads, "We, once conquered by William, have now set free the Conqueror's native land." This reflects a complex relationship with the past, where the memory of conquest and liberation intertwines, shaping the national identity in ways that resonate even centuries later. Many English people today tend to identify more with the conquered Anglo-Saxons than with their Norman conquerors, even though both groups are part of their ancestral heritage. When examining the works of modern historians, one can observe that British authors often emphasize the legitimacy of Harold II's claim to the throne and the heroism of the Anglo-Saxon defense. In contrast, foreign authors might provide a more balanced account or one supporting William's claim, giving equal weight to William the Conqueror's strategic prowess and the inevitability of Norman success. I always stress the importance of reading sources from as many points of view as possible and coming to your own conclusions based on the available source material. This variation in historical interpretation enriches the discourse, offering multiple lenses through which to view this pivotal event in English history. Understanding these differences can provide a more nuanced and comprehensive view of the Norman Invasion and its lasting impact on England.

The eleventh century was a tumultuous period for England, as the nation faced numerous conquerors and would-be conquerors. A compelling comparison can be drawn between two of its most successful rulers, both of whom managed to reign for roughly two decades until their deaths. One might wonder how the Danes, under King Cnut the Great, maintained a relatively stable and peaceful rule from 1016 to 1035, compared to the more turbulent reign of King William from 1066 to 1087. Several explanations account for the differences in the stability of their reigns. King William hoped to recreate an empire similar to the Anglo-Danish one ruled by King Cnut the Great. However, unlike Cnut, William faced waves of rebellions and insurgencies against his rule. The Anglo-Saxons accepted Cnut's reign but refused to accept the conquest imposed on them by William. One reason for this may be that Cnut the Great legitimized his reign by marrying Emma of Normandy, the widow of Æthelred II, the former Anglo-Saxon king of England. This connection legitimized Cnut's position in the eyes of the Anglo-Saxon nobility and populace, creating a sense of continuity rather than outright conquest. William, on the other hand, had no interest in mingling his family with the Anglo-Saxon nobility. None of his sons married into English nobility, and he kept his French-born wife, Matilda. Cnut the Great also had Anglo-Saxon supporters who served as powerful allies during his invasion of England. In contrast, William's invasion force consisted solely of soldiers from Normandy and surrounding French-speaking duchies, with no local allies rallying to his side upon his arrival on English shores. Furthermore, when Cnut became king of England, he swiftly executed Anglo-Saxons whose loyalty he did not trust, replacing them with trustworthy natives. William, by contrast, installed his own followers in powerful positions, distributing land, wealth, and power to his foreign allies while systematically dismantling the existing Anglo-Saxon nobility. This disregard for the pre-existing ruling class likely strained William's relationship with his new subjects further. Another important point is that while Cnut the Great was a foreigner like William, the Danes were already a visible and influential minority in Anglo-Saxon England, particularly in the Danelaw region. Even Harold Godwinson, traditionally seen as the last Anglo-Saxon king, had a Danish mother. Moreover, Cnut's father, Sweyn Forkbeard, had briefly ruled England from 1013 to 1014. Thus, Cnut's coronation as King of England was not a groundbreaking event that broke with tradition. Many who had served in Sweyn's royal court retained their allegiance to the Danish royal house and quickly sided with Cnut when he launched his invasion. William the Conqueror, on the other hand, came from a semi-autonomous duchy in France, where he was already a vassal of another king. Although the Normans were well-known, they were not a significant or established minority in Anglo-Saxon England, unlike the Danes. The Anglo-Saxon population likely viewed Cnut the Great as a Scandinavian ruler who would continue the existing rule established by his Anglo-Saxon predecessors, whereas William the Conqueror was seen as a hostile adversary—an outsider who laid claim to the English throne based on contested inheritance claims. William also changed the court and governance language to Norman French, while Cnut the Great sought to balance Danish and Anglo-Saxon interests and largely kept Old English as the language of his court and administration.

This cultural divide between the foreign ruling class represented by William and the subjugated Anglo-Saxons likely hindered the Normans' ability to assimilate into English society as seamlessly as their Danish predecessors. Nonetheless they ultimately remained in England. Over the decades and centuries that followed, the cultural divide between the Normans and the English gradually diminished, and in time, they came to be seen as one unified people, blending their traditions and identities into what would become the foundations of medieval England. Despite this, while William the Conqueror is celebrated in Normandy, he holds a mixed reputation in England. Many British historians acknowledge the significant contributions the Normans made to England, but he is often viewed as a successful tyrant who ruled the English nation with an iron fist and responded to any hint of dissent with great cruelty.

In hindsight, the Norman Conquest of 1066 emerges as a defining event that significantly altered the trajectory of English history. Its legacy reflects the intricate dynamics of power, national identity, and territorial conflict. This event was neither the first nor the last instance of warfare sparked by competing claims to rule or disputes over territorial ownership. Such issues persist in shaping political conflicts to this day. While the Normans brought forth innovations in governance, language, and culture, they also sowed the seeds of division and resentment that would echo through the ages. Understanding the multifaceted nature of their conquest of England allows us to appreciate the intricate tapestry of English history, where the past continually informs the present. As we reflect on the enduring impact of this transformative event, it becomes clear that the interplay of conquest and legacy, legitimacy and resistance, continues to resonate within England's collective memory and the social identity of its citizens today. This highlights that history is not just a ledger of events but a vibrant conversation spanning generations, connecting those who came before us with those who will follow.

BIBLIOGRAPHY

Articles and Websites

Bates, Stephen. 2016. Eric Christiansen Obituary, 13 November, 16:53 GMT. https://www.theguardian.com/education/2016/nov/13/eric-christiansen-obituary.

Cannon, John, and Robert Crowcroft. 2015. "Stamford Bridge, battle of." *A Dictionary of British History*, 3d ed. Oxford: Oxford University Press. https://www.oxfordreference.com/view/10.1093/acref/9780191758027.001.0001/acref-9780191758027-e-3256.

Dockray-Miller, Mary. 2021. "The Failed Masculinities of Tostig Godwinson." *Writers, Editors and Exemplars in Medieval English Texts*, ed. Sheryl M. Rowley. The New Middle Ages. Cham: Palgrave Macmillan. https://doi.org/10.1007/978-3-030-55724-9_12.

Douglas, D.C. 1042. "Rollo of Normandy." *The English Historical Review* 57, no. 228: 417–36. http://www.jstor.org/stable/554369.

Encyclopedia. 2018. *Dacia*. Last updated May 8. https://www.encyclopedia.com/history/ancient-greece-and-rome/ancient-history-northern-europe/dacia.

Fell, Christine. 1974. "The Icelandic Saga of Edward the Confessor: Its Version of the Anglo-Saxon Emigration to Byzantium." *Anglo-Saxon England* 3: 179–96. https://doi.org/10.1017/S0263675100000673.

Finch, Paul. 2003. "Viking Dust at Stamford Bridge." *Military History* 20, no. 1: 34. https://search-ebscohost-com.esc-web.lib.cbs.dk/login.aspx?direct=true&db=afh&AN=9156900&site=ehost-live&scope=site.

Härke, Heinrich. 2011. "Anglo-Saxon Immigration and Ethnogenesis." *Medieval Archaeology* 55, no. 1: 1–28. http://dx.doi.org/10.1179/174581711X13103897378311.

Haslam, Jeremy. 2021. "The Settlement and Landscape Context of the Battle of Hastings." *Medieval Archaeology* 65, no. 1: 126–50. https://doi.org/10.1080/00766097.2021.1925007.

Hewitt, Christopher Macdonald. 2018. "Mapping the Pevensey Area Back to 1066: The Historical Environmental Evidence." *Cartographica* 53, no. 2: 75–85.

Izzard, Natalie. 2023. "Matilda of Flanders." Historic UK. https://www.historic-uk.com/HistoryUK/HistoryofEngland/Matilda-of-Flanders/.

Jennings, S., and C. Smyth. 1990. "Holocene Evolution of the Gravel Coastline of East Sussex." *Proceedings of the Geologists' Association* 101, no. 3: 213–24. https://doi.org/10.1016/S0016-7878(08)80006-5.

Jones, Michael John. 2018. "Domesday Book: An Early Fiscal, Accounting Narrative?" *The British Accounting Review* 50, no. 3: 275–90. https://doi.org/10.1016/j.bar.2017.10.002.

King, S.H. 1962. "Sussex." *The Domesday Geography of South-East England*, ed. H.C. Darby and E.M.J. Campbell, 407–82. Cambridge: Cambridge University Press.

Livingston, Michael. 2024. "The Arrow in King Harold's Eye: The Legend That Just Won't Die." Medievalists.net. https://www.medievalists.net/2022/10/arrow-king-harold-eye/.

Lyons, Mathew. 2021. "Months Past June." *History Today* 71, no. 6: 26–27. https://search-ebscohost-com.esc-web.lib.cbs.dk/login.aspx?direct=true&db=afh&AN=150192303&site=ehost-live&scope=site.

Manley, Brendan. 2008. "Last of the Vikings." *Military History* 25, no. 4: 38–41. https://search-ebscohost-com.esc-web.lib.cbs.dk:8443/login.aspx?direct=true&db=afh&AN=34183563&site=ehost-live&scope=site.

Mark, Joshua J. 2018. "Rollo of Normandy." World History Encyclopedia, 8 November. https://www.worldhistory.org/Rollo_of_Normandy/.

Morton, Catherine. 1975. "Pope Alexander II and the Norman Conquest." *Latomus* 34, no. 2: 362–82. http://www.jstor.org/stable/41533253.

National Museum of Denmark. n.d. *The Grave from Mammen.* https://en.natmus.dk/historical-knowledge/denmark/prehistoric-period-until-1050-ad/the-viking-age/the-grave-from-mammen/.

Oldroyd, David. 1997. "Accounting in Anglo-Saxon England: Context and Evidence." *Accounting History* 2, no. 1: 7–34. https://doi.org/10.1177/103237329700200102.

Oxford English Dictionary. 2024. "Propaganda." https://www.oed.com/dictionary/propaganda_n?tl=true.

Parker, E. 2014. "Siward the Dragon-Slayer: Mythmaking in Anglo-Scandinavian England." *Neophilologus* 98: 481–93. https://doi.org/10.1007/s11061-013-9371-3.

Rollason, Nikki K., and Michael J. Lewis. 2020. "Harold-as-Aeneas? The Influence of the Aeneid on a Rescue Scene in the Bayeux Tapestry." *Speculum* 95, no. 3: 665–703. https://doi.org/10.1017/S0017383520000066.

Strickland, Agnes, and Elizabeth Strickland. 2011. "Matilda of Flanders, Queen of William the Conqeuror." *Lives of the Queens of England from the Norman Conquest*. Cambridge Library Collection, British and Irish History, General, 21–105. https://www.cambridge.org/core/books/abs/lives-of-the-queens-of-england-from-the-norman-conquest/matilda-of-flanders-queen-of-william-the-conqueror/D8F0DB7DA781013F5FF75FF247D5F20E.

Winkler, EA. 2020. "Imagining the Medieval Face of Battle: The 'Malfosse' Incident and the Battle of Hastings, 1066–1200." *Historical Research* 93, no. 259: 2–22. https://ora.ox.ac.uk/objects/uuid:c0ad0921-af2e-455c-abe9-9ad944495ab8.

Books

Abbott, Jacob. 1902. *Makers of History: William the Conqueror.* New York: Harper & Brothers.

Anlezark, Daniel. 2017. *Alfred the Great.* Kalamazoo: Arc Humanities Press.

Barlow, Frank. 1970. *Edward the Confessor.* Berkeley: University of California Press.

Bates, David. 2016. *William the Conqueror.* New Haven: Yale University Press.

Blake, Norman. 1992. *The Cambridge History of The English Language: Volume II: 1066–1476.* Cambridge: Cambridge University Press.

Brandon, Peter. 1974. *The Sussex Landscape.* London: Hodder and Stoughton.

Brownworth, Lars. 2014. *The Normans: From Raiders to Kings.* London: Crux.

Burgess, Glyn S., trans. 2004. *The History of the Norman People: Wace's Roman de Rou* [originally written ca. 1160–1174]. With notes by Glyn S. Burgess and Elisabeth van Houts. Woodbridge: Boydell.

Butler, Denis. 1966. *The Story of a Year.* New York: G.P. Putnam's Sons.

Clanchy, M.T. 2014. *England and Its Rulers.* Newark: Wiley Blackwell.

Cole, Teresa. 2016. *The Norman Conquest: William the Conqueror's Subjugation of England.* Gloucestershire: Amberley.

Crouch, David. 2007. *The Normans: The History of a Dynasty.* London: Continuum.

Crowcroft, Robert, and John Cannon. 2015. *The Oxford Companion to British History*, 2d ed. Oxford: Oxford University Press.

Daniell, Christopher. 2003. *From Norman Conquest to Magna Carta: England 1066–1215.* London: Routledge.

David, Charles Wendell. 1920. *Robert Curthose: Duke of Normandy.* Cambridge: Harvard University Press.

DeVries, Kelly. 1999. *The Norwegian Invasion of England in 1066.* Woodbridge: Boydell & Brewer.

Douglas, David C. 1999. *William the Conqueror.* New Haven: Yale University Press.
Dudo of Saint-Quentin. 1015 [1998]. *History of the Normans.* 1998. Edited and translated by Eric Christiansen. Introduction by Felice Lifshitz. Woodbridge: Boydell & Brewer.
Fleming, Robin. 2009. *Domesday Book and the Law: Society and Legal Custom in Early Medieval England.* Cambridge: Cambridge University Press.
Garnett, George. 2007. *Conquered England: Kingship Succession, and Tenure 1066–1166.* Oxford: Oxford University Press.
Gravett, Christopher. 1992. *Hastings 1066: The Fall of Saxon England.* London: Osprey.
Hicks, Carola. 2007. *The Bayeux Tapestry: The Life Story of a Masterpiece.* London: Vintage UK.
Higham, Nicholas J., and Martin J. Ryan. 2013. *The Anglo-Saxon World.* New Haven: Yale University Press.
Hjardar, Kim, and Vegard Vike. 2019. *Vikings at War.* Oxford: Casemate.
Holman, Katherine. 2007. *The Northern Conquest: Vikings in Britain and Ireland.* Luton: Andrews UK.
Howarth, David. 1977 [1993]. *The Year of the Conquest.* Illustrated by Gareth Floyd. New York: Barnes & Noble Books.
Hudson, John. 2018. *The Formation of the English Common Law: Law and Society in England from King Alfred to Magna Carta.* London: Routledge.
Huscroft, Richard. 2013. *The Norman Conquest: A New Introduction.* London: Routledge.
Kapelle, William E. 1979. *The Norman Conquest of the North: The Region and Its Transformation, 1000–1135.* Chapel Hill: University of North Carolina Press.
Karkov, Catherine E. 2020. *Imagining Anglo-Saxon England: Utopia, Heterotopia, Dystopia.* Woodbridge: Boydell.
Kay, Helen. 2020. *The 1066 Norman Bruisers: How European Thugs Became English Gentry.* Barnsley: Pen and Sword History.
Koziol, Geoffrey. 2018. *The Peace of God.* Kalamazoo: Arc Humanities Press.
Larsen, Karen. 2015. *A History of Norway.* Princeton: Princeton University Press.
Lausten, Martin Schwarz. 2002. *A Church History of Denmark.* London: Routledge.
Magnus, Olaus. 1555. *Historia de Gentibus Septentrionalibus.* Giovanni M. Viotto.
McLynn, Frank. 1999. *1066: The Year of the Three Battles.* London: Pimlico.
Morris, Marc. 2013. *The Norman Conquest.* London: Windmill.
Mortimer, Richard, ed. 2009. *Edward the Confessor: The Man and the Legend.* Woodbridge: Boydell.
Mueller-Vollmer, Tristan, and Kirsten Wolf. 2022. *Vikings: An Encyclopedia of Conflict, Invasions, and Raids.* Santa Barbara: ABC-CLIO.
Musset, Lucien. 2002. *The Bayeux Tapestry.* Translated by Richard Rex. Woodbridge: Boydell.
Neveux, François. 2006. *A Brief History of the Normans: The Conquests That Changed the Face of Europe.* London: Constable & Robinson.
Pastan, Elizabeth Carson, Stephen D. White, and Kate Gilbert, Kate. 2014. *The Bayeux Tapestry and Its Contexts.* Woodbridge: Boydell.
Paul, Nicholas L. 2012. *To Follow in Their Footsteps: The Crusades and Family Memory in the High Middle Ages.* 1st ed. Ithaca: Cornell University Press.
Rex, Peter. 2011. *A New History of the Norman Conquest.* Stroud: Amberley.
Rex, Peter. 2012. *William the Conqueror: The Bastard of Normandy.* Stroud: Amberley.
Rippon, Stephen. 2000. *The Transformation of Coastal Wetlands: Exploitation and Management of Marshland Landscapes in North West Europe During the Roman and Medieval Periods.* Oxford: Oxford University Press.
Smiley, Jane, ed. 2001. *The Sagas of Icelanders: A Selection.* Translated by Katrina C. Attwood, George Clark, Ruth C. Ellison, Terry Gunnell, Keneva Kunz, Anthony Maxwell, Martin S. Regal, Bernard Scudder, and Andrew Wawn. New York: Viking Penguin.
Snorri Sturluson. c.1230 [1964]. *Heimskringla: History of the Kings of Norway.* Translated by Lee M. Hollander. Austin: University of Texas Press.
Swanton, Michael, ed. and trans. 2000. *The Anglo-Saxon Chronicles.* London: Phoenix Press.

Szabo, John F., and Nicholas E. Kuefler. 2015. *The Bayeux Tapestry: A Critically Annotated Bibliography*. Lanham: Rowman & Littlefield.
Tinti, Francesca. 2021. *Europe and the Anglo-Saxons*. Cambridge: Cambridge University Press.
Tombs, Robert. 2016. *The English and Their History*. New York: Vintage.
Vincent, Nicholas. 2011. *A Brief History of Britain 1066–1485: Birth of the Nation*. London: Robinson.
Whitelock, Dorothy. 1972. *The Beginnings of English Society*, 2d ed. Harmondsworth,: Penguin. Revised eds., 1965, 1972.
Williams, Ann. 2003. *Athelred the Unready: The Ill-Counselled King*. London: Hambledon and London.
Williams, Gareth. 2007. *West Over Sea: Studies in Scandinavian Sea-Borne Expansion and Settlement Before 1300*. Edited by Beverley Ballin Smith and Simon Taylor. Leiden: Brill.
Wood, Harriet Harvey. 2008. *The Battle of Hastings: The Fall of Anglo-Saxon England*. London: Atlantic Books.
Yorke, Barbara. 1990. *Kings and Kingdoms of Early Anglo-Saxon England*. London: Taylor & Francis Group.

INDEX

Abbaye-aux-Dames 137
Abbott, Jacob 60, 61, 63, 68
Abegg Foundation 137
Abingdon Chronicle 148
Abingdon Manuscript 45
Adela of France 65, 66, 134
Adelaide of Normandy 66
Adelinus 148
Ælfgar, Earl of Mercia 38, 45
Aelfwold 148
Ælla, King of Northumbria 26
Ælle (South Saxon leader) 23
Aeneas (mythological figure) 72
Aesop's fables 129
Æthelbert of Kent 22
Ætheling, Edgar 38, 115, 116, 139, 147, 148, 150
Æthelred II 33, 34, 50, 51, 76, 179
Aethelsige, Abbot of St. Augustine 148
Æthelstan (brother of Alfred the Great) 28, 31, 32
Aethelwold (nephew of Alfred the Great) 31
Æthelwulf, King of Wessex 27, 28, 29
Aimeri de Thours, Viscount 98
Alain, Earl of Brittany 5
Alaric, King of the Visigoths 18
Albert I, Count of Vermandois 8
Albinus of Canterbury 23
Alcuin of York (theologian) 25, 49
Alençon 67
Alexius I Komnenos 122, 123
Alfred (Edward the Confessor's brother) 34, 35, 36
Alfred (1740 opera) 31
Alfred the Great 3, 27, 28, 32, 38
Algar, lord of Gloucester 65
Aller 30
Alstem (Guthrum) 12, 13
Ambrières 69
Anchises (mythological figure) 72
Andelle, River 13

Anderitum (Roman fort) 90
Andredsweald 90
Angelcynn (term for Englishkind) 30
Angles 16, 20, 23
Anglo-Saxon Chronicle 20, 21, 23, 28, 29, 30, 40, 43, 49, 88, 91, 95, 102, 118, 121, 126, 139, 144, 145, 147, 154, 155, 156, 157, 164, 167, 168, 173, 174
Anglo-Saxon England 20, 101, 120, 121, 163, 180
Anglo-Saxons 3, 12, 16, 19, 21, 22, 23, 27, 30, 31, 32, 33, 45, 50, 55, 59, 75, 85, 91, 94, 95, 96, 98, 103, 104, 105, 106, 107, 108, 109, 110, 112, 113, 116, 118, 128, 135, 168, 173, 175, 179, 180
Anjou 66, 67, 69, 71, 80, 82
Anlezark, Daniel 27, 28, 29, 30
Anselm, St. 71
Ansgar 115
Aquitaine (France) 80
Archil 148
Arthur, King 19, 21, 22, 32
Asbiorn, Jarl 147, 150
Ascanius/Iulus (mythological figure) 72
Ash Wednesday 142
Ashdown, Battle of 27
Asser (biographer of Alfred the Great) 28, 29, 30
Augustine of Canterbury 22, 25
Augustus 17, 114
Aurelianus, Ambrosius 21
Axholme, Isle of 149

Baldwin V, Count of Flanders 47, 65, 66, 70
Baring, Francis 81, 82
Barlow, Frank 34, 35
Barn, Siward 148
Bassebourg Hill 70
Bates, Stephen 8, 35, 60, 61, 62, 63, 65, 66, 88, 165, 166
Battle Abbey Chronicle 104, 105

INDEX

Baudri of Bourgeuil 112, 134
Bayeux Tapestry 6, 40, 72, 73, 76, 80, 81, 83, 100, 103, 104, 105, 106, 107, 108, 110, 111, 112, 113, 128, 129, 133, 134, 135, 136, 138, 170, 178
Beachy Head 84, 86, 87
Bede 20, 21, 22, 23, 24, 31
Benoît, Antoine 111, 134
Beorhtwulf, King of Wessex 28
Beorn (Leriz) 147
Berengar, Count of Bayeux 12
Berkhamsted 116
Berlin State Library 9
berserkers 9
Bessin 14
Bexhill 87
Black Sea 123
Blake, Norman 119
blood eagle (Viking ritual) 25
Bodiam 96
Boethius 31
Bogdan Serai 123
Bonaparte, Napoleon 128
Bonneville-sur-Touques 37
Boston (Lincolnshire) 163
Boulogne 35, 67, 80, 83, 100, 112, 140
Brandon, Peter 88
Bras, Charles de 171
Bremen 48
Bretons 14, 80, 97, 105, 106, 107, 108, 139, 144
Brevis Relatio 61
Bristol Channel 144
Britannia 17, 31
British Isles 3, 16, 25, 26, 31, 49, 135, 174
Brittany 8, 13, 14, 15, 37, 72, 73, 74, 79, 80, 149, 170
Brønsted, Johannes 9
Broughton 125
Brownworth, Lars 174, 175
Bructeri 20
Brunanburh, Battle of 31
Buckland cemetery 21
Burgess, Glyn S. 87, 88, 91, 92, 93, 94, 95
Burgundy 14, 64, 80
Busac, William, Count of Eu 67
Butler, Denis 48, 58, 59, 66, 84, 85, 86, 90, 94, 97, 107, 108, 109, 112, 116
Byron, Robert 123
Byzantine Empire 78, 122, 123

Caen 64, 65, 134, 137, 169, 170
Caesar, Julius 17, 82
Caldbec Hill 97, 98
Camelot 19
Camlann, Battle of 21
Cannon, John 50, 58

Canterbury 25, 35, 36, 37, 39, 75, 115, 119, 120, 125, 126, 128, 174
The Canterbury Tales 119, 126
Cap d'Antifer 84
Carmen de Hastingae 80, 92, 95, 100, 110
Carmen de Hastingae Proelio 79, 81, 92, 100, 105
Carolingian Empire 32
Cerdic (West Saxon leader) 23, 24
Charles the Bald 29
Charles III of France 12, 13, 14
Chaucer, Geoffrey 119
Cheshire 31, 149, 159
China 17
Chippenham 30
Chrétien de Troyes 21
Christian of Aarhus 147
Christianity 13, 14, 18, 33, 77, 100, 167
Christiansen, Eric 8
Chronicle of St. Maixent 98
Cirencester 17, 30
Clanchy, M.T. 121, 126, 139
Claudius, Emperor 17
Cleveland 152
Cnut, King 34, 35, 36, 38, 42, 48, 51, 52, 76, 103, 115, 116, 127, 147, 148, 154, 157, 164, 166, 179, 180
Cole, Teresa 167, 169, 170
Combes, Pamela 91
Conan II, Duke of Brittany 72, 73
Consanguinity 66
Consolations of Philosophy (Boethius) 31
Copsig, Earl of Northumbria 146
Corinium 17
Cornwall 17, 28, 65, 144, 145
Cospatric 43, 148, 150, 152
Coutances 13, 117, 149, 160
Crimea 123
Crouch, David 69, 70, 71, 116, 117
Crowcroft, Robert 50, 58
Cumberland 44, 126, 155, 158
Cumin, Robert 146
Curthose, Robert 71, 164, 165, 168, 175
Cynric (West Saxon leader) 23
Cynuit, Battle of 30

Dacia 10, 11, 12
Danegeld 50, 150, 158
Danelaw 27, 34, 50, 147, 180
Danes 10, 12, 19, 31, 42, 48, 50, 51, 52, 94, 127, 139, 143, 147, 148, 149, 150, 151, 153, 158, 166, 167, 179, 180
Dania 10, 11
Daniell, Christopher 115, 128, 134
David, Charles Wendell 71, 72
De Excidio et Conquestu Britanniea 20
de Chernet, William 159, 160

Index

Denmark 1, 9, 10, 11, 12, 22, 34, 36, 43, 48, 49, 50, 51, 52, 58, 94, 115, 122, 141, 148, 149, 150, 164, 166
De Obitu Willelmi 60
Derwent River 57
DeVries, Kelly 43, 46, 47, 48, 52, 54, 57, 58
Dinan 72
Dives-sur-Mer 84
Dockray-Miller, Mary 46, 47, 48
Domesday Book 6, 81, 88, 92, 102, 121, 125, 144, 154, 155, 156, 157, 158, 159, 160, 161, 162, 177
Domesday Tables for the County of Hertford 81
Domfront 67, 69
Dominican Order 10
Douglas, David C. 159, 164
Douglas, D.C., 10
Dover 21, 89, 115, 124, 140, 147
Dragon ships 54
Droitwich 18
Dublin 26, 31, 144
Dudo of St. Quentin 3, 7, 8, 9, 10, 11, 12, 13, 14, 35
Duke Geoffrey of Brittany 14
Dumville, David 23
Duncan I, King of Scotland 44
Durham 43, 146, 152, 155, 158
Duval, Georges 137

Eadmer 39, 173
Ealdgyth 143
Ealdred, Archbishop of York 40, 115, 117
East Anglia 12, 20, 26, 27, 30, 38, 147, 148
Eastbourne 87
Easter 24, 29, 41, 144, 147, 164, 166
Eboracum 17, 18
Ecclesiastical History of the English Peoples 23, 31
Edgar (King of England) 33
Edington, Battle of 30
Edith of Wessex 36, 37, 38, 39, 46, 143
Edith Swan-Neck 143
Edmund of East Anglia 27, 126
Edward the Confessor 32, 33, 34, 35, 36, 37, 39, 41, 43, 47, 48, 65, 73, 74, 77, 83, 98, 116, 118, 126, 129, 140, 145, 148, 159, 178, 183, 184, 185
Edward the Elder 31
Edward IV of England 81
Edward's promise to William 39
Edwin, Earl of Mercia 45, 47, 55, 106, 115, 116, 145, 151
Egbert, King of Wessex 28
Egil Skallagrimsson 53
Elnochus 148
Emma (mail shirt) 54

Emma (Queen of England) 34, 35, 41, 148
Encomium Emmae 34
Englalond (medieval name for England) 17, 32
England 1, 3, 4, 6, 11, 12, 13, 15, 16, 17, 18, 19, 20, 22, 24, 25, 26, 27, 28, 31, 33, 34, 35, 36, 37, 38, 39, 41, 42, 43, 47, 48, 49, 50, 51, 52, 54, 55, 56, 57, 58, 60, 63, 65, 73, 75, 76, 77, 78, 79, 80, 81, 83, 84, 85, 86, 87, 88, 91, 95, 98, 101, 102, 115, 116, 117, 118, 119, 120, 121, 122, 123, 124, 125, 126, 127, 128, 129, 130, 133, 134, 136, 137, 139, 140, 141, 142, 145, 146, 147, 149, 150, 151, 152, 154, 155, 156, 157, 158, 160, 161, 162, 163, 164, 165, 167, 168, 169, 171, 172, 173, 174, 175, 176, 177, 178, 179, 180, 181
Enguerrand II, Count of Ponthieu 66
Essex 20, 28, 94, 158
Estrith 148
Eustace II, Count of Boulogne 83, 107, 112, 140, 141, 142
Excalibur 21

Falaise 60, 62, 63
Fécamp 61, 62, 71, 89, 93, 94, 165
Fell, Christine 123, 124
Feudalism 124, 125, 136, 161, 177
Finch, Paul 9, 52, 57
Finehair, Harald 11
Finland 11
FitzNigel, Richard 121
FitzOsbern, William 74, 78, 79, 87, 121, 124, 147, 149, 160
Flanders 14, 29, 35, 43, 45, 47, 65, 66, 70, 77, 80, 146, 164, 166, 167
Flat Holm (island) 144
Fleming, Robin 161
Flemish 13, 80, 97, 140, 146
Florence of Worcester 44, 148
Forkbeard, Sweyn 34, 51, 52, 180
Foucault, Nicolas-Joseph 134, 135
Fragmenta Vetusta 5
France 8, 9, 11, 12, 13, 14, 29, 36, 48, 51, 62, 63, 64, 65, 68, 69, 80, 82, 84, 119, 122, 136, 138, 152, 163, 164, 167, 173, 175, 176, 180
France, Kingdom of 14
Francia 12, 63, 79, 154
Franciscan Order 10
Franks 13, 14, 20, 29, 173
Freeman, Edward 135, 136
Frey (Norse god) 33
Friesland 48
Frisians 20
Frutolf of Michelsberg 173
Fulk II the Good, Count of Anjou 66
fyrd (Anglo-Saxon militia) 30, 84, 85, 94, 97, 101, 102, 103, 104, 107, 109

Gamal 148
Gaul 17, 18, 22, 80
Geoffrey Martel, Count of Anjou 67, 68, 69, 70, 71, 176
Geoffrey of Coutances 117
Germanic kingdoms in England 20
Gesta Guillelmi 37, 76
Gesta Normannorum 7, 8, 95
Giffard, Walter 74, 79
Gilbert of Brionne 62
Gilbert of Lisieux 75
Gildas 19, 20, 21, 23
Giroie, William 62
Gisla of France 13
Glaber, Ralph 62
Glastonbury 126
Glima 53
Godwin (Earl of Wessex) 35, 36, 37, 38, 39, 43, 97, 152
Godwinson, Gyrth 92, 93, 95, 105, 107, 108, 124, 133, 142
Godwinson, Harold 6, 33, 37, 38, 39, 42, 43, 46, 47, 48, 55, 56, 57, 58, 66, 73, 83, 85, 113, 115, 116, 118, 122, 125, 129, 130, 134, 136, 142, 143, 144, 159, 176, 178, 180
Godwinson, Tostig 38, 41, 42, 43, 44, 45, 46, 47, 48, 52, 54, 55, 56, 57, 80, 91, 95, 141, 142, 144, 176
Goebbels, Joseph 136
Goscelin 122, 124
Gotland 10
Gough Map 89
The Grave from Mammen 9
Gravett, Christopher 99, 102, 104, 115, 117
Great Heathen Army 26, 27, 29
Gregorian Mission (597) 22, 23
Gregory I (the Great), Pope 22
Gregory VII, Pope 76, 166, 173, 174, 177
Gruffudd ap Llewellyn 38, 46
Gruffydd (son of Maredudd) 160
Gueriir, Saint 28
Gunhilde 51
Gurim 11, 12
Guthrum 12, 27, 30
Guy, Bishop of Amiens 79, 111
Guy of Ponthieu 39, 129
Gyða of Denmark 43
Gytha (mother of Harold Godwinson) 142, 143, 144

Hadrian's Wall 17
Hakon 74
Hákon 37
Halfdan (Viking leader) 26, 27
Halfpenny, Joseph 5
Halley's Comet 133
Harald Bluetooth, King of Denmark 50
Hardrada, Harald 3, 6, 41, 48, 51, 52, 54, 55, 56, 57, 58, 83, 85, 86, 90, 94, 95, 100, 106, 176
Harefoot, Harold 34, 35, 36
Härke, Heinrich 20, 23
Harold's oath to William 39, 93
Harrying of the North 6, 95, 139, 153, 172
Harthacnut 34, 35, 36, 148
Haslam, Jeremy 91
Hastings 6, 80, 81, 85, 87, 88, 89, 90, 91, 93, 95, 96, 97, 98, 100, 102, 104, 113, 114, 115, 128, 133, 140, 146
Hastings, Battle of 3, 6, 40, 59, 79, 80, 81, 89, 96, 100, 102, 111, 112, 113, 121, 129, 133, 135, 136, 140, 143, 147, 176
Hauteville, Roger de 77
Heidarviga Saga 52
Heimskringla 10, 104
Hengist (legendary founder of Kent) 23
Henry I, king of France 62, 63, 65, 67, 68, 70, 82, 127
Henry of Huntingdon 112
Henry V of England 81
Herbert II, Count of Maine 71
Hereward the Wake 121
Herfast 125
Herleva (Arlotte) 60
Hewitt, Christopher Macdonald 88, 89, 90, 102
Hibernia 18
Hicks, Carola 136, 137, 138
Higham, Nicholas J. 16, 18
Himmler, Heinrich 136
Historia Brittonum 23
Historia de Gentibus Septentrionalibus 11
Historia Ecclesiastica 80
Historia Gruffydd 11
Historia Langobardorum 16
Hitler, Adolf 128, 136
Hjardar, Kim 52, 53
Hobbes, Thomas 21
Holderness 149
Holy Grail 21
Holy Land 15, 61, 77
Horace Round, John 95, 136
Horsa (legendary brother of Hengist) 23
House of Godwin 36, 37
Howarth, David 74, 78, 83, 84, 85, 86
Howden, Roger of 88
Hudson, John 120, 121, 124
Hugh of Fleury 81
Hugh of Grandmesnil 74
Hugh of Montfort 74
Hugh the Ass 160
Hull 163
Humber, River 31

Index 191

Huns 18, 20
Huntingdon 46
Huscroft, Richard 125

Iceland 11, 53
Inventio et miracula sancti Vulfranni 34
Iona 49
Ipswich 147, 163
Iran 17
Ireland 11, 49, 143, 145, 174
Ironside, Björn 26
Ironside, Edmund 38, 51, 115
Isidore of Seville 10
Ivar the Boneless 26
Izzard, Natalie 67

Jelling 50
Jerusalem 20, 61, 68
John of Worcester 39, 46, 80, 143, 144, 145, 165, 167
Jones, Michael John 154, 159
Judith (daughter of Charles the Bald) 29
Judith of Brittany 15
Jutes 20, 22, 23, 118

Kapelle, William E. 42, 43, 44, 45, 46
Karkov, Catherine E. 19, 20
Karli 148
Kay, Helen 156
Kent 20, 22, 23, 24, 27, 28, 29, 88, 115, 124, 140
Kentish Chronicles 23
Koziol, Geoffrey 64, 65
Kuefler, Nicholas E. 128

Lamellar armor 54
Lancelot 21
Lancelot, Antoine 134
Lanfranc 70, 75, 76, 125, 126, 155, 169
Larsen, Karen 36
Lausten, Martin Schwarz 50
Le Mans 14, 165
Lejard, André 136
Leo IV, Pope 28
Leo IX, Pope 66
Leofric, Earl of Mercia 38, 152
Leofwine, Earl 38, 105, 107, 124, 133, 142
Leominster 37
Lewis, Michael J. 72, 73
Lillebonne 77, 78
Lindisfarne 25, 49, 50
Lindsey (Lincolnshire) 27, 149
Lindum 17
Livingston, Michael 111
Lodbrok, Ragnar 26
Londinium 17
London 17, 27, 30, 35, 46, 81, 85, 87, 92, 93, 94, 96, 105, 111, 115, 116, 117, 118, 123, 142, 149, 163
Longships 54
Longsword, William 13, 14
Lord Tennyson 21
Lyne, Malcolm 91
Lynn 163
Lyons, Mathew 49

Mac Mael n'Ambo, Diarmaid 144
Macbeth, King of Scotland 42, 43, 44
Maclagan, Eric 136
MaerleSweyn 150
Magnus, King of Norway 36, 37
Magnus, Olaus 11
Maine 67, 69, 71, 72, 79, 80, 139, 165, 167
Majorca 123
Malcolm III, King of Scotland 43
Malet, William 149
Malory, Thomas 21
Manley, Brendan 52
Marcus Aurelius, Emperor 30
Maredudd, King of South Wales 160
Margaret of Maine 71
Margot, Hugh 92, 93
Maria Haraldsdottir 55
Mark, Joshua J. 11, 12
Martigny, Charles de 171
Marx, Karl 1
Matilda of Flanders 47, 65, 66, 67, 70, 76, 79, 116, 117, 133, 137, 138, 144, 145, 164, 165, 171, 179
Mau, Brihtric 65
Mayenne, Geoffrey of, Lord 72
McCollum-Oldroyd, David 157
McDonald, John 158
McLynn, Frank 55, 56, 57, 71, 74, 75, 77, 78, 79
Mercia 20, 24, 26, 27, 30, 34, 47, 116, 145
Meulan 12
Middle English language 118, 119, 126, 176
Mill, John Stuart 1
Minorca 123
Modern English language 118, 119
Monmouth, Geoffrey of 19, 21
Mont-St.-Michel 8
Montacute Castle 149
Montfaucon, Bernard de 111, 129, 134, 135
Montfort, Hugh de 140, 141
Montivilliers Abbey 61
Mora (Ship) 79, 84, 86, 87
Morcar, Earl of Northumbria 45, 46, 47, 55, 106, 115, 116, 121, 141, 145, 151, 168
Morris, Marc 41, 62, 63, 64, 75, 79, 108, 112, 116, 124, 125, 141, 142, 144, 146, 147, 153, 155, 157, 167, 169, 171, 172, 174
Mortimer, Richard 33, 34, 35, 36

Morton, Catherine 75, 76
Mount Badon, Battle of 21
Mueller-Vollmer, Tristan 26, 27
Musset, Lucien 134

National Museum of Denmark 9
Nennius 23
Neveux, François 8, 13, 14, 15, 35, 61, 62, 64, 66, 67, 68, 69, 70, 72, 73, 85, 97, 105, 106, 118
Newcastle 157, 163
Nicaea 61, 122
Nicholas, abbot of St-Ouen 79
Nicholas II, Pope 66, 76
Nietzsche, Friedrich 178
Norman Conquest of England (1066) 1, 3, 6, 16, 19, 33, 39, 40, 41, 45, 47, 71, 79, 81, 84, 85, 86, 87, 89, 91, 94, 118, 119, 122, 126, 127, 128, 129, 133, 135, 136, 138, 141, 143, 154, 159, 160, 161, 164, 177, 178, 181
Normandy 3, 7, 8, 10, 11, 13, 14, 15, 33, 34, 35, 36, 37, 39, 41, 47, 49, 50, 58, 59, 60, 61, 62, 63, 64, 65, 66, 67, 68, 69, 70, 71, 72, 74, 77, 80, 81, 82, 83, 84, 85, 88, 91, 92, 93, 116, 117, 120, 124, 129, 133, 134, 139, 142, 146, 155, 165, 167, 168, 175, 176, 179, 180
Normans 1, 3, 7, 8, 14, 15, 19, 35, 37, 41, 51, 54, 59, 62, 63, 65, 66, 72, 75, 77, 85, 87, 90, 92, 94, 95, 96, 97, 98, 99, 100, 103, 105, 106, 107, 108, 109, 113, 114, 117, 118, 119, 120, 121, 124, 125, 127, 128, 129, 133, 135, 136, 142, 144, 145, 147, 148, 149, 150, 155, 161, 163, 164, 171, 172, 173, 178, 180, 181
Norse 7, 24, 25, 26, 33, 49, 52, 54, 55, 56, 57, 83, 122
North Sea 18, 51, 58
Northampton 45, 46
Northumbria 20, 23, 24, 26, 27, 38, 42, 43, 44, 45, 46, 47, 85, 116, 141, 145, 148, 151, 152, 153
Norway 9, 10, 11, 20, 26, 34, 36, 41, 47, 48, 49, 53, 56, 58, 106, 133, 166
Nova Anglia (New England) 123

Odda, Earl 38
Odin (Norse god) 33
Odo (brother of King Henry I of France) 68
Odo of Bayeux 74, 121, 132, 133, 140, 141, 165, 168
Odo of Penthièvre 73
Olaf III, King of Norway 55, 166
Old English 16, 17, 50, 56, 118, 119, 126, 162, 176, 180
Old Saxons 20
Oldroyd, David 158
Orderic Vitalis 39, 47, 62, 76, 80, 113, 117, 124, 140, 142, 143, 144, 145, 147, 148, 149, 151, 152, 164, 165, 168, 169, 170, 171, 172
Orne Valley 69
Orosius, Paulus 10
Orri, Eystein 55, 57
Osbeorn 42
Osberh (mother of Alfred the Great) 27
Osbern of Crépon 62
Osulf of Bamburgh 46
Oswiu (Northumbrian king) 24
Oswulf of Bamburgh 141
Oxford University 8

Paris 12, 13, 29, 122, 137
Parker, E. 43
Passais 67
Pastan, Elizabeth Carson 135
Paul the Deacon 16
Peace of God 64, 65
Perceval 21
Peterborough Manuscript 45, 156
Pevensey 59, 87, 88, 89, 90, 91, 95, 96
Philip I of France 164, 167
Picts 18
Poitou 80
Ponthieu 39, 66, 80, 84
Popa of Bayeux 12, 13
Port, Hugh de 160
Portsmouth 163

Radbod the Frisian 12
Rædwald (East Anglian King) 24
Ragnar Long-Neck 12
Ralph, Earl 38
Ramsay, Sir James Henry 81
Raphael, Sir Herbert Henry 4
Rechru 49
Regenbald 125
Reginald 125
Rennes 73
Repton 27
Rex, Peter 47, 48, 52, 63, 77, 78, 79, 81, 87, 88, 89, 97, 98, 105, 106, 108, 109, 110, 113, 114, 118, 125, 141, 142, 145, 147, 148, 149, 151, 152, 170, 171, 172, 173
Riccall 55, 56, 57
Richard I (the Lionheart) 21
Richard I of Normandy 8, 14, 62, 67
Richard II of Normandy 14, 15, 34, 41, 67
Richard III of Normandy 15, 66
Richardides 67
Ringulf of Oby 148
Rippon, Stephen 89
River Couesnon 72
Robert, Archbishop of Rouen 62, 63
Robert, Bishop of Hereford 158
Robert, Count of Mortain 74, 149, 168

Index

Robert I of Normandy (the Magnificient) 15
Robert II, Archbishop of Rouen 11
Robert II of France (the Pious) 14
Robert of Jumièges 35
Robert the steward 39
Robin Hood 121
Rodulf of Gacé 62
Roger of Beaumont 74
Roger of Hovedon 151
Roger of Montgomery 74, 79, 109
Rögnvald, Earl of Möre 9
Rollason, Nikki 72, 73
Rollo of Normandy 7, 8, 9, 10, 11, 12, 13, 14, 15, 41, 62, 66, 83
Roman conquest of Britain 17
Roman de Rou 80, 81, 87, 91, 93, 95, 113
Roman Empire 3, 18
Roman Republic 17
Romania 10
Romans 17, 18, 19, 20, 151
Rome 11, 18, 25, 28, 29, 44, 61, 75, 76, 77, 171
Romney 88, 89, 115
Rother, River 96
Rouen 12, 13, 14, 37, 61, 165, 168
Ruallon, Lord of Dol 72
Rugii 20
rune stones 9
Russia 11
Ryan, Martin J. 16, 18
Rye 87, 89

St. Albans 126
St. Augustine 148, 166
St. Brice's Day Massacre, 1002 50, 51
St. Valery, Ponthieu 84, 85
Saint-Wandrille 34
Salisbury 149, 157, 167
Sandwich 89, 147
Saxons 16, 18, 19, 20
Scandinavia 1, 18, 27, 31, 50, 52, 54, 58, 83, 143
Scania (Skåne) 12
Die Schlacht von Hastings 80
Scotland 11, 18, 27, 43, 44, 47, 122, 147, 148, 149, 152, 153, 174
Scots 18, 31, 42, 44, 139
Scutari 123
Sedlescombe 87, 96
Seine, River 14, 35, 68
Senlac Hill 96, 97, 104
Senlis 29
Sewell, Brian 137
Shepard, Jonathan 123
Ship List 79, 80
Sicily 77, 122, 176

Sigurd Snake-in-the-Eye 26
Simeon of Durham 146
Siward, Earl of Northumbria 42, 43, 44, 46, 152
Skye 49
Sledd (East Saxon dynastic founder) 24
Smith, Adam 1
Sogne Fjord 52
Southwark 115
Spain 76
Spatz, Wilhelm 80, 81, 82
Staffordshire 149
Stamford Bridge, Battle of (1066) 55, 56, 57, 58, 86, 95, 104, 176
Stigand, Archbishop 39, 40, 75, 117, 125, 131
Stiklarstaðir, Battle of (1030) 48
Strathclyde 27
Strickland, Agnes 65, 66, 67
Strickland, Elizabeth 65, 66, 67
Stuf (founder of Isle of Wight kingdom) 23
Sturluson, Snorri 10, 48, 51, 54, 104
Summarlithr 148
Surrey 28
Sussex 20, 28, 87, 88, 89, 96, 97, 98
Swanton, Michael 45, 88, 102
Sweden 11, 12, 26, 58
Sweyn, Earl 37
Sweyn II 36, 48, 58
Szabo, John F. 128

Tacitus 17
Taisson, Ralph 64
Tamworth 24
Tarsus 25
Telham 96, 97
Thames, River 37, 50, 85, 94, 96, 115, 140
Thanet, Isle of 26, 29
Theodore of Tarsus (Archbishop of Canterbury) 25
Thetford 27
Thor (Norse god) 33, 120
Thorbrand 148
Thorbrand the Hold 148
Thorney 94
Thouars 80
Thurkill, Jarl 147
Thurstan Goz 62
Tillières 63
Tinti, Francesca 16, 25
Tolkien, J.R.R. 22
Tombs, Robert 17, 18, 20, 21, 22, 24, 26, 30, 31, 32, 33, 36, 122, 126, 154, 155, 156, 163
Tosny, Berengar de 125
Tower of London 118
TRE (Tempore Regis Edwardi) 160

INDEX

Treaty of Saint-Clair-sur-Epte 14
Trondheim 52, 54
Turold 62

Ubba (Viking leader) 26
Uhtred, Earl 148
Ulf Ospaksson 52
University of Copenhagen 10

Varaville 69
Varaville, Battle of 70
verba novissima 40
Vertue, George 4
Vexin 167, 168
Victoria and Albert Museum 136
Vike, Vegard 52, 53
Vikings 3, 7, 8, 9, 11, 14, 25, 26, 27, 28, 29, 30, 31, 33, 50, 52, 53, 54, 77, 78, 100
Vincent, Nicholas 31, 50, 51, 126, 127, 140
Vita Ædwardi Regis 38, 39, 40, 46
Vita Wulfstani 41, 166
Vitalian, Pope 25
Vortigern 18

Wace 64, 67, 78, 79, 80, 81, 87, 88, 91, 92, 93, 94, 95, 106, 111, 113, 114, 173
Wales 18, 38, 77, 155, 160, 174
Waltheof 43, 46, 122, 148, 150
Wantage 27
Wareham 27
Weald 18
Wenric of Trier 173, 174
Werlenc, William, Count of Mortain 67
Wessex 20, 26, 27, 28, 29, 30, 31, 34, 35, 36, 38, 43, 50, 72, 104
Western Roman Empire 18
Westminster 33, 94, 116, 117
Westminster Abbey 33
Westmorland 155, 158
Whitelock, Dorothy 19
Wighard (bishop-elect of Canterbury) 25
Wihtgar (founder of Isle of Wight kingdom) 23

William of Jumièges 10, 35, 36, 62, 64, 80, 95, 96, 110, 142
William of Malmesbury 11, 15, 19, 39, 41, 46, 61, 65, 75, 76, 110, 143, 144, 166, 167, 168, 170, 172
William of Poitiers 37, 40, 64, 65, 67, 73, 74, 75, 76, 80, 81, 85, 92, 93, 95, 96, 100, 108, 109, 110, 111, 113, 116, 118, 121, 140, 141, 142, 143, 144, 147, 152
William of Warren 74
William the Conqueror 3, 4, 35, 37, 38, 39, 41, 47, 59, 60, 63, 64, 65, 66, 67, 68, 69, 70, 71, 72, 73, 74, 75, 76, 77, 78, 79, 80, 81, 82, 83, 84, 85, 86, 87, 88, 89, 90, 91, 92, 93, 94, 95, 96, 97, 98, 99, 100, 105, 106, 107, 108, 109, 110, 112, 115, 116, 117, 118, 121, 122, 123, 124, 125, 126, 129, 130, 132, 133, 136, 139, 140, 141, 142, 143, 144, 145, 146, 147, 148, 149, 150, 151, 152, 153, 154, 156, 157, 158, 159, 161, 163, 164, 165, 166, 167, 168, 169, 170, 171, 172, 173, 174, 175, 176, 177, 179
William II Rufus, King of England 169, 175
Williams, Ann 51
Williams, Gareth 11
Winchelsea 89, 142
Winchester 65, 144, 145, 146, 147, 149, 150
Winkler, Emily A. 113, 114
Witan 75, 154
Wolf, Kirsten 26, 27
Wood, Harriet Harvey 105
Worcester Manuscript 45, 88
Wuffa (East Anglian dynastic founder) 24
Wuffingas (East Anglian royal dynasty) 24
Wulfnoth 37, 143, 168
Wulfstan (Anglo-Saxon writer) 33, 41

York 5, 17, 24, 25, 26, 27, 36, 40, 41, 42, 44, 45, 55, 58, 90, 94, 115, 117, 123, 139, 147, 148, 149, 150, 151
Yorke, Barbara 20, 22, 24
Yorkshire 19, 55, 141, 148, 149, 151

www.ingramcontent.com/pod-product-compliance
Lightning Source LLC
Chambersburg PA
CBHW032045300426
44117CB00009B/1197